Book of Pieces

Robert Roth

Book of Pieces

AND THEN PRESS
NEW YORK • NEW YORK

Some pieces included here first appeared in: *And Then; Central Park; Cultural Correspondence; Curare #9; 5 Minutes of Fame; Hawansuyo; Health Proxy; Home Planet News; HPN Online; Language Crossings; Palabras Luminosas; Quartsiluni; Shadow of the Geode; Social Text; Socialism and Democracy; somedancersandmusicians.com/5operas; St. John's Review; Through the Cracks; White Rabbit; Who Seeks Finds; widdershins.*

Contents

Acknowledgments

When my book *Health Proxy* (Yuganta Press, 2007) came out I wanted very much to show it to my mother. I wanted her to be proud of me. But I also knew some of the content might disturb her. And maybe even disturb her in a big way. But since she was frail, had a lot of trouble with her eyesight, I thought why not. I could have the best of both possible worlds. She would be proud of me publishing the book and most likely not be able to see much of anything.

So I gave her the book. One time on a visit I saw her in the kitchen wearing her glasses, a magnifying glass in one hand, a flashlight in the other, a bright light overhead, reading every word in it.

She turned to me with a smile she could barely suppress and said, "Just because you say it's so doesn't make it so."

Book of Pieces is dedicated to the memory of my mother, Kato Laszlo Roth, and my oldest and dearest friend, Arnold Sachar. The losses of my mother and Arnie have been wrenching. Two basic pillars of my life pulled out from under me.

Book of Pieces is also dedicated to the memory of Shulamith Firestone, Charles Pitts, Muriel Dimen, Ray Korona and D. H. Melhem, all people I loved who died in recent years. People who engaged the world with such intensity, power, imagination and commitment. Each has been ripped away from me. But each also is woven deep into the fabric of my very being.

Over the years Myrna Nieves and Michael Szpakowski, with a determination and focus they bring to their own work, cajoled, encouraged and finally convinced me to put this book together. Myrna in fact many years ago sat me down in a restaurant, took out a piece of paper and had me list things I would like to include. Then I got to writing *Health Proxy* and put all that to the side. One advantage and disadvantage of waiting so long in doing this is that the book is significantly longer than it would have been then.

The work included here covers decades of my life. It is a combination of fiction, personal/political prose, an interview and some poetry. I wrote the first piece, "In the Audience," in the late '70s when I was 37. The last this year at 72. The pieces aren't put in chronological order. The only time I mention when something was written is if I think there is something significant about the date.

Actual paragraphs occasionally repeat themselves. Over the years I would just borrow, steal, plagiarize from myself. I seriously didn't think anybody would notice. And I knew even if someone did they wouldn't particularly care. But 25 years in this case might just be 25 pages. So if something sounds familiar there is no need to go back and check.

A few of the pieces have been taken from two longer works I am still working on. The first of the two is "Fear Led to Fantasy," which is about the last four years of my mother's life. My mother and I worked on it together. "You write about the outside, I'll write about the inside," she said to me one time I visited her in the hospital. The other is called "Lousy Boyfriend," several parts of which most likely will not see the light of day for another hundred years or so.

In putting *Book of Pieces* together I discovered patterns that I was barely aware of. Something that might feel like a faint thread running through any particular piece becomes more than faint as it repeats itself throughout the book. Seeing places I am emotionally stuck or even intellectually stuck is quite interesting and humbling to me. On the other side of that is how wild and fantastic some of it feels to me. "I wrote that! From where? How? Wow!"

I want to thank Carletta Joy Walker for writing the foreword to this book. From the very first moment I even heard about her (Arnie spoke with such enthusiasm about her radio show months before we actually met) I felt that we were going to be the best of friends. When we actually first met it was like a wild chariot ride through the heavens. Such passion, such insight, such contagious charismatic energy. We have collaborated on many extraordinary things over the years. Included in this collection are some of those collaborations.

And thank you Myrna for writing the afterword to the book. Thank you for being my friend. Thank you for reading your work to me over the phone. Thank you for being a part of my life. Over the years it has been vitally important to me to be able to get Myrna's response to something I have just written. All that brilliant energy focused in on it. But even more important is the privilege of hearing her read something she has just written. Being brought into her creative process. Her poetry, her essays, the chronicling of her dream states. Such an extraordinary writer—serious, playful, sensual, meditative, deep. And such a special friend.

I've also included four pieces in the body of the book written by other people. Each piece connects to something I've written— enhancing the book immeasurably.

Two friends after reading my essay "Shooting Baskets" independently recommended I read "Shooting Hoops" by their friend Tobin Simon. It is about two people with Parkinson's shooting baskets. Toby, thank you for letting me include that poem here.

Anne Forer, close friends with Shulamith Firestone (Shulie), writes a description of when she first met Arnie and me. She casts a whole other light on our friendship. How it was seen from the outside. She also discusses, with such profound insight, the deep similarities between Arnie and Shulamith, both of whom I write about in the book.

I also include a piece by my mother just because. But not entirely just because. It follows a eulogy I wrote about the great D. H. Melhem whose attention to my mother's work gave my mother much sustenance during some of the most harrowing moments in those last years of her life. I wanted to have them next to each other as a way to express my gratitude to D. H. for both her concern and her kindness. In addition my mother's piece "Two Faces of a Nazi Sympathizer" is one of my all time favorite pieces ever. So it just feels terrific to have it in here.

Then finally there is Bernie Tuchman's comment that appeared in the comment section of *The New York Times*. It was an addition to a comment I had written earlier in the same section in response to an article about hospice care. Together (certainly more than mine would have been by itself) they form an important addition to the discussion about hospice care. Bernie pops up in different places in my book. A poet/economist, he has been a powerful presence in my life for decades.

I also want to thank Kika Stayerman—dancer, filmmaker, actor, poet—for her wonderful interview of Carletta and me about *And Then*. Her probing, sensitive and insightful questions issued into a flow of response and self-reflection that helped me understand even better what it is that we have been doing all these years.

I want to thank Michael Szpakowski for creating the cover art. Also for the camera-ready score of *Smart and Tart Juicing*, a 90 second children's opera he, Carletta and I collaborated on. It would take two books to describe the impact Michael has had on both my life and the political/cultural life of the planet. Michael, a great big thank you.

I want to thank Jim Stoller and Carol Jochnowitz for all the ways they helped bring this book to fruition. They have been there for me in big ways over the years. I do feel at times that I may have gone to the well once too often. And that even my gratitude is one part added burden.

Jim first read many of the pieces in this collection soon after they were written. Jim's multiple angles of perception, deep insights and subtle understanding of the nuances of words have been almost a staple of my life for decades.

As for Carol, I never understood what being the "cat's meow" meant until I saw the glow on people's faces whenever they would pull me aside and almost spontaneously start singing her praises.

Thank you Bill Cofone for the beautiful photo you took of me for the back cover. Such patience. Hours and hours and countless photos just to catch one moment in time. Also thank you for the photo you took of my mother and me which is included in the book. Those photoshoots of her in her apartment were something else again.

Stephanie Hart, Frank Murphy, Louise Rader, Ralph Nazareth, George Spencer, George Snedeker, Howard Pflanzer, Safiya Bandele and ibin Kenyatta who toil in the Vineyards of Creation, who often have persevered in the face of great hardship, who do the most magnificent work imaginable, I want to thank you all for taking the time to help me with your suggestions, advice and support.

Thank you Shelley Haven, painter, photographer, dear friend who was there in the beginning with her special genius to help create—with Marguerite Z. Bunyan and Arnie Sachar—*And Then* magazine, the most important ongoing project of my life. And for still being a part of it after all these years. We are now joined by Ralph, Myrna and Carletta who have helped expand the scope of the magazine and intensify even further the depth of exploration that takes place in its pages.

And as for you, Marguerite, thank you for everything and for more than everything. Thank you for putting your love and enormous talents into designing this book. And thank you most of all for your remarkable gift of friendship.

When I wrote "In the Audience" $10 was a lot of money. It is still a fortune if you don't have it. But next to nothing if you do. As I write this three friends have been driven out of their apartments by huge rent increases. In the late '70s the gentrification of neighborhoods was just beginning. It was alarming and destructive and portended a very bleak future. Still I had no idea how far my neighborhood, Greenwich Village, would devolve. It has become a soulless hell where absentee billionaires have asserted their will over distraught and embittered millionaires. A class struggle like nothing I could have imagined. All this while the rest of us try to make do with whatever minimal protections we still have left.

When I peered into the future I thought the struggle, if you want to call it that, would be between a deeply engaged enlightened humanism and a powerful transcendent wildly humane radicalism. Not between a life-deadening imperial corporate liberalism and a world wide sweep of fanatic, clashing, reactionary fundamentalism.

Not all is gloom and doom of course. And so now I want to thank people who are vital to my life. Whose very being and commitment bring joy and possibilities both into the present and into the future.

I want to thank David Neiditch for the depth of his knowledge, his breathtaking curiosity, his ability to master a wide range of interests as well as his ability to help me out of huge holes I often find myself in—either out of my own making or not.

Thank you Fredy Roncalla, a poet in three languages (Quechua, Spanish and English), a musician, a singer, God what a singer, and maker of funky jewelry. We meet every Sunday before the opening of the flea market in Chelsea where Fredy has a booth. Each time we meet we cover the whole gamut of existence. Fredy always making sure we never get too full of ourselves.

Thank you Nadina LaSpina and Danny Robert, two of the most glamorous people I know. Whether at Occupy Wall St. or marching with them at the first Disability Pride Parade or seeing them on the evening news or having a picnic with them by the water their special combination of resistance and panache is something to behold. And I have no shame at all basking in the reflected glory I feel whenever we are together.

Thank you Jens Magnussen in Denmark who five years ago suggested we write an ongoing poem, later named "Transatlanticity" by our dear friend Lennox Raphael. Jens writes something and I respond. Stanza upon stanza over the years. I want to thank Lennox also for inadvertently coming up with the name for this book. I sent him a couple of pieces I had just written. He e-mailed me back "Enjoyed reading this. you must put these pieces together in BOOK OF PIECES." I liked how that sounded, thought it was a suggestion for a title and that's how the title came into being.

My friend George Jochnowitz entitled his book of essays "The Blessed Human Race." I indeed feel blessed to have encountered so many people over the years who have allowed me to be part of their lives. Political allies, a couple of political adversaries (unusually kind ones), friends, a whole range of people so diverse and so special that whenever I can stop and take a breath I am flooded with gratitude and awe.

Thank you Sohnya Sayres, Jim Story, Mark Blumberg, Nanette Funk, Marlene Nadle, Margaret Mercer, Ana Lopez Betancourt, Laura Liben, Michael Kranish, Fred Kramer, Pam Carter, Steve Sprung, Marianela Medrano, Ian Vollmer, John Marcus Powell, Richard Crasta, Rozanne Seelen, Margaret Yard, Michael Sahl, Luis Benitez, Nancy Ross, Ahmed Abdullah, Dyske Suematsu, Arlene King, Christine Grant, Monique Ngozi Nri, Karen Ogulnick,

Sonia Robbins, Marvin Schwartz, Victor Wallis, Maria Arias, Ann Snitow, Herb Perr, Sam Swartz, Carole Rosenthal, Daniel Goode, Bruce Morris, Sheri Gibbings, Ildi Tobias, Alix Kates Shulman, Lee Cronbach, Walter O. Beaton, Judith Ward, Donald Lev, Ronna Weinberg, Norm Alster, Jenne Vath, Ned Bateman, Richard Kutner, Andrew Field, Chloe Smolarski, Dorothy F. August, Lynn Kutner, Zaadia Colon, Lonnie Fairchild, Richard Roth, Connie Peretz, Michael Wrought, Jos Kraay, Akosha, Lotte Jaspers, Susan Sheldon, Sofia Marrero, Frank Castronova, Mimi Bluestone, Laurie Roth, Vincent Giangreco, Gary Sheinfeld, Elsa Rizzi, Gene Brown, Bill DiFazio, Greta Hoffmann Nemiroff, Steve Bendich, Harilyn Rousso, Jane Heil, Neil Heims, Ellen Aug Lytle, Marta Lukacs, David Berger, Rosalie Calabrese, Gerald Williams, Charles Winter, Rosemary Drescher, Barbara Garson, Vincent Tomeo, Trudy Silver, The Sticker Dude, Susan Goodman, Sabrina Foley, Mike Usyk, Oliver Ogulnick, Aton Archer, Patty Wolff, Regina Eisenberg, Gabbie Regalado, Paul Meyers, Judith Ghinger, Ralph Pessah, Amber, Jill Hochberg, Milt Polsky, Albert Waugh, Barbara Petrizze, Kamala Mottl, Sy Safransky, Alejandra Mandelblum, Ernest Russell, Michael Lytle, Legacy Russell, Taira Akbar and Joan Greenbaum.

In 1992 while on the subway I wrote this poem:

> An old Jewish face
> One day will appear
> Where this middle aged face
> Looks back at you with such love

I didn't know then and I still don't know now who that "you" is.

But this old Jewish face is definitely beginning to appear.

And whoever that you is, I guess it can be whoever wants it to be, this book has been put together for you.

Foreword by Carletta Joy Walker

An act, an inning, a chapter—a puzzle, a quilt? Space, vast space, in conversation, interaction, emotion on the journey, path, life walk.

Two friends on a see-saw, they sit at various angles in relationship with each other and the thingy you hold onto. On the other side of the plank, past the balance point is complexity—up and down we go.

I am closely familiar with most of the pieces comprising this book, having heard many of them as they were forming into coherent and sharable wholes from the places where they resided in notebooks, on scraps of paper and in the ethers of Robert's mind, body, spirit. In compiling these pieces into a book we get to view each in relationship to itself and to the other pieces. With much familiarity, I had no idea how I would respond, engage with this volume. Once started, I was drawn to continue reading. Not to find out what happens next—I know what happens has happened. Complex honesty: gentle/strong/meandering/precise self-exploration—and consequently exploration of others also—choices, options, opinions, thinking; the political up-close and personal; the personal enmeshed in the political. Essays, stories, poems, reviews, journals, fragments past to present.

For years we, Carletta and Robert talked for hours, yet it seems that we also almost immediately knew how to sit with silence, tuning into emotional subtleties inhabiting the exchange around us.

I am more and less experiential than Robert
I am less and more intellectual than Robert
I am more and less emotional than Robert
I am less and more exacting than Robert
If possible, I live in even more vast undefined space than Robert
If possible, I live within even more bound and edged space than Robert

All with same and difference allowing us to co-write a libretto for an opera for children, answer complementarily questions for an interview about *And Then* magazine, sit in a restaurant post the close and consecutive deaths of my parents, walk through the final days of Arnie's life, sit with the Leading Lady filled with life in the midst of her negotiating with death. And now we are here in shared reflection of a Robert Roth life that is rising from his life rebalancing as players on the plank ascend, descend—many in quantum physics reality: on the seesaw, the merry-go-round and slide, the basketball court and in a classroom all in the same space in time. Many have transformed their molecules—spirits released from the tangible: works, words, memories left to stir up air, the complexity of breath.

Book of Pieces is a hologram; you need a lot of integrity to really believe the stuff Robert believes!

"Coming into political consciousness I had imagined a radical movement similar to the beggars' march in The Threepenny Opera. *It would be a home, a place to gather for the despised, the grotesque, the disenfranchised, people in pain, outcasts. Together we would menace the society in our very being, in our very acceptance of each other's humanity, in our essential beauty and defiance."* (Robert Roth, *&then*, 1987)

Health Proxy, Robert's first "…dynamic collage of consciousness—bits and pieces of perception, insight, observation, dialogue, interviews, monologues, commentary, tirade…" [Ralph Nazareth 2007 Yuganta Press] ends with a fantasy. "Verdi reported that while walking in Venice he heard his tune on everyone's lips. I have a fantasy of me walking in Brooklyn and hearing some girls around a corner skipping double-dutch singing words that sound vaguely familiar. *We are wild berries singing…* And then I recognize it as our opera transformed by being passed from child to child, *We are canter berries lying…*, street to street, *blackberries brooding…* neighborhood to neighborhood, *Robert is one thirsty man* village to village, city to city, country to country, continent to continent—all across the globe. Until finally here in Flatbush they own the song, *we are girls with braids flying.*"

Book of Pieces is necessary for the fullness, completeness of the social political personal record: picture, song, dance, story—not the finish of it, rather the wholeness of it. Once again I am thankful and appreciative for the song on the girls' lips, the gathering of the marchers, for being seen and written into the record, for Robert's risking the stillness of love to share and share in life creation.

Leading Lady

MY MOTHER AT 89 pounds, dehydrated, emaciated down from her regular 130 or 140 lbs, looked from the distance like a pre-pubescent girl of maybe twelve. Having used the bedpan that had been shoved under her, she was there trying to wipe herself, her ashen pubic hair and genitals revealed to the entire ER.

She wanted to leave, insisted on leaving. "I'm not going to rot on this street corner. Get me out of this drugstore."

She said if we did not help her she would go herself; she opened her pocketbook and pulled out a couple of dollars so she could get herself home. She would not let the pocketbook out of her sight. All the time she was in the hospital, the three hospitals really, and the two rehab centers, that pocketbook was always within reach.

My brother stood on one side of the bed and I on the other as we tried to prevent her from getting up and falling. She then started kicking and punching in two directions at once; not flailing out of control punches and kicks, but well placed and ferocious. She was fighting for her life. "I'm not going to rot on this street corner. Get me out of this drugstore," she kept saying over and over again.

Adrenaline flowing, her body was lithe, coordinated and supple much like the young gymnast she had once been. If we had backed away from the bed she would have gotten off and fallen. I begged a doctor I had known from her nightmare ordeal at Elmhurst to give her something to calm her down. The doctor had actually spoken to me on the 6th floor of Elmhurst a few days after her time in the ER and apologized to me and then to my mother for how she had been treated. With not much prodding he and a nurse came over with a syringe. "I know what you're trying to do." My mother squirmed away shrieking, "No you're not. No you're not" as they tried to raise her sleeve. She wouldn't let them. Finally the curtain was drawn. A bloodcurdling scream came from behind the curtain. When they opened the curtain the kicks and punches still came at us precise and

1

perfect but slower and slower and then slower still. Only when she fell completely asleep did they stop.

The next day.

"Why would they choose a skeleton to be the leading lady in their play?" my mother asked as my brother and I walked into her room. At first I thought she was joking but she asked it again.

"Why would they choose a skeleton to be the leading lady?"

"You are quite beautiful, you know," I answered.

"But why now?"

"Don't knock it," I said. "You never know when you get your break."

She was sure a coffee company was bankrolling the film. But had no idea as to why. I had no idea either.

"Why would they make a skeleton into the leading lady for their play?" she asked. Her long hair flowing freely, her gestures broad and dramatic. "Do you think all those doctors will be in the movie too? Or do you think they're too busy?"

She paused.

"What about that scene in the drugstore where I was hitting and kicking both of you? Are they going to include that in the movie too?"

"Well, if they want the movie to be a hit they will have to."

"A mother shouldn't do that to her children," she said.

She paused again. And then with more than a little pride, "Were you as impressed as I was with how energized I became?" ■

Homunkulus

STANDING ON SHERIDAN SQUARE I watched the World Trade Center on fire. Powerful symbols of global economic domination burning right in front of me. Should I be excited? Was I excited? Thousands of people working in those buildings. Was I horrified? I should be horrified. I was watching and not knowing what I was feeling. My emotions buried deep beneath my face, as my mind ran on a thousand tracks.

Two very round, big, sexy men were standing on the corner. Hmm they're the chefs on Channel 13. A kind of pleasure raced through me. Two Italian chefs with accents from the American South who, without a trace of shame, cook dishes made with cream and butter and sugar. Good-humored and sexy men. Both a lot of fun to watch. The smaller of the two in a deep burgundy silk shirt talking on a cell phone. The other, the bigger of the two, turned in circles looking stunned.

I listened as the smaller of the two spoke to someone in the crowd. He had no southern accent. One eye on the burning towers, one ear stretched towards the chef. A loud van blasting staticky official dispatches. They don't have southern accents!

A young gay black man screamed and fell to the ground. I turned towards him then back as the first tower fell. Oh look at that! Hmm!! God thousands of people dying! I hate those buildings. Really I'm indifferent to them. Thousands of people dead. For the man who fell there was no space between him and the horror a couple of miles away. For me all I had were thoughts that were keeping me from feeling.

A Latino man listening to a radio said they hit the Pentagon and the Capitol and the White House. The war of 1812 the White House burned to the ground, I thought. And here was a cruel and vicious assault against a cruel and vicious adversary. Life negative forces unleashed against each other. What was my connection with the people who did this?

3

What was it to the people in the buildings? To the people in the Pentagon?

That night I walked in semi-shock on a very dark street in Greenwich Village, a street that was being torn up. A crazed dark-skinned man was jaggedly pacing back and forth. We were alone on the street. I was frightened of him, though he didn't really seem dangerous. I tripped over some debris, hurt my shoulder, my knee, my ribs. The man barely noticed I was there. A block away was St. Vincent's Hospital.

There were scores of hospital workers and a street full of gurneys waiting outside the hospital for victims of the attack. No one would be coming. I thought about going into the emergency room, then thought better of it and went home to clean up.

●

It was less than a month earlier that I first met Benno Schmidbaur. He invited me to his studio in Saugerties, N.Y. Sculpture work of horror, torture, pestilence and death. Pieces made from wood, metal, stones, feathers. There was a harshness and a delicacy to it. Looking at the work, surrounded by it really, I flashed on the ugly intimate knowledge that the torturer has of the inner psyche of his or her victims. The peculiar erotic dimension to its cruelty. We can see this in the soft poetic face of Osama bin Laden. Or in the heavy breathing, flushed, almost adolescent face of George W. Bush. In the spectacular brilliance of the World Trade Center attack. Or in the relentless and brutal response to it.

And there off in a corner of the studio, was a figure half human half devil lying somewhat on its back somewhat on its side. It was called Homunkulus.

Homunkulus had hooves and pointed ears and a red face. He was lying on something that looked like a platter with protruding nails around its edges. He looked half asleep. I felt a surge of tenderness towards him. A kind of protectiveness as I wondered what his life would be like. And I wondered what type of relationship I could have with him.

4

A friend once told me a story of seeing a boy holding a scorpion in his hand. Neither was afraid of the other. And neither hurt the other.

Was this being a danger to me. Was I a danger to it. How much of my life could I give to it?

Many years ago I was invited by a friend to come to a school she ran for "disturbed" children. A boy, maybe seven, caught my eye. He was someone none of the staff had ever been able to communicate with. He made a face at me. I made a face back. He made a face back at me. And I at him. And we did this for maybe ten minutes.

He knew I was not mocking him as we kept moving inside this very real and extraordinary space. I remember how powerful our face conversation felt. I can still feel the fragility of the boundaries. So clearly defined. So easily violated. I knew I didn't have the emotional capacity or the imagination to sustain it. I knew I needed to be released from the intensity of the contact. And how easy it would be for me to obliterate my own vulnerability by punishing the boy for both his fragility and his trust.

I had to disengage. And we slowly and very gently moved outside the space we inhabited together. Each taking care of the other as we did.

My friend and her colleagues were stunned. They asked me if I wanted to come back. I said I couldn't. I knew if I came back I would have to be with this person forever. It was a basic life choice I was far from ready or capable of making. So the rest of my life has been lived without him.

Homunkulus. What do I need to surrender in myself in order to be open to this being. Is it even dimly aware of my presence? Maybe it couldn't care less. Or maybe it cares very much. Maybe it wants to eat me. Maybe it wants to love me.

At a consciousness raising group of people involved in S&M a woman, a middle-aged dominatrix, talked with pain about a series of relationships she had had with men. The men had approached her asking if they could be her submissive. She agreed. At first the men seemed very happy with how things were going. At some point however they would panic. They had entered a transformative process that they were not prepared for. They had promised her a commitment. But they could only be visitors into her world. She had poured much of herself into these relationships. She brought to each man her imagination, her commitment. She gave them the full creative force of her love. And then they bailed out on her. The experiences had left her demoralized, depleted and if not bitter, very cautious of what she could expect from people and their enthusiasm. Half human half devil. How did Homunkulus come into being? An illicit affair? A moment of passion? A rape? Did it materialize fully formed? Did it come from Benno's imagination only to enter my own?

Do I need to give Homunkulus human attributes in order to love him? Maybe some mechanism will kick in and make him a mortal enemy. Can I only feel safe if he is contained inside boundaries set by me?

I think of white people, white people from the United States who adopt children of color from around the globe. Often they are people themselves painfully marginalized in the world. Jews, lesbians. All kinds of people. Many of whom have deep consciousness, powerful commitments and enormous ability to love. And here they are benefiting in a real sense from the misery their country has helped create. A pool of children has been created out of that misery. And from a very bitter lens their children are the spoils of oppression. And what do people do with that? Half human half devil. How are these children seen? What powerful racial and imperial scripts played out inside the deepness of their contact?

Half human half devil. Homunkulus lies on his platter. Is he being offered up to us as food? A sacrifice? A burnt offering? He looks half asleep. Resting. I feel a tenderness towards it. What will his life be like? Will he move inside the shadows? Have to sleep under bridges? Will it be humiliated and hunted down? Will it turn vicious? Will he seek revenge? Will it float through the universe lost inside the beauty of its own mystique? Will he survive? Will it die? Maybe he Maybe it Maybe

Maybe Robert just maybe you should just shut up and listen! ■

We Want to Know

Written with Carletta Joy Walker and Arnold Sachar

1. WHERE DO WE LEARN to compare ourselves to other people?

2. What does it mean to be brilliant?

3. How does enjoyment become talent become something to be utilized become a job? How does enjoyment become no talent and one become ignored, encouraged to try something else, encouraged to keep on trying?

4. Is it more difficult to say one is angry than to act angry? If so why?

5. When is it, is it, ever okay to make a mistake? When is it, is it, ever okay to "organically" self-discover mistakes?

6. How do people work collectively when they are separated by racial, gender, class, status realities?

7. Is it always necessary to have an opinion?

★ What does it mean when a good friend enthusiastically asks me to join them in a creative project and then when I go with them to public events such as films or poetry readings they consistently make harsh criticisms of whatever is going on using terms such as boring, unmoving and uneven?—Arnie

8. What is respect?

9. If we know Kent State, do we know Jackson State?

10. Are the effects, the realities, of a society that is socially, culturally, economically and politically white dominated the same as the effects and realities that result from people's individual racial bias or prejudice?

11. What is beautiful?

12. Where do we learn to devalue/put down ourselves and others? What, if any role does this play in the function of our lives? Do we, why do we miss the irony/contradiction between these attitudes and the ones that believe in the equalizing of power relationships and the dissolution of hierarchies?

★ What happens when you're brimming with enthusiasm, make an offering to the world and no one listens?—Robert

13. Do we seek approval? From whom?

14. What does it mean when you get a grant/prize/award? Does it help finance your work? Does it exercise control over you? Does it affirm that you are on the right track? Does a "gift" to one come at the "expense" of another? What does it say about you if you don't get one? Who are the people making the decisions? Who do they represent? Do your answers change based on your receiving or not receiving one?

15. What is a bad neighborhood?

16. What is ordinary?

17. What is the difference between the 10 to 15 ivy league schools; the colleges that are not that, but are not considered community colleges; historically Black colleges, Jewish colleges, Catholic colleges, Women's colleges; and the colleges considered community colleges?

18. Are oppositional movements in large part a quest for excluded people to achieve power and prestige roles in mainstream institutions and frameworks?

19. How do we celebrate someone without diminishing ourselves or someone else? How do we celebrate ourselves without diminishing someone else?

20. How do we choose who to sit next to?

21. How does setting (classroom/gallery/media program/public forum/?) affect response (critical/supportive/encouraging/competitive/disparaging/?)? How does presenter (adult/child/student/peer/co-worker/boss/teacher/male/female/black/white/English-speaking/Asian/?)?

 ★ What does it mean that every time I write and speak I hear voices saying boring, unmoving and uneven? I freeze into terrified paralysis? Do these function as control words?—Arnie

22. Is critiquing, evaluating, etc. inherently critical?

23. What is a good neighborhood?

24. How do we define a person such that we can do something to them?

25. Why do we compare people?

 ★ Is there an aspect of definition/of defining that is inherently stifling? When it involves a person is it always to some extent limiting and is the opposite true i.e., is definition liberating? Which came first; where is the balance?—Carletta

26. What are functions of intermediaries and middlepeople as they relate to art, literature, business, sports, film, etc.?

27. What does it mean to be called upon as an expert?

28. Why do people purporting to challenge old values, build new values, often adhere to evaluation concepts like good and bad or average which reinforce/bolster the very system they oppose?

29. Does someone feel confirmed or negated when they are celebrated by the cultural machine?

30. If museums have better representation along racial, gender and class lines how are they transformed? How do they remain the same? Does a transformation reinforce the ways they either remain the same or change?

31. Why is someone "good enough," "interesting enough" to be assaulted, jailed, economically compromised for attending a demonstration, but "not good enough" or "not interesting enough" to be on, or have their own radio spot or television program or newspaper column, etc. within the same alternative movement?

32. Why is competition acceptable in certain areas and not in others? Which areas are acceptable to you?

33. Is there a difference between an informed and knowledgeable business manager and a skilled and inspired poet?

34. How does improvement relate to what one enjoys doing? Who is improvement for?

  ★ Why do I Robert have no questions to ask myself?—Robert

35. How does it feel to be always told one's place either directly or indirectly?

36. Is refusal to adjust to standard definitions and roles a form of maladjustment and immaturity or oppositional protest? What is the ability to adjust?

* Why do I ever respond/act on answers to questions that have neither been asked or answered?—Carletta

37. How do we perceive people's race, gender, class that is different from ours? How do we perceive height, hair color, skin shade, accents that differ from our own?

38. Does your voice change when you talk to a person you consider famous? Does it change mid-conversation if you recognize the person as famous? How does it change?

39. What is the difference between a "work of art" and the expression of someone's joy and sorrow that is not considered a work of art? Who makes these distinctions? Why are they made? ∎

Irving Wexler

OFTEN WHEN PEOPLE GIVE eulogies what they are saying about the other person is what they secretly wish would be said about themselves. Albeit under better circumstances. And so the wonderful things I want to say about Irving Wexler are really the wonderful things I want said about myself, the wonderful things he made me feel about myself.

He made me feel passionate. He made me feel compassionate. He made me feel that my life mattered and that it mattered deeply. He appreciated my written work, affirming it and understanding it in ways few people have. He made me feel as if my words had special significance. He made me feel that I had great analytic gifts and a deep sense of poetry and powerful political commitments. He made me feel that I was a person of enormous sexual power or at least a person of enormous sexual wishes. He made me feel beautiful. He made me feel each time we met, each time we spoke, each time we did anything, each time we argued, something important and historic was occurring.

I could say he made me feel elegant. But that would be stretching things. But Irving in fact was elegant. He was dapper, rakish. He had a real sense of style. He was also funny, funny in the way people with larger than life personalities can be funny. For he had the writ large, comic presence of unfettered genius.

Often when Irving would enter a room a field of energy would surge towards him. However sour and critical his disposition might have been just seconds before, and very sour it was likely to be, he entered a room like a superhero from the cosmos, totally delighted to see anyone and everyone. His enormous capacity to appreciate and delight in people, in the end was stronger than his disappointments and what to me, at least, was his overly critical disposition.

I visited Irving shortly before his death. To see him in his hospital bed, his own world shutting down just as the outside world was entering into its new stage of cruelty, was excruciating for me. Yet inside the magnitude of the present horror I looked at him and felt a strange comfort.

We live. We die. We live and we die. And to think that I was placed on earth at a time I would meet Irving Wexler filled me with gratitude. ■

October 20, 2001

Notes of an Unknown Writer

Excerpted from a journal I kept from August 1988 to March 1989.

TRIP TO BOSTON COMING to a close. Had chance to see every close friend. Met one or two new people. For the most part the trip was quite nice. Sitting in newly discovered park. No one here, just birds.

•

How is someone feeling when flattered in a way that someone else might see as offensive, but who seems to be enjoying the appreciation? At April's party, an actress, long legs, short dress, nasal high-pitched voice, situation comedy voice, appeared genuinely flattered when a man she had known, whose name she didn't remember, whom she had known in Hollywood ("LA") said that his name for her was "precious." She said that was sweet. Someone else might have thought the guy was creepy. But then he might not have said it to someone else. It had taken him a while to gather the nerve to tell her the nickname he had for her.

When someone is patronized but feels flattered—smiling face lighting up—how is this different from the emotions a person feels when the compliment is altogether genuine? What I'm getting at is that if a person is patronized, insulted, unconsciously mocked—do they understand it deep inside even if they think they are being complimented? Do they think the person is friendly? Appreciative? Or do they perceive, however dimly, that deep down the flatterer is, even in ways not intended, hostile, bigoted, and unfriendly? How many lifelong contacts—friendships, love affairs—fall inside this pattern? What subterranean understandings at play? What did I feel towards the actress? Towards the man? What did I want them to think of me?

•

I look through my notebook—a lot has happened since we last spoke. Your phone number always here at my fingertips. For six months I haven't been able to dial your number. Much has happened in between. Yet it is almost like yesterday that I haven't been able to dial your number.

•

I am now at an age where I have watched people grow old. There is a shock. I sometimes blame someone for looking older, maybe more feeble, their body thickening, their bones feeling more frail or their body a little stooped, their face worried in a way I have always associated with older people. I see my friends looking more and more like my aunts and uncles had when I was a child. I find myself blaming people as they take on those forms.

•

The people in their forties when I was in my twenties are dying in their sixties. This is the first generation I have seen grow old. And it is a shock. I feel a surge of hostility whenever I see people take on mannerisms or even physical characteristics that I associate with people who are older. I think it is willed and I am angry.

•

Waiting for Harvey at the Municipal Building with Arnie.

•

Waiting for Marguerite and her friends to celebrate her birthday at Prince St. Restaurant.

•

Waiting for Marilyn on the Staten Island side of the Staten Island ferry. Not exactly sure where we are to meet. Hope we don't miss each other. Hot sun on this miserable summer day. Nice ride on ferry. It was actually cool. Had to wear cotton sweater Mark gave me as a present. Mark injured back trying to help Linda move. He offered to help after long exhausting double shift work week in the unbearably hot stacks of the Harvard Business School library. No air conditioning. The stacks are maybe twenty degrees hotter than the rest of the building. Mark's work partner just recently retired. The full burden of his absence falling on Mark's shoulders. All this while he is also working very hard on the union drive there. Not exactly sure where Marilyn and I are supposed to meet. If we're both early then one of us is waiting in the wrong location.

•

Hiroshima Day: Can't talk to Akemi. Today the separation is particularly painful. Probably permanent.

•

"Free Sherman McCoy" his T-shirt read.

"Are you Sherman McCoy?" I thought to myself.

What if I wore a T-shirt that read "Free Robert Roth"?

•

The hottest day has not turned into the hottest of nights. In fact it is almost cool.

Anyone with any money sits in cafés. Those without sit in small parks.

•

Sitting in this triangular park [Greenwich Village] surrounded on three sides by cars. "I feel like a poodle fucking a Great Dane." The sentence jumps into my head as I wonder to myself what sex would be like with a man that big.

•

I see so many fewer people I know in the streets. I no longer run into people I know. For years I was often the one person any number of people would on occasion run into. There was much more of a street culture of people I was friends with. I can still see people at events. But not walking the streets. All day I can walk and not run into a person I know. Years ago I could just take a walk and let each person I would meet usher me through some part of the day. Now I have to make phone calls for appointments. Very rarely does someone just drop by.

•

Friday night 10 PM: In the street. Man lying unconscious, beaten up in a fight. Cops and paramedics attending to him in rubber gloves. Discard gloves in the street. One woman goes over to complain. Clearly she feels all pleased with herself. AIDS hysteria breaking out everywhere.

•

Sarah Kendall came into the Magic Carpet Restaurant for lunch. Looking very tired or depressed. Clearly in some type of pain. Her legs looked thin. Are they old lady's legs? Or are they young dancer's legs, thin and well muscled? She did seem connected to her notebook in a way much different than me. Then again she is Sarah Kendall!

•

I can hear my own voice, that tired depressed sound. I don't feel a connection, more it is I don't feel able to challenge what people have to say when I'm in disagreement with them. I go along with what they say—not agreeing—but keeping my differences muted. I don't engage the person. This is not quite right. Can't quite get it. Don't feel an excitement.

•

Work won't resume for another month. More like six weeks. My money is dwindling. Have been on an austerity budget. Eating maybe too little. Losing weight.

17

Magazine not coming together. I'm always coming back to Akemi, my father, my trip to Israel, my job as newspaper distributor, playing basketball in the church. My father's death. Hostile Christian faces staring at me during basketball game at the church.

Park clean-up welcome. But each improvement could be laying the groundwork for further gentrification. August is almost over. Two months go by. I do nothing. The days just disappear. The park is filled with people. The park attendant spraying pigeons with his hose, playing with them. They scatter in panic. A man in a suit is eating a banana. Another man is talking to himself, making a speech. Two women are complaining about the people they're working with. Fences around parks are springing up throughout the city. Want to make parks safe—want to keep "undesirables" out. Too many pigeons here right now. I have to leave.

•

Joan's pregnancy so far very difficult. She has a very hard time keeping food down.

•

After my father slipped back into a coma they attached an external pacemaker to him. This operation took a number of hours to perform. It was supposed to be a simple operation, but it wasn't.

On the day he died, I had visited him in the morning. The doctor I had spoken to said he had improved. He in fact seemed a little better. I left the hospital feeling somewhat hopeful. Later that day his pacemaker malfunctioned and everything went haywire. They brought him to the operating room but after a number of hours he died. I saw him in a viewing room. Blood was dripping from beneath the sheet covering him onto the floor. The blood was dark, watery, with little air bubbles. I wanted to stick my hand into the blood and then rub it all over my face. But I didn't.

My father died with a white beard and a peaceful face. For two and a half weeks no one shaved him. Slowly as his beard grew in, his personality transformed. He died as a man with a white beard—a poet? a peace activist? a prophet? He did look different. Only his forehead was the same. I didn't even know that his beard would be white. His lips had been stretched (maybe into a smile) by the respirator shoved down his throat. And so he died a man with a white beard and a peaceful smile and very long nails that no one would cut. I looked at my father's wise peaceful face and kissed his forehead. His forehead was cool but his body was still warm. I felt his death as an offering, a present. It was a present I could not accept. My whole life I have not allowed the full force of experience to affect upon me. I have always been too numb, too frozen by life-shock.

•

A worker from Con Edison saw my father's car swerve and knock into a lamppost. He pulled my father out of his car and gave him CPR and brought him back to life. The ambulance came and took him to Elmhurst General Hospital (Queens) where they worked over him, stopped him from dying and gave us two and a half more weeks to be with him.

To prevent him from dislodging the various tubes inside him, my father's hands were tied with a soft cloth to the railings on the side of the bed. When I entered his room the first thing I saw was his chest heaving in and out, the respirator expanding and contracting his lungs. Toothless, his blue eyes unfocused, his skin still remarkably smooth, his head moving from side to side I pictured him as the marathon swimmer he had been in his youth.

Struggling for breath, his head moving from side to side, weighted down by the water-logged swimsuit his mother had made from an old pajama top, I could actually see his small, firm, immigrant body fighting the waves, the water, the exhaustion. This time however it seemed as if he might be defeated. He looked so vulnerable lying there in his bed. What I mean by vulnerable is that he seemed like a rare and gifted athlete with a will of iron, faced with maybe just one obstacle too many. Not a man who might be dying.

•

After two days my father emerged from the coma. He was in an altered state of consciousness. An almost stoned, blissful state. He was playful and affectionate. "She's very pretty," he said of the nurse across the room. "Go, go tell her you're a writer."

He could not grasp where he was. And if he did he would immediately forget. Every ten minutes he wanted to go home. He wanted to be moved to New York Hospital. He would ask my mother to call up doctor friends long dead to rescue him. At one point it occurred to him that he had blacked out. He mused as he said the word "blackout." It was almost as if he were delighted to have experienced something he had always heard about.

The first words he spoke, no one could understand. Impatiently he gestured for paper and pencil. He scrawled "kosher" on the paper. Then "roll and coffee." The only thing he was allowed to eat was ice. "Here's your roll and coffee," I said. His tongue thirstily drank in the ice. "You know, this is manna from heaven," I said to him. And whenever I or my brother fed him ice we would imagine it to be the most delicious of foods.

Lying in the bed next to my father was a young black prisoner in critical condition.

He had complained of fatigue at Rikers Island. They did not take his complaint seriously. He soon fell into a coma. Young interns on loan from Mt. Sinai Hospital, those clean-faced, energetic, "brilliant" young doctors slavishly worked over him. Supervised by the "top" doctor-teachers, they used every modern device and instrument on him. While they worked on him, his wife and family waited outside the room.

When my father emerged from his coma, joy overcame my family. White Jewish family, momentarily joyous. Black family grim and resigned. A very painful and confusing moment.

The doctors took great pains to explain to the prisoner's wife exactly what they were doing, what his condition was, what they were going to do next. They were extremely gentle with her. At one point she turned to me and said, "Now they treat me like a queen."

•

The cop's face looked like it was in a state of transition, moving either from youth to middle age or from middle age to old age. I could not tell which. It's when the small changes not quite yet

•

The face of the cop looked like in the process of fixing into a

•

A police sketch artist can alter a face, add years onto it, project how it might look after it has aged fifteen years. Subtle alterations and the face of the person in the sketch is altered. The cop's face was caught in transition before a new face set in place. You could almost see the face rearranging itself. I think how frightened he must have been, how frightened I would be, if that moment of transition was so sharply revealed on my face.

The changes are so subtle, so slow, and one day the face has rearranged itself and your face is that of an older person.

•

The NYU clerical workers are going on strike. Will have to deliver school papers there. What will be the best way to do it? Leave the papers outside the buildings? How to do this right. I wonder how long it will take them to settle. The nurses were on strike at Mt. Sinai where my father had been transferred a few days before he died. Julian Beck was also there the same time. A call was made over WBAI to send all the healing energy towards Julian. No one of course mentioned my father's name. No one knew him. I need this strike like a hole in the head.

Carl's more compulsive patterns seem suspended this year. Fell in love. Joan is pregnant. No-nonsense person. Carl is kept in check. Problems with her pregnancy intensifying a deep sadness. There they are, two wonderful, sensitive, aware people, after a wedding, inside state of pregnancy confusion. Now there is the reality. Not easy to handle.

Akemi/Robert: Race, gender, class. Japanese/Jewish. Inside that reality. All the good will, hard to overcome social divisions, neurotic personalities. Deep love not always enough. Strong enough to join us, not strong enough to sustain us. Pain in this disappointment. Boredom. Both hearing each other's stories once too often. The most nightmarish experience is waking up next to someone after three years, seven years, ten years wondering who that person is. Only knowing that person inside the dynamic that has been established. In five minutes you might know more about Akemi than I do after two years. "Let's start from the beginning. Do you have any hobbies?" Akemi asked me after our first really big fight. I see similarities between Akemi trying to get her green card and Joan and her pregnancy.

•

Akemi's family upper middle class. Her father, a former table tennis star, is a banker. Her mother was tennis champion of a whole region of Japan. Akemi intimidated by her mother's ferocity would lose, still lose, any game she would play against her.

As a young girl she discovered a book by Mao and read it and studied it. Her two favorite political figures were Mao and Rosa Luxemburg. Akemi became a student leader in college. Started her own sect, a women's liberation sect. She designed a shocking-pink helmet for its members to wear. Akemi would make speeches in front of 40,000 people. She said though that they weren't speeches, but agitations. The difference being that an agitation was an engagement of equals while a speech was talking down to people. Her agitations could last as long as forty

22

minutes. Wearing a helmet and kerchief over her face, as well as not being able to see individual faces from the podium, made it much easier for her to speak in front of a huge crowd. She was in fact a painfully shy person.

I asked her once to do an agitation into her telephone answering machine. It sounded quite impressive. "Ladies and gentlemen under my command," was how she translated the beginning of her agitation. It was only when she started working with peasants and had to break her ideas down into a simpler language that she began to understand her own politics.

•

The weather has gotten colder. I am back in the park. Some of the same people sit around. The pigeons are still here. An old man carrying some mechanical device goes through the garbage picking out things for his shopping cart. Another man is feeding the pigeons. The Presidential election. Three conservative candidates and one slightly left of center candidate who is both a homophobe and a xenophobic racist. Very, very depressing.

•

Over at Carl and Joan's. Three heterosexual couples eating dinner. Sex turning into comfort. I don't want to be that comfortable with anyone.

•

Met Marybeth on her way to design T-shirts for new Mexican restaurant. Project she is working on, a book on condoms, not getting off the ground. Similar problems we're having with *And Then*. Hard to pull everything together.

•

I need sex. With whom I don't know. Very demoralized of it ever happening again.

•

It seems to have happened almost overnight. My face seems to have rearranged itself into a markedly older face. I don't know how this face is seen by others. It is not a face that will drive people away. But I don't know if anyone will ever again be drawn to it.

•

Dark Filipino nurse attended to my mother right after she learned that my father was dead. Lolita and Monica, two good friends I met in Israel. They were working as servants to make enough money to send back to their families in the Philippines.

•

I touched my father's nipple while leaning over his hospital bed. "I hope he doesn't die this minute," I thought to myself laughing.

•

The memorial service for Carol's father Louis Klein at Alternative [the radical school located in Brooklyn]: Carol who for ten years has presided over countless events at the school was presiding over this one also. People were dressed mostly in black, black suits, black dresses. Many older people, family members mostly, and friends of Louis. I didn't see too many of Carol's friends there. Just her best friends. A left-wing family, part of a counterculture, here the counterculture being that of the old left, rather than the counterculture of the '60s. There was an expansive humanity in the room. People there who for decades had worked for social change. Some unfortunately I suspect had also been part of a sordid history of betrayal and the rationalization of awful governments and fucked-up political movements. The people there were not all that different from some of my father's sisters and brothers. Louis Klein brought his children on demonstrations. My father was a Jewish small business-man. I remember how angry I was at my uncle Sandor when he described my father that way as a child. I remember sitting in Sandor's car thinking furiously that my father was a "big" businessman. My father was an orthodox Jew and a political liberal. He also knew (they I think would see it differently) that in the crunch his brothers and sisters would always come back to him for help. This gave him a certain smugness as well as a certain insight into the world. Anyone venturing too far afield with whatever flair or independence would when they fail fall back on the security offered by a world they held in contempt. So in a sense my father knew me all too well. He had seen me before in some of his seven brothers and sisters. He could not understand what it was that we were trying to live for. He understood us in terms of our defeats and humiliations and our dependence on him. Everyone coming back to him for protection. So there was pride in his son's accomplishments, also a certain vindication in his son's defeats. There was also a largeness to my father, a warmth and a wild sense of humor. He was very generous. Once when I needed to borrow a large sum of money he did not ask me what it was for. He knew it was for something important and both trusted my judgment and knew I would pay it back. My father was compassionate, neurotic, filled with confusion and hysteria, told I suspect to take cold showers or long walks to cool off desire. He could however step out of his own prejudices when it mattered and attend to the problem that presented itself.

Louis Klein seemed stern and demanding. He was a war hero and a fighter, a real fighter for social change. He was hot-tempered but always yielded to the wishes of his children if they pressed him enough. Had fond memories of the Party, struggled for justice till the very end. Carol stood in front of the room composed and articulate. There was no memorial service for my father, though hundreds came in a summer rainstorm to fill the chapel. He had always made time for people, paying a special attention to anyone he might know. Neither my mother nor brother nor I spoke at the funeral. Jonathan Berger and his journalist friends all spoke at his brother George's funeral. He introduced all the speakers in a deep, resonant voice. "George was a genius of a father," he said at one point. "Then why did he die before his son was ten?" I thought to myself, surprised by my own bitterness.

•

The magazine still in chaos. I haven't heard from Bruce or David yet.

•

David Truong's piece has come in. Harvey gave it to me. Short and very important. Puts us 50% there. We are in better shape now. Arnie and I have to concentrate on what to do next.

•

A beautiful change in the weather. Two days ago I wrote a letter to Z [a libertarian left-wing magazine]. The only really or almost really good thing I have written in a while. Then I had a cappuccino. I should have written more. Caffeine is a powerful drug for me; it brings up feelings that could be released in writing. Instead I spoke to Arnie on the phone. I was jittery, depressed, and a little sick for a day and a half. I think it was triggered by the caffeine. I think if I had better used the caffeine high it might not have happened. Somehow half my emotions surfaced. Or more precisely my emotions surfaced halfway and then got stuck. Next time I drink coffee I'll try not to squander it.

•

My aunt Irene would sleep with a black mask over her eyes. She loved to dance when she was young. I only knew her when she had multiple sclerosis. The mask kept the light out of her eyes so that she could sleep. I remember the mask and the smell of witch hazel that she would rub on her body. I loved that smell and would be surprised, in fact not believe, how strong it smelled up close. Or how awful it tasted. She would love to tell me that the song "Goodnight Irene" was written for her. In Israel Lolita cried herself to sleep each night listening to love songs sung by English and American rock musicians. I felt enormous gratitude towards those singers for the solace they gave her. On a farm in South Carolina, my friend Emmet Durant kept his sanity as a child by reading Rimbaud and not feeling like a total freak.

•

Received Greta's piece in the mail as well as the poem by Mike Sahl's friend. The magazine is taking its own form.

•

The elections are coming soon. Bush is gaining strength. A tired, demoralized country is voting in another conservative President. They are doing it without much passion. He could be President for the next eight years. Why not? The country is even more distant to me than ever before.

•

The leaves are falling outside my window which is why they call it the fall.

•

I constrict my cheeks, squint my eyes as if by an act of will they will catch on fire.

•

Now that the weather is cold I have to find somewhere inside to write. Today it is the library. The Jefferson Market Library which had once been a courthouse.

•

Woke up with a cold and a swelling around my asshole. Two years ago when I had the same thing the doctor told me it was hemorrhoids.

•

The library is filled with school kids from I don't know where. Some older people. More eccentric types. My academic friends use the NYU library. They use personal computers and credit cards. They write books, work hard, and make money. They are always on the move when they haven't collapsed.

•

The intense sexual longing no longer in Akemi's face. I remember the moment love left her eyes. A loss, a loss so enormous.

•

I wake up. My nose hurts; my ass hurts. I wish I got this from a nighttime of pleasures. Not from doing nothing.

•

I came home to an apartment filled up with steam. The whole building complaining. Something wrong with the boiler. This building can be a living hell. Had to organize against the landlord a couple of years ago. Conditions improved somewhat. While I was working on the truck Carlos came to fix the toilet. What he did was build a huge mound to secure the toilet to the floor. He mixed the cement in two pots of mine, ruining them both. I have to piss on an incline now.

•

Rashes all over Akemi's body the last time I saw her.

•

I look a wreck. Dark circles under my eyes. I am fatigued and feeling depressed. A deep, deep sadness.

•

Election Day: It looks as if Bush will win. Though nothing is certain. I hope it's not a landslide. There is a remote possibility of a landslide. The weather is not too cold. I am not voting.

Feel a little left out of things. There would be some satisfaction in voting against Bush and joining whatever might be decent in the population that is voting for Dukakis. Maybe even voting for whatever is remotely decent in him.

•

The day after Bush's victory. Anyone reading this will know whatever has transpired since this has been written. His victory I think is slightly less than awful.

•

High-energy blond comedian whom I saw last night in the restaurant talking with her friends. If I had gone home with her, with my hemorrhoids and upscale cement-mounted toilet, I would not want to know of the jokes she would tell her audience.

•

Coming to see Harvey I stopped at a Most Wanted display and looked at the criminals at large. The photos are constantly changing. Only one white face among all the black and Hispanic faces. Most of the people are younger than me. But they look like older men.

•

Again I'm here at the Municipal Building waiting for Harvey. It seems I'm almost always waiting here for him. Certainly it's true in relation to this journal. I've worked five more hours with Alice, reading her book out loud. It is totally exhausting. We still have three chapters to do—all considerably shorter than the ones we have already done. How many pages will the book be altogether I don't know. I want to beat this cold that is coming over me. I see Claudia tomorrow night. If anything develops I don't want it interfered with by a cold. I think some deep romantic feeling killed off by ending with Akemi. Akemi a more recurrent theme in this journal than Harvey. So is my father. I suspect they are the only two people mentioned more often.

Harvey's ankle is swollen. He is being driven very hard at

work. Like Mark, Harvey takes on a huge load of work. They both do slave away under the burden of useless work. Work which in another context would be far from useless, though probably still exhausting. But maybe less exhausting than now. Mark works in the stacks of the library of the Harvard Business School. Harvey for the Department of Environmental Protection. Mark lugs books around all day, fetching them for students and faculty. It is an endless job. This along with helping to organize the union has left him depleted. He just got a promotion. But since he doesn't have a degree he can never be a full librarian. Harvey is an economist who continually does paperwork and has to make suggestions. Any real suggestion he might make of course would never be taken seriously. A clean environment and a well-functioning library. Two essential needs of our future society can be helped brought into existence by my two close and tired friends. What they can't do now they can do then.

•

The night Hirohito died: I don't have Akemi to drink a glass of sake with and then have Arnie tell me how he never celebrates the death of another human being.

•

Hirohito's death a historical moment that could not put me back in touch with Akemi. What a waste!

•

I think of Akemi sitting in the darkened kitchen of my apartment early one morning, taking long drags on her cigarette. Very lonely person in a new and strange country. Deep anxiety momentarily relieved with those drags. Italian and Japanese radicals smoke cigarettes differently. For the time being I'm going to leave it at that.

•

My nerves are on edge. In addition, Gorbachev is visiting New York. Traffic could be hell. Job could get all fucked up. I remember leaving funeral services for James Baldwin. I went with Gary and another friend to an Italian restaurant near St. John the Divine where the services had taken place. As we walked in Gorbachev had just arrived at the airport and was being greeted by Reagan. This was being shown on TV in the restaurant. The service had been overwhelming. The love in that room and the grief! And then to see these two white men ready to figure how best to divide the world. The contrast was sharp.

•

Max ran into Akemi at the post office this morning. She is very thin but looking well. She had been in the hospital for a month with a bleeding ulcer. She is no longer working in the restaurant, having been sick since October. She is moving out of her apartment. Her English, according to Max, has improved considerably. She has a friend, a professor, whom she speaks to a lot. Possibly a lover. I think I will call her later. Or write her a card. It has been a long time. I need to put some kind of closure or a different continuation on this. Too much pressure on her. Too much pressure. It was easier for her to meet someone than it has been for me. I do feel estranged. I did feel a special bond to her—I still do. But this I think might free me. I hope we can meet. Probably for lunch. She was in the hospital for a month without calling me. So clearly I've been placed way out of her mind. I have no need to place myself back in. But if possible I want some contact.

I don't feel there was bitterness towards me, more a falling out of love. A disappointment in who I am. More I think when she saw me so close up she stopped seeing me altogether. Both disappointment and relief, more than horrible panic, marked our breakup for me. And some guilt in not having the imagination to bridge the gaps which separated us. Probably she's with someone who doesn't "respect" her feelings as much as I did. So the person in a way is probably relating to her better. For both good and bad, I always take people at their word regardless of what I think they're feeling. This sometimes provides me with an out.

I avoid engaging the person. Sometimes it is just that I am bored with the drama that often ensues. The cut-off with Akemi, her not calling me when she was sick, having a new lover maybe will allow us to be friends. Because I do respect a person's decisions, maybe to a fault, maybe we can be friends.

For a year now I haven't called. Her number just at my fingertips. I myself might have thought of a way to heal the rift. I think I didn't want to. I don't like resuming love affairs. For me it usually means the extension into a lot of pain. I would like to see her, and see if, in a very tentative way, we can check in with each other every so often—till we have some type of contact. I'm talking too much. My disappointment has been severe. And clearly my life will be lived without her being an important part of it.

•

This feels almost too important to write down. But if I don't I'll have to stop writing in my journal. I spoke to Akemi Wednesday. When she answered the phone we moved right into the conversation. It was clear that she was happy to hear from me. Clearly she had expected me to call. From Oct 23 to Nov 23 she was in and out of the intensive care unit of the hospital. They gave her codeine which she thinks was too strong for her. She threw up blood and twice fainted in the street. I don't remember the exact sequence of events. This morning, thank God, was to be her last visit to the doctor. She was much better.

Her English is much improved. She speaks with great beauty and poetry. Very melancholy and sad. She has a boyfriend whom she wants to live with. They are looking for a place to live. A bigger place. In Manhattan. She said she is too frightened to live in Manhattan alone. She doesn't want to give me her new address because she wants to keep me in her past. Very sad, very sad. I was sick Wednesday night. My stomach was aching. I hardly slept. Thursday night I went to bed at 8 and felt much better in the morning. This was an extremely sad experience for me. I remember when we first met. I did feel we should be careful. She did seem very young—naive. It did scare me. Then

32

to have such absolute passion come towards me. And then have her history unfold. Someone similar to Rosa Luxemburg—still naive and crazy—Rosa herself very crazy. Trembling lips. Discovering sex for the first time—an explosion.

The happiest day turned into the beginning of the end. She invited me for lunch at her restaurant. Sweating, working so hard she served Harvey and me a banquet. The bill was the equivalent of an appetizer. We didn't know what type of tip to leave. Harvey thought three times the tax. It came to less than five dollars. We should have left ten. Akemi thought we left less than twice the tax. The meal was so exquisite. Her rage so deep. We should have spoken before about what to do about the tip. I should have put more money down in any case. The beginning, really, of the end. No way to undo it. I bought a ten-dollar record for Shizo, the other person waiting on tables that day. He was surprised and very happy. Still, a wall between us was now there.

Over our last year together Akemi started to scapegoat me. I was the only person she could yell at. I was the only person she could say "no" to. I think she enjoyed fighting. I just couldn't get angry back when she insulted me. I thought her rage grew largely out of circumstance. I didn't like to be a target of her rage. But it didn't seem to have that much to do with me. She could make me guilty but not angry. I still hope there will be a time when we can be close again. This has been a hard time for her—a hard time for me. Maybe the degree of love she felt for me—though it didn't feel entirely personal—though often that is the case—I never quite trusted it and maybe that is how I lost it—I feel almost as if I'm being faithful—proving my love by not meeting anyone else. But everyone I know—and clearly she also—wants to live with someone. That someone can't be me. I'm too restless, too claustrophobic. Being with me does create problems. I don't have something to offer besides sex, love, and empathy. Day-to-day life becomes a bore with me. I do have too many moments when I grow edgy or withdrawn. I can die when I see Carl and Joan or Alice and Martin. There does seem to be genuine love and concern there—but I would be dead before I would be in that situation. It is what they want. I think the degree of alienation and separation I would feel—the deadness I would feel—would overwhelm me. They have all lived through hard times, difficult times. They seem happy with their choice. Released from a certain type of struggle. One type of loneliness abated. I can't now imagine anything resembling a sexually free world anymore. I mean even a place where people wish to take such a concern seriously. So really my decision is to be alone. People getting married in droves. Others getting into "relationships." The Institution of Marriage. The Institution of Relationships. No one even talks about marriage as an oppressive patriarchal institution anymore. Here again I'm talking about the institution, not about individual choices.

Now Akemi wants to live with a man. Something she never thought she would do. She sounded so knocked about on the phone. Her dreams so flattened. Protection so dear to her now. She has thrown herself into another dangerous situation.

I can give someone intimacy, love, sexual pleasure. But I can't help structure a life. Carl and Martin are able to help create an environment where life exists: work space, living space, entertainment, friends, cooking, vacations, a home, a shelter, and they certainly are interesting and intimate enough. There is something about those lofts, those meals, those vacations—the ability to "create" a life that until now I thought was nothing. And it is not something that I want. Still it provides a buffer so people can be together without necessarily bumping up against each other. Though all those dramas are played out there too. But still there is something there that I can't provide. I can't enter the routine, but I have no real substitute. Except for my refusal to participate! Alice is much happier than when she was alone. I don't know what I'm talking about. The fire has been knocked out of Akemi. Bravado may have hidden certain needs or maybe didn't allow her to see what risks were involved in certain decisions. The society will extract its price wherever there is real life. Living in the United States has taken its toll. A person almost from another planet. A Japanese woman outside her culture, a Jewish man outside his. Yet she's Japanese and I'm Jewish. The way we're outside our cultures was as remarkably similar as it was different. I think the problem of understanding was as much hers as it was mine. Martin, Alice, Carl, Joan all have an abundance of energy. The structure of their lives somehow allows their lives to continue. Something is going on that I don't understand. To me that type of contact is death. There is something positive there that I just don't see. It seems like death to me.

· · ·

A small leap forward.

A couple of weeks after the election of George Bush, friends and I went to see the political folk group Bright Morning Star at the Somerville Theatre. The concert was part of their tenth anniversary tour. The group seemed at first a little depressed and tired. Years of political struggle had clearly taken their toll. Jokes about Quayle, statements of defiance, could not offset a deep sense of defeat. The audience, mostly older Movement people, had about it a weariness mixed with a genuine spirit.

The previous night we had gone to the same theatre. The opening performer sang political folk songs while the featured performer sang more raucous "personal" songs. The audience was somewhat younger. On both nights there was a large women's/lesbian presence.

One section of the theatre seemed reserved for deaf people. The first night two different women, one for each singer, stood in front of that section, translating songs and spoken words into sign language. Sign language is very expressive and powerful. The women, both wearing black, while clearly in a subordinate role to the singers, were also spectacularly independent of them. After each performance, when the signer's name was mentioned, she received long, sustained applause.

The next night there was a change. The signer actually

entered into the performance itself, doing a dance number with one of the bright morning stars. At one point a group of deaf people from the corner of the auditorium started to sign back at the stage as their voices rose into a beautiful chorus. The signer, through her gestures, encouraged the rest of the audience to join in the singing. New voices. Then suddenly new hands were gesturing in the air. The whole audience was then asked to sign. One deaf woman just exploded in delight.

I remember once playing basketball in Tompkins Square Park with a group of black players. In between games, five or six transvestites, a rainbow coalition of transvestites, black, Hispanic and white, all powerfully built and gorgeously dressed, walked by the basketball court in their high heels. Some of the players ran to the fence that enclosed the court and started hooting at the procession. There was no threat of violence and the transvestites didn't seem at all fazed by it. Still, it was very unpleasant. But what struck me most was how these most graceful of athletes, through bigotry and panic, had suddenly frozen into the most rigid and ridiculous of people.

My friend Harilyn Rousso recently read a poem as part of a performance given by women with disabilities. There were many people in wheelchairs in the room. Some people were missing limbs, some were blind. All types of disabilities. One woman read a poem of her adjustment to her double mastectomy. It was a powerful evening. As a person from the outside I entered a space where oppression was being responded to, where solidarity was strong, where communication was deep. I was part of the alien and hostile world of the able-bodied or more accurately, as it is now being defined, part of the world of the temporarily able-bodied. I was a visitor into a world rising in spirit. I felt incredibly awkward moving about. My legs felt like encumberments. To write about this sounds like an indulgence. It might be an indulgence. But the experience was real.

The deaf people that night in the Somerville Theatre were excited by the signing of the rest of the audience. But I didn't know what I was doing. The stupidity one can feel learning a new language! They seemed to genuinely appreciate our attempt to sign as well as enjoy how funny many of us looked in trying. A significant change, I think, had taken place that night— a change growing out of years of collective and communal experience and struggle: a genuine small leap forward. ■

Defiance

THE MAKE-UP ALMOST DRIPPING from her face, she stood with defiance in front of the mirror. Her straightened hair with its reddish tone fell softly over her shoulders giving her, she felt, a sexy elegance.

"You must show and not tell." The narrator hears his friends' voices echo in his brain. Most of his friends, like him, are at the bottom of the heap. Still they feel that they must keep their critical apparatus intact. They function as the street cops of the cultural machine. Much like the most beaten down father who must teach his children obedience to authority, they must preserve a structure that is deeply humiliating to themselves. The narrator cannot concentrate on the story. The voices are telling him to know his place. As a result the narrator identifies strongly with the character as she looks into the mirror. Her boyfriend is coming home after a long absence. Where has he been? How long has he been away? That will come later. The character had planned to meet the boyfriend at the airport wearing the sexy new outfit she had made for the occasion. "Could you pull your hair back when you greet me at the airport?" The boyfriend had said this on the phone just the night before. "I want to be able to see your whole face. It's so beautiful." She had just walked into the apartment after spending two hours at her hairdresser getting her hair done just right. She was stunned by the request and somewhat bewildered by it. He had used the very same words once to prod her gently to use less make-up.

Unlike the character, the narrator was less than bewildered by the boyfriend's request. He remembered his own response when his beautiful radical Korean girlfriend came home with her hair permed. "How could someone who could shake the foundation of Korean society want to look so westernized!" He told her how lovely she looked and brooded about it for two days.

Like the narrator, the boyfriend won't look too deeply into himself. He focuses instead on his lover. Her hair being straightened means that she has internalized her oppression as a black person. Wearing make-up means she feels bad about herself as a woman. Shaving under the arms means she is ashamed of her body. Why is he so drawn to her? Why does he want to change her?

Political and psychological categories can help make one understand feelings that are deep and bewildering. They can explain for example why you might wake up each morning in a state of dread or why something that should seem like a compliment can create a deep sense of humiliation. But even the most powerful and accurate categories can freeze one into a place of partial understanding. The boyfriend's love is very deep. Four months away has created an unbearable longing. Instead of writing letters they had sent drawings and sketches back and forth communicating on levels each never before thought possible. What about her appearance is so threatening to him? How does he feel about the heads that she turns whenever she walks down the street? Is he trying to help release her into some deeper state of consciousness (probably) or attempting instead to control her sexuality (probably also)?

The narrator suddenly scribbles on the side of the page: "Teenage mothers remain outside everyone's control. Social workers, right wing clergy, even feminists have all given it their best shot. It is their inability to be managed that generates such fear. Certainly more than any real concern for their situation."

The black woman, in her late twenties, stands in front of the mirror, her hair pulled back, her face well scrubbed. After an absence of four months her lover is returning. Momentarily stunned by a comment he had made on the phone the other night, any hurt that may have lingered has receded with the excitement of his anticipated arrival. She remembers the serious face she wore as a teenager, as turbulent erotic energy was just about to burst from under her skin. "Yes, I think I'll dress like a slightly risqué schoolgirl. Maybe I'll even bring a notebook with me to the airport," she thinks to herself smiling.

The narrator turns on his friends with a fury. They sit around like pundits on television. They sound like articles in magazines. "Trembling Asian lips," he once wrote while describing sex with his Korean lover. He took out the word Asian and closeted his sexuality. After any event they stiffen into critics. Even a rare accomplishment of a friend cannot be fully appreciated. They hold on for dear life to the right to have an "honest opinion." Movements for autonomy wind up as the right to an honest opinion. It is with their honest opinions and multiple critical structures that they police each other and themselves.

As you might have guessed by now, since he did not mention his own race, the narrator must be white. White narrators only identify those who are not white by their race. But he did mention that the boyfriend was white. Or did he? Maybe not. But if he did it would only be to make a point. If he were writing about the boyfriend alone he probably would not mention it.

What about the narrator's own feelings about the woman character? I think I will give her self-inflicted scratch marks on the back of her hand. Why is he so drawn to her? I think I will keep her face scrubbed clean when she goes to the airport. What scores does he want her to settle for him? No, I think she'll put on thick make-up out of spite. How deep is his love?

Like the boyfriend the narrator is stuck in a partial consciousness. He himself becomes fixed to two-dimensional explanations. He can't enter into the space of the woman. Her insecurities, her strengths, are well beyond his understanding. He, like the boyfriend, wants her to represent him in some way. So there is a struggle going on between them.

As for the character herself? She just stands in front of the mirror with the make-up dripping from her face, scratch marks on her hands, furious at them both. ∎

The Tower of Babel

Written with Arnold Sachar

And the Lord said, "Come, let us go down, and there confuse their language, that they may not understand one another's speech."
(Genesis 11:6-7)

Israel has a right to exist
The self-determination of the Palestinian people
The PLO terrorists are two-legged beasts
Israeli atrocities outrage the American people
They always blame the Jews
Well, that's the nature of war
The Begin and Sharon government
The idea of Palestine
The Soviet Union protests Israel's naked aggression. It is a threat
    to all peace-loving peoples
It's good that Jews are not acting like victims anymore
I'm anti-Zionist, not anti-Semitic
Why don't they ever blame the PLO
Begin and Sharon aren't Jews
Never again
The PLO are two-legged beasts
Judeo-Nazis
The 1967 borders
Israel is the best defense against Soviet penetration of the Middle
    East
The Palestinians have a backward culture
The positive elements of the Reagan Plan
Our national interest
The Jews made the desert bloom
Judea and Samaria
Security
Arafat is hinting at a two-state solution
Blood libel

The Jews are struggling over their souls
Zionism is racism
The self-determination of the Palestinian people
The protest in Israel over the massacres shows the vitality of
    Israeli democracy
Palestine is Arab land
Israel has a right to exist
We are all Semites
We have to get back to the Camp David accords
The Zionist ideal
We have to wait until after the inquiry and get all the facts
The Israelis are alienating world opinion
How could such an atrocity occur in the twentieth century
We can't be even-handed
The Arab states should have absorbed all those refugees for years
Operation Peace for Galilee
The PLO doesn't speak for the Palestinian people
A homeland
The peace process
Christian militiamen
Jews should not criticize each other in public, because we are all
    part of the same family
The self-determination of the Palestinian people
Israel has a right to exist
Mopping-up operations
Revolution till victory
We are not terrorists
Occupied land
What about the arms caches
PLO fighters
Don't blame the Jews
The violence of the oppressed is of a different order than the
    violence of the oppressor
We expect a higher standard from a democracy
Israeli Defense Force
Jews have used up the moral collateral of the Holocaust

The PLO charter

A free and independent Lebanon

What the Israelis did to the Palestinians is the same as what the
Germans did to the Jews

A great victory for the Palestinian people

Begin equals Hitler

UN Resolution 242

We had to do it in order to survive

The West Bank and the Gaza Strip

The excesses of people driven to desperation

What do they want from one little nation surrounded by a sea of
hostile nations

Who is Reagan to tell us what to do

The Fez Peace Plan

The Camp David accords

It has become a Goliath; it no longer is a David

Israel has a right to exist

Arafat is the same as Hitler

Weinberger and Shultz

The last bargaining chip

Decades of tribal warfare

The return of the Golan Heights

A confederation with Jordan

The Red Crescent estimates

Never again

The root cause is

The soldiers showed great courage

The self-determination of the Palestinian people

An outpost of democracy

A democratic secular state

Everyone is entitled to a homeland

Arafat is loved by his people

The oil interests

The Jews have lost their souls

Israel is a light unto the nations

The idea of Palestine will never die

We are all Semites
Revenge
Israel has a right to exist
The self-determination of the Palestinian people
The Golan Heights
They overestimated the number of casualties
Dr. George Habash
How come the media always favors them
What about the arms caches
Civilians are always killed in wars
The PLO hides behind the skirts of women and children
We admire moral Jews
They held Israel to a standstill
How could Christians do such a thing
We are grateful to our Soviet allies
We are grateful to our American allies
Israel has a right to exist
The self-determination of the Palestinian people
Because of all the years of suffering... ∎

November, 1982

In the Audience

For Pete Wilson

1

A MAN IN HIS late forties sits on a bench in Washington Square Park. He is disheveled and out of sorts. He gestures casually in the air as he makes his point. Ideol, ideology, ideol, he says over and over again. His manner is that of a teacher in front of a small class. Or that of a man, a man of opinion, being interviewed on television. A woman not yet old rocks violently back and forth a few benches away trying to release some violent inner pain.

2

It is Christmas time. On sale, green shower soap in the shape of a microphone.

3

Maxwell throws Allison's book aside. It is a study on language. He is jealous and in a rage. Perceptions formalized. Thoughts codified. Maxwell Berman cannot follow what is being said. His mind is in a blur. A real emptiness is slipping through those structures, he thinks angrily. No, a passionate heart is beating through those structures. His own heart beats wildly. And he lies stricken, almost as if in love.

Inside a car. A scene remembered. In the front seat a dialogue. Karla, dark, intense, a fine public speaker, turns to her friend Norman and says, "You can always interpret what I have to say. You make clear sense of it." Norman suddenly pink faced answers, "You're the one with so much to say."

Short little outbursts. Short political essays. That is the limit of Maxwell's work. A year of thought into thirty words, maybe three hundred, maybe twelve hundred. And the words definitely need an easily recognizable context to give them any sort of meaning. For by themselves they do not create a world. He cannot "invent" a world. In such a way is his imagination limited. So he cannot call himself a poet. He is a marginal polemicist, attached to the moment, engaged in obscure skirmishes.

Maxwell picks up Allison's book again. Why does she want him for a friend? Why would any of them want to know him? It was as if he were a girl who had learned how to flatter, smile, be bright. And they could imagine him to be as they wished him to be. Those of the world of books. Resigned caretakers of Knowledge, he thinks; suddenly he is angry again. Why do they take it for granted he knows what they know?

Maybe they are drawn to him the way social scientists are drawn to shrewd peasants or bright-eyed black children: to accumulate and codify and pepper their works with vignettes and little quotations of life. He is repelled and he is frightened. He wants their acceptance.

4

The shutters are closed bringing the room into darkness. "For final relaxation, everyone in the corpse position," the voice of the Yoga instructor, authoritative, reassuring. "On your back, eyes closed, feet a foot and a half apart, arms slightly away from your sides, palms up, turn your head from side to side until comfortable." The voice changes: "By the process of auto-suggestion..." It is no longer authoritative, rather it is mechanically commanding. A mind control machine, thinks Maxwell. More precisely it is as if a small cassette recorder had been implanted in his brain. "By the process of auto-suggestion you will relax, completely relax. My toes will relax," the voice continues, "my toes will relax, my toes are relaxed. My ankles will relax, my ankles will relax..."

Allison lies alongside Maxwell. Her toenails are painted bright orange. The room is at rest. Maxwell lies still, sweat from his forehead running down the sides of his face. Subtle smells released by the sweat from his groin enter his nostrils. Maxwell remembers resting after masturbation: Licking my semen from my fingers, I relax, completely relax.

But for the voice, the room is silent. And the voice soon will disappear. This is the part of the class Maxwell most looks forward to. The *asanas* are arranged to bring one into a state where consciousness is altered. And the room itself is transformed into a sanctuary, a place for meditation, reflection. Occasionally the silence will be broken, and Maxwell jarred, by a loud noise from the street or by the sweet chiming front doorbell of the *ashram* itself.

Allison's thin arms rest by her side. Her fingers are relaxed, completely relaxed. She is aware of the absence of pain. Deeply etched lines on her forehead disappear during final relaxation. Life force energy flows through her body and she feels herself young and supple.

From the very first moment they met, Maxwell had felt a powerful, though peculiarly limited, almost compulsive pull towards Allison. It was as if Allison had drilled two fingers through his chest, touching his heart but for an instant, then pulled her fingers out as quickly as she could, leaving the part that she touched burning with love. And so a part of his heart no bigger than a quarter was totally in love with Allison. And for the full year they have known each other it has never increased or diminished in size.

During the first months of their friendship Maxwell and Allison would meet every couple of weeks for half an hour or forty-five minutes, usually in the late afternoon in a coffee house or restaurant. They would meet in a space in Allison's tight, carefully structured schedule. Maxwell who had less to do could more or less be the one to accommodate.

Their meetings were often tense and peculiar. They would speak past each other. They would both be dull. Allison would look up at the ceiling. Maxwell would talk past her shoulder. Allison would withdraw. Maxwell would grow panicky and start speaking compulsively, speaking loudly with uncharacteristic bravado. And the more Maxwell would talk the more Allison would withdraw. And the more she would withdraw the more he would talk. Allison would feel she was drowning or she was being consumed. Once, in the street, she grabbed her chest and grew faint. "Please, no more," she demanded. Whenever he left her Maxwell would feel relieved. It's not worth it, he would think. And then a half hour later he would be flooded with affection and longing.

The tension between them in part was over aspiration and life style. Allison, the author of a book on linguistics, though in the grip of a tenure struggle, was in a partial way being rewarded for her work. She felt, however, that she did not allow herself free rein, either in her work, for her theories always seemed to stop at the point of breakthrough, or in her life style, which was subtly but significantly upwardly mobile. Allison in short was the very good student who had grown up to be the very good scholar. In turn she was to receive the proper social rewards. She was extremely competent in her work and she defended her areas of competence with a ferocity that she hated, for it symbolized her own complicity in the limits placed on her imagination. She could not allow herself to imagine herself as more than competent. She was the Prisoner of Competence. She wanted to break free.

Maxwell in turn was not able to write a book or produce a body of work. He didn't even try. He was the poor student who had either been broken by the system or had somehow managed to cut himself free from its socialization and was brilliant and daring. His essays were usually very short, condensed, and often beautiful. They were small meditations. To Maxwell they seemed alternately slight and deep. He wrote them only occasionally. There were long periods of inertia.

"You are either a writer or you are not," someone once told him. "And you write thirty variations of the same fantasy," he replied, rupturing their friendship.

His short pieces, while having a validity of their own, symbolized for Maxwell his own imprisonment. They legitimated his passivity. They suggested unusual potential and yet they hid the full range of Maxwell's concerns and understandings which if revealed might be less significant than he wished to imagine.

And Maxwell always imagined himself on a grand scale. Important thinker, huge recognition, tremendous respect and influence.

Maxwell and Allison, two talented insecure people, symbiotically locked, would meet fairly regularly. One day Maxwell blew up. "I'm always in the interstices of your life," he said with a flourish. "I'm neither your friend nor your colleague. I'm neither in your public life nor your private life."

Allison answered, "There are certain things, very intimate things, that I can tell you. Other things I make a conscious decision not to. It must be painful and confusing. Our conversations are stilted. There is something twisted in our friendship." And with a flourish of her own, "From now on I will be consistently less intimate."

Except for an occasional chance encounter where they would both be polite and formal, Allison and Maxwell did not speak for two months. One cold dismal afternoon marching in a demonstration Allison came over to Maxwell and after a few moments asked him if he would like to take Yoga with her. "It might help center you," she said with a smile. She herself had been taking it for a couple of months and was feeling very good about it.

Maxwell came to Yoga initially to be near Allison. But their meetings in class have only been random and occasional. Maxwell came alone more often than not and the classes themselves have taken on a certain importance.

There are moments of unease, even dread. He always enters the room with caution. Painful memories surface as body tension is released. Maxwell is not very loose yet or supple. He has trouble with the *asanas*. His legs feel like match sticks, thin, brittle. And he can feel naked in his awkwardness.

"This is not a competitive environment," an instructor inevitably says when either Maxwell or someone else is particularly clumsy or slow. And Maxwell can always hear the unease barely concealed by these words. The instructors' startling grace, thinks Maxwell, is not the result of inner quiet but is achieved by sheer will. They fear abandonment as persons and are ashamed of their bodies.

The experiences in Yoga are charged and dangerous. Bodies sweaty, vulnerable. Intense awareness and the suggestion of common understanding. Something powerful is taking place. Strange unexpected feelings surface and consciousness is altered. Possibilities for betrayal hang heavy in the room. A chance word, a foolish observation, can be particularly painful. Comments such as "We are not a Mickey Mouse organization. The weekend retreat is well organized and efficient," or "Yoga sure can make your day," can be particularly jarring. They underline the split in consciousness of people who are deep within a common experience.

Contemplation, silence, community, a dark sexuality are at the core of Maxwell's social vision. Fear of death and of life freeze the body and the spirit. Destruction, war machines, grinding social injustice, brutal nation states grow out of this terror. And the social structures take on a life and history of their own, and constrict human and social possibilities even further. In Yoga, as in absorbing conversation, or in an intense sexual encounter, one briefly is able to glimpse a state different from what is. It is terrifying and often not very clear. But one has stepped outside everyday experience and consciousness. Things can be different. And even if only that has become clear, something significant and dangerous has taken place.

And so when Maxwell distances himself too sharply from the people in the room, seizing on their vulgarity or their narrowness, he does so as much out of his own fear of illumination as out of desire to protect himself from false experience.

Our fingers will touch, our fingers will touch, our fingers touch, a hidden smile forms inside his restful face.

Loud disco music from the street, loud frantic voices from the street break into the room. And across Maxwell's mind an exuberant Christopher Lasch, wearing silver pants and a scarlet jersey, skates and dances to the pounding disco beat. And as suddenly as he had appeared, he disappears as the music and voices fade up the block.

And somewhere in the corner of his mind a long forgotten scene emerges. And he watches as it passes before him.

A fund raising for the then faltering now defunct Free University. Allison, whom he had not yet met, was being introduced by Joan McBride, economist, workplace organizer, movement heavy.

"I would like to introduce my very dear friend who will sing some songs she has written."

They theorize, they organize, and they sing their very own songs, Maxwell remembers thinking.

Allison's hair, dark blonde, was cut much shorter then. He noticed her gold wedding ring as she played her guitar. She wore a dark blue work shirt with a red star on her collar.

Maxwell remembered how uneasy he felt as he watched her. He hoped her songs would be good. He hoped her songs would be bad. Never quite comfortable with the people at the school, he would often make clumsy attempts at friendship. He, however, was very difficult. He was insistent, often unyielding. He would polarize and provoke. He felt beleaguered. But if there was one thing that defined the Free University it was that everyone felt that they were part of a beleaguered minority. There was much unease and rancor. But little lasting bitterness. People without much social power had gathered to form a place to share ideas, study, and in some cases work out political strategy. The people were often paranoid and defensive. And Maxwell was no exception. He admired some of the people, basically he respected everyone, but more often than not he was in a state of agitation.

Maxwell remembers how his mind strained that night as he juggled hollow perceptions, idle perceptions to make himself feel important.

Wedding ring. Worldly. Adult. Domesticated. Complacent. Worn out. Defeated. Red star. Adventure. Break from domestic

51

stranglehold. Identification with people in struggle. Anger at injustice. Sexy. Sexy symbol of entrenched state power.

The event took place three years ago, two years before he met Allison, one year before the break-up of her eight-year marriage. It is the impressions of her songs, more than the actual words, that have remained with him.

The songs could not be easily categorized. They had within them conflicting strains. One would emerge, then fade, quickly replaced by another. It was as if some conflict and struggle were taking place within the songs themselves. The songs would cut deep and then pull back, becoming almost compulsively light hearted. Her songs had a sad playful humor, but it was a humor more debunking than radically subversive. Maxwell sensed at the time a tension between an almost timid venturing forth and a wild yet inhibited rage.

Later in the night the room broke into a chorus of song. Folk songs, political songs, popular songs, religious songs. As is often the case, the folk and political songs were sung with an earnest animated enthusiasm. And the pop and religious songs with an ironic, self-satisfied, near manic frenzy. There was plenty to drink, dope to smoke, food to eat.

And in walked Joe DePerri. Short and round, rosy cheeked from the cold winter night, Joe DePerri joined the chorus of voices. Someone handed him a beer. "Sonorous music," he once wrote in an essay on mass culture, "maintains routine perception by being sweet and soothing." Joe DePerri took a drink from his beer, hitched up his pants, deepened his voice, giving it a rough edge. But his voice soon became melodious and high pitched. Occasionally it would crack. And he would collect himself and his voice would deepen then grow high again.

Joe DePerri's presence charged the room. Singing became more animated. People more alert. This was often the case. Even rooms that were dull often became transformed when he entered.

Joe DePerri had a galvanizing personality. He set things in motion. He started magazines, political organizations. He helped start the Free University. Joe DePerri was a fine public speaker, a good careful inspiring teacher, with an acute social imagination and powerful analytic gifts. He had if not a deeply poetic nature, a forceful and almost joyous polemical style. His written work could be dense, even labored, but more often than not it had the feel of a working-class ballad. If there was one major flaw in his character, it would be that he was morally obtuse. He could not be trusted.

Maxwell enjoyed watching Joe DePerri when a serious new problem arose: sensing the confusion and the shifting opinion in the room, Joe DePerri would panic at his loss of control, and then make up arguments on the run, leapfrogging ahead to resume his place of leadership. There would be a slight break in his voice, a slight color to his cheeks, revealing to Maxwell just when Joe DePerri had lost his integrity.

Round, long-winded, shiny-faced men have always had a special place in Maxwell's heart. He would for example make it a point to be home whenever Hubert Humphrey would defend the Vietnam War on television. Something in his enthusiasm, in his earnestness, would draw him to the man. Hubert Humphrey would say and, more importantly, believe whatever it was that was required of him. He was in the fullest sense the suppliant. Maxwell imagined him as the servant of the people.

One night in a heavy rainstorm, Hubert Humphrey greeted President Johnson at the airport. He stood there so erect, holding his umbrella over President Johnson's head, the rain pouring down his beautiful wet face, the floodlights shining off his shiny bald head. He had given himself over totally to his President. Hubert Humphrey looked almost saintly that night, deeply transformed by sacrifice.

Joe DePerri, charismatic, inspiring, morally obtuse, occasionally abusive, generated resentment as well as admiration. People felt manipulated by him. "It's as if we were puppets on a string, here to play out his fantasies," was a common complaint.

In one rare and revealing outburst, Joe DePerri answered a room full of people angry at what they perceived to be his

cavalier treatment of them by saying, "The movement is frag-
mented and there is no sense of community. I know almost
everyone here. I brought you all together and there is no other
way you would have met. This project grew out of my imagina-
tion and out of my inspiration. It had to grow out of someone's
imagination. I'm limited, I'm just a person. This project can be
redeemed, transformed by all of you working together. I'm tired.
And God damn it leave me alone." And he dashed out of the
room and sat on the steps trembling.

Arbyne all night stood off to one side. She did not join the
singing. Looking through slightly tinted glasses, her eyes, clear
and excited, would dart curiously from person to person, taking
in everyone in the room. Her curly hair, black and gray, formed
a bluish halo around her.

The communal singing ended. Allison had left much ear-
lier, but she was not all that important to Maxwell that night.
People moved about starting conversations. Others went to
another room where there was music to dance to. Joe DePerri
moved from person to person, speaking intimately and with ani-
mation. Each conversation, however brief, would end only after
a small but significant catharsis. Arbyne came up to him. He
greeted her warmly. "What did they think about my piece?" she
asked before even saying hello. "We decided that it wasn't quite
right for our purposes," he said officially.

"What do you mean by 'we'? Two days ago you said that
you liked it. Well I'm upset."

"That's tough," he said suddenly, his face freezing into the
face of a tough guy. He grew silent as he savored the force in his
voice.

Arbyne wanted to cry but wouldn't. The thought of him
trying to console her, of his putting his arm around her made her
almost shake with disgust.

"I'll bring it elsewhere then."

This was not what he wanted. "If you only rework it," said
Joe DePerri. He panicked, his voice softened. "I think you just
have to fix up the beginning."

54

Liar, she thought. Her head pounded. She said, "I like the beginning. And I don't want to talk about it anymore. Besides I don't like you."

Joe DePerri grew despondent and started to speak very fast, charmingly.

Arbyne felt herself weaken. She tightened up her body and her face became a mixture of anger and disdain.

Joe DePerri crumbled into sudden depression. Arbyne walked away. Joe DePerri looked quickly, anxiously around the room. He settled upon a young man, a psychiatrist, and soon they became locked, absorbed in conversation.

"Feel the awareness come back into your body," a distant voice reaches Maxwell. "Everybody sit up. Om. Om. Om. Om shanti, shanti, shanti." One final prayer. Maxwell's eyes are still half closed and he smiles at Allison. It is not so much desire he feels, thinks Maxwell, but the need to be near her, wake up next to her. Still imagining himself just waking up, he brushes her shoulder as he passes. Allison quickly thanks the instructor for a very fine class. Whoever is dressed first will wait for the other on the stoop outside.

5

Allison, alone in her bed, strokes her belly gently. She touches a nipple playing with it until it is firm, licks her fingers, sucking them half unconsciously.

It is still raining hard as it had all weekend. "To be in bed with someone on such a rainy day, huddled together under the covers, doubly emphasizes the idea of shelter," she thinks as she pulls the covers over her head. "Lovers always rush to meet in the monsoon season. It is a relief from the bareness."

Her face flushes with sudden erotic feeling. And as suddenly she feels broken, dried out. "Burned out," she thinks. Pain grips her stomach. And she does not want to come out from under the covers.

The paper she will deliver comes into focus. Important faculty members will be there. To displease them might jeopardize even further her chances for tenure. But some students of hers will be there as well as some faculty members who support her. She won't be totally alone.

Her hair feels stringy, damp. The fingers on her hand ache. Arthritic hands and I'm so young. It can only get worse. And the pain in her fingers, though not often severe, appears to foreshadow a lifetime of pain. It is something she does not often think about. She has put it to one side. But it is there, muted but continuous.

The weekend had been one of controlled panic. She would look at her paper, then type up whole new pages at a time, only to discard what she had just written. She would read sections of her paper into her tape recorder, and play it back imagining herself a member of the tenure committee, sitting in the lecture hall, holding the frightened candidate's future in her hands. And she even read the beginning of her paper into her own telephone answering machine. "This is Allison Kramer, the subject of my paper is patterns of speech differences according to sex and class in the urban Northeast, if you wish to critique me please wait until you hear the tone." She had actually done this and would not answer the phone for five hours. She smoked dope on and off all weekend. Her mind would float out into reverie and then crash back into anxiety.

Allison washes her hair, combing it out slowly, relaxing herself. She smokes a cigarette, and then puts it out quickly. She makes toast and tea. She puts on a little eyeshadow, a little rouge and some lipstick. She puts on hooped earrings, a silver necklace and an elegant if not extravagant blouse. She flirts with herself in the mirror, touches her cheek. Allison's hands begin to tremble. The pain in her fingers increases, an intense throbbing pain. She swallows two aspirin. Throws on her raincoat. And leaves for school.

On the subway Allison carefully observes the passengers. She divides them into age, sexual, and racial groupings. She imagines who she would like to sleep with, what combinations of people and where. She knows the stations by heart, but starts testing her memory. She feels a brief satisfaction as each predicted station comes into view. It was a game she played with her brother as a child. They would compete with each other over whose memory was better. They liked to make faces at the passengers on the subway and at each other. Their faces so beautiful and rubbery.

Allison's mind unexpectedly focuses on the last night she and Joe DePerri had ever spent together as lovers. It was not a love affair that she often thought about. It was brief and not very memorable or painful. And it had been well over a year since it ended. And now she can think only of that night. The scenes of that night replaying themselves with astonishing clarity. She has almost completely forgotten they had been lovers. There is a casualness and affection and mutual regard that they now have for each other. But she feels bitter as she remembers that night.

Joe DePerri answered the door carrying a saucepan. I'll be with you in a minute, he said rushing back into the kitchen. Allison walked into the living room, and she noticed herself gazing upon it as if for the first time. She had been there four or five times before. Now she was seeing it in a totally different light.

The tenure pressure had been severe that week. She had come here in order to be catered to, waited on, to luxuriate in being attended to. Joe DePerri had said, "Tonight you will just sit and relax. And you will see what a really good cook I am."

But Allison could not relax. She found herself rather detached and anthropologically observant. She looked around the room and for the first time had a real sense of unease. For the first time the bookshelves, the art objects, everything about the room seemed to be arranged for effect. The room in fact was impressive. Everything about it suggested a person of genuinely serious and critical intelligence, a person of fine taste.

The books were arranged by topic. Excellent books, serious topics. Allison felt cold as she made her observations. The mahogany stained bookshelves were bracketed to the walls. The shelves on one wall contained fiction, both contemporary and classical, while on another wall were arranged scholarly and critical works of history and social science. Previously she had been impressed by the range and taste of his reading, but now she felt, and for reasons she could not fully understand, that there was something manipulative about it all. She tried to pull herself away from her perceptions. But she could not do so for more than a few seconds. She felt not so much that Joe DePerri was trying to manipulate her or any passing stranger into outright subservience, but rather as if the structure of the bookshelves provided a framework or scaffolding for his own egotism. This reflected not a conscious desire to control or manipulate, thought Allison, but rather a massive self-absorption whose effect was the same.

Allison thought of Joan McBride, whose books were piled helter-skelter on her bookshelves, other books lying on tables or chairs. And she thought of Joe DePerri's own work room, his bedroom with papers scattered on his desk, his clothes thrown on the floor and chairs. But it was the living room that he presented to the world. Allison became upset again. There is nothing wrong with beautiful books, she told herself. His books are not detached from his main concerns, thought Allison, they are books he has read, books he has studied.

Joe DePerri called from the kitchen. "I'll talk to you in a minute," he said. "Why don't you pick out a record." She was relieved to be able to perform a task. But similar thoughts came to her as she attempted to choose a record. The records were not arranged in such impeccable order. But they were placed on a beautiful shelf. There were fewer records, but well chosen. The best jazz, best rock, best blues, best classical. Pairs of names as if mocking her flashed in front of Allison's eyes. Vivaldi and Mozart, Charles Mingus and Charlie Parker, Bessie Smith and Billie Holiday, Bob Dylan and The Rolling Stones. A new thought made her smile: occasionally Joe DePerri would spend hours listening to records of social protest, mostly militant workers' ballads, and he would sing along with them, his voice breaking whenever he would get too excited.

Allison picked Vivaldi's *The Four Seasons.*

"Oh, *The Four Seasons*," Joe called from the kitchen. "I particularly like Neville Marriner's performance."

Allison checked the cover quickly with annoyance to see if it was the Neville Marriner recording. It was. She was both curious and upset, suspicious and off balance. Was he patronizing her, she wondered. Was he just showing off his general knowledge of music, or, as she wanted so badly to believe, was he just expressing simple enthusiasm about the recording?

She smoked a cigarette but could not listen to the music.

"I'm making lemon and garlic salad dressing. Come in and smell it as I put it together. I discovered the recipe just a couple of days ago."

Allison went into the kitchen. "Do you like your roast beef rare?" asked Joe.

"Yes," she answered.

Joe looked at the clock. "I'd better take it out within five minutes then. While I'm making the salad dressing do you think you could pull apart the lettuce leaves and slice the tomatoes."

The roast beef, the fresh lemon and garlic, the olive oil carried her along with the impetus of their good smells. She found herself separating the lettuce leaves and quartering the tomatoes. He said he was going to do it all himself. "I'm going to do it all by myself from scratch," he had said. And for an intense moment, Allison felt resentful and constricted. But Joe looked so engaged and earnest, even loving, as he prepared the dinner for her. But the ambiguity of the situation did not leave her. For once she was aware of the disparity between Joe's genuine concern and interest and his massive egotism, subtly manipulative while hardly noticeable.

Allison had been uneasy in the living room, and now she was standing in the kitchen preparing the meal. She was confronted by false promises subtly broken. Allison turns over the phrase in her mind as she sits on the subway, still not halfway to school.

"I spoke to Robert Laszlo," Joe DePerri said as they sat down to eat. "I told him how excited I was about your book. He told me that he remembered Fischer's review in my magazine and was interested in it. And he'd meant to get around to reading it. And now that I brought it up, he will definitely review it for *The Nation*."

"Robert Laszlo will review my book," Allison screamed out, her whole face lighting up.

Joe smiled at her, a smile mixed with delight and pleasure.

So that's my reward for being a good lay. The thought sprang suddenly and unexpectedly. It almost choked her. God, that's unfair. And her face turned into a mask. But quickly the pleasure and excitement of Robert Laszlo reviewing her book returned.

Taking a chance, she asked, "Did you finally work things out with Arbyne?"

"She's a very bright woman," answered Joe, "but she is being totally unreasonable."

"What do you mean?" asked Allison.

"Each new manuscript becomes crazier and crazier. A whole new section of this one is devoted to the occult and astrology. She calls them the female sciences. It's pseudo-spiritual nonsense. She won't change a sentence. And she is not writing metaphorically. She means every word of it."

"Well, I'm sure there is more to it than that."

"I don't care if there is more to it. It's regressive and it's empty."

Allison grew stone silent. You boorish pig, her mind screamed, any creative woman is going to be driven crazy in this culture.

As Allison now remembers her thoughts she is filled with shame. She had been thinking like a stupid social worker. Who was she to imagine Arbyne as crazy? Nine out of ten times Arbyne will make wild bizarre leaps and land on her head. Her theories are often half-baked and compulsively thrown out. But she has also illuminated the darkness, if only briefly, and she has penetrated, if only randomly, areas of concern seldom if ever explored.

Allison returns to that night.

"It will be a long hard haul," Joe said, speaking of tenure. "The cutbacks, the firings, make each opening that much more precious and difficult to secure. As radicals and as Marxists it is difficult enough. They tell us," his voice grew indignant, "that our ideology," he said the word with a bitter mockery, "informs and distorts our objectivity. They have no ideology, right? Their ideological hegemony is so taken for granted. They think *that* is the world." Joe's face grew soft. "And as a woman," he continued, "it is doubly and triply oppressive. Only so many positions can be filled. No one will say it outright. But we all know that it's true."

"Well," he said trying to be kind, "security can be its own prison." He paused for a moment and then smiled. "Well, if you don't get it, you can always raise a family."

Allison laughed. She answered with a retort that she cannot remember.

And the next morning she woke all knotted inside.

Where did he get the nerve to put up bookshelves that would be so imposing. To have such impeccable taste. To know that it was Neville Marriner. He asks me over to dinner and I have to help him prepare the salad. I can always raise a family. Very, very funny.

Jokes like that blunt the edge of sexual hatred, thinks Allison as she nears her stop. They allow us to get through dangerous situations. But they camouflage the social conflict and they obscure the true extent of oppression. She thinks how often she would joke back, share a laugh, be petulant. But deep down she always felt humiliation and rage. Filled with embarrassment and self-loathing, she thinks of how she has acquiesced to such a process.

One more relationship down the drain, Allison remembers thinking as she left Joe DePerri's apartment.

Allison pulls out the paper she is to deliver. This whole fucking nightmare is going to go on forever. Any mistake, a wrong word and it all can explode. She always has to be careful. She has to flatter but not be too obvious about it. Every moment she is on edge. Every step is like being on a minefield. Every sentence is a semantic minefield. She must mute her radical perceptions, reducing them to scattered insights. She must keep her prose stiff and dense and be scrupulous with her references. Why don't I ditch the whole thing, she constantly asks herself. But security is very important to her. She does not want to float, to flounder about. And jobs are not that easy to come by.

Allison has become edgy and paranoid. She read a crucial paragraph to four different friends. Three said it should stay in. One said she should cut out the whole paragraph, that it was too politically charged. And Allison screamed that her friend was just out to kill her.

The rain has turned into a gentle drizzle. Somewhere between dream and nightmare Allison Kramer walks the five blocks to the campus. Twenty minutes early the lecture hall is already half filled.

6

Sarah Kendall is giving a reading. The crowd is steadily filling up the spacious auditorium of the Greenwich Village school. Maxwell Berman stands by the door watching people as they enter.

"Are you still an intellectual?" Suzanne says approaching Maxwell. She leans forward, "Or are you now into using your hands?" She has always been this way. She would ask a question, aggressive and intimate and totally unpleasant. Suzanne's face looks gaunt and haunted. "God, she's aged," thinks Maxwell. He has not seen her during the two years since the Free University folded. "Some of us from the old school have taken over an old precinct house," says Suzanne. "We're going to build a garden on the roof." "That sounds nice," answers Maxwell, sneaking a look around the room wondering who else had come.

"I just recovered from a nervous breakdown," she continues. "The tranquilizers have dehydrated my body. I've lost twenty pounds." "Are you okay?" asks Maxwell, wishing she would leave. He knows he should feel concerned but he can't. "Do you know that I just got out of the hospital," Suzanne says, moving to a new person. "I had a nervous breakdown. They put me on tranquilizers that dehydrated my body. I lost twenty pounds. Did you hear that we've renovated the old precinct house? We don't know whether we should concentrate on theory or practice. I think we should do both. Don't you?"

It was already twenty minutes after Sarah Kendall was scheduled to read.

"There's Joe DePerri," someone shouts out. Joe DePerri nods to the voice and scans the room.

Allison walks in with a group of friends. She waves casually to Maxwell. He has the feeling she is still annoyed with him. He had spoken to her on the phone yesterday and read her a statement he had written. It called for the release of Dan White, the murderer of gay rights leader Harvey Milk, on the grounds that the type of hatred which leads to murdering "deviants" and the fear which leads to locking up murderers amount to the same thing. When Maxwell asked Allison if she would sign the statement she explained, "God, Maxwell, you're always trying to provoke people. Well, this statement I'm not going to sign." Robert Laszlo also would not sign the statement. He told Maxwell that he didn't disagree with it, but he said that as a gay man he wanted to talk about institutionalized homophobia, not about the nature of punishment. Maxwell sees Joan McBride. He goes over to her and asks, "Have you read my Dan White statement?" "I thought it was basically amoral," she answers.

Her comment makes no sense. There is too much noise, too much activity to ask her what she means.

Sarah Kendall enters the auditorium. The applause is heartfelt. She responds to the greeting with a slight, almost timid wave. She seems both shy and overcome as she makes her way to the stage. Sarah smiles broadly to a friend, hugs two or three people, squeezes an arm. Throughout the room people turn to friends and say, "God, isn't she wonderful." Affection and love pour out to her as she approaches the microphone; there is a sense of well-being. The people this night have come as much to celebrate her for the person she is as to hear her read. She is an artist of rare gifts and a public figure of rare courage. She speaks with wisdom and simplicity and this has endeared her to her public. And it is these very qualities that Maxwell Berman will focus on this night with such dark and bitter rage.

There is a terrible defensiveness, analyzes Maxwell, as she introduces the first story she is planning to read. He understands the source of her defensiveness all too well. The projected wisdom of her persona, like his own stumbling incoherence, protects her from the academicians and the intellectually accomplished; people she at once fears and is greatly drawn to. They in turn are often struck by her vitality and her intelligence. But she knows that she is not one of them; they fear her. And she herself fears her own vitality, thinks Maxwell. She has let her folksiness limit the full range of her subversive spirit.

When Sarah Kendall speaks, a simple anecdote, a shrug of the shoulder can unravel the most sophisticated apologetics for injustice and death. Yet somewhere within the simplicity of her manner there lies a rigid ideological mind, thinks Maxwell, a mind that negotiates its way through the world along a narrow corridor of concerns. And for Sarah Kendall to venture outside this narrow corridor causes her terrible anxiety. In the face of a politics that challenges her own, she can turn vicious.

Maxwell remembers a night many years before when Sarah Kendall was asked how young men should respond to the draft. Her voice grew thin as she answered, "It is our moral obligation to do whatever is necessary to stop this war. Look at the terrible sacrifices of the Vietnamese people. It is a moral obligation for young men to turn in their draft cards." And her tone implied that there was something unforgivably self-indulgent about not exposing oneself to danger in the struggle against injustice. Whether vicious or puritanical, it was very cruel, thinks Maxwell, suddenly re-experiencing the sense of guilt he felt while listening to her answer. And he knew there would have been no way for him to challenge her that night without being humiliated, for Sarah Kendall, in moments of panic, could treat even people of vision as if they were agents of death.

The room has grown very hot. People throughout have remained very attentive, engaged in the experience, deeply responsive. And the more enthusiastic the response the more Maxwell withdraws into himself. Each turn of phrase repels him. Each word, each gesture, each response. The appreciative laughter makes him cringe. The affirmation of community further separates him from the rest of the audience.

He thinks of Arbyne secluded in her vision, driven to near madness by abuse. "The differences between what you and others have to say are significant," Maxwell would tell her, "but not all that significant." "You'll see some day how serious they are," she would answer. Tiny seemingly obscure skirmishes, she would insist, might very well determine the whole direction and spirit of a movement.

Sarah Kendall's voice breaks as she reads. There are sobs in the room, then laughter.

Headlines shape your consciousness, Maxwell's thoughts accuse the audience. Code words substitute for thought. You rest so secure in a closed arena of consciousness. Half of you are always filled with new concerns: nuclear power plants, sterilization abuse, medical cutbacks. Always instant anger, instant all the facts, instant full of opinions. Instantly mobilized. And the rest of you, the independent-minded, can't get absorbed in anything that is new. You choose so carefully which issues will engage you, at which injustices you will draw the line. You remain so complacent with explanations worked out so long ago.

Maxwell's eyes grow distant as he remembers two recent scenes.

At a conference on pornography a civil liberties lawyer was talking to a small group of people who had gathered around him. He took his pipe out of his thin, slightly opened mouth and said, "You should have seen the response when I defended the Klan." There was a twinkle in his eyes. The civil liberties lawyer was very pleased with himself. "I recognize all the dangers

and complexities of the situation, but nonetheless I believe..."
Nonetheless he remains so manly, willing to risk all for a principle. And in the face of women acting so irrationally against pornography, he knows how to maintain a consistent point of view.

Three women against pornography appeared on morning TV in front of a studio audience made up largely of midwestern housewives. "We have some trouble with the civil libertarians," one of them said to a whole roomful of people who had no sense of freedom. One woman from the audience spoke about how pornography pollutes. The three women against pornography nodded encouragingly. They would not speak about the hidden violence of the family. They would not speak of the everyday sexual and psychic dread of the women in the audience.

Maxwell is enraged by his recollections. He takes out his notebook that he always carries with him and writes: "The civil liberties lawyer does not understand the pervasive social madness, the manipulation of consciousness. He is secure in his homilies, for way down he thinks this is a free society. He thinks passing ERA will solve the problem of misogyny. He goes through life with his little formulations. He turns red in the face during heated discussion. Basically he is complacent."

Maxwell continues writing: "In the society of docile, frightened people, largely without will, the three women against pornography offer mind control as their program for social transformation. Destroy dangerous images, they say. They manipulate the fear and bigotry of imprisoned midwestern housewives. This to build a movement!!"

The reading will go on forever. His head spins, tears fill his eyes. He is slumped in his seat. The common understanding. The common pain. The common outrage. So deeply connected to the people. So split off. Everything is unraveling, unraveling. They are being thrown into different worlds. It is a rupture of love. The bond between Sarah and the audience grows stronger. "This is my favorite story," he hears a voice whisper. The separation is permanent.

The air in the auditorium has grown oppressively hot

and damp. Suddenly the reading is over. He files out with the crowd. He lingers outside, breathing in the cool spring air, resting against a car. The light from the street lamps comes from far overhead. He feels less enclosed.

Some people gather about in small circles, others leave quickly. He waits a while longer. Joe DePerri walks outside talking excitedly with two friends. Suzanne looks needfully from side to side. Joan McBride, busy as always, walks away with a strong determination.

"This is the community in resistance," thinks Maxwell. "The comic individuation of people," he writes in his notebook. "The comic individuation of the people in the community of resistance."

What does that mean, wonders Maxwell. Each person is ludicrous, partly distorted yet partly free. Does it matter? For a moment the people he knows seem like figures in a landscape of buildings and human activities. They were shaped by the society, they shaped the resistance to the society—well, he thinks, it can't be otherwise. He laughs at himself. He feels calm.

Allison calls over Maxwell. Clearly she is no longer annoyed at him. She and a few friends are speaking with Sarah. "Hi," says Maxwell. Allison extends her cheek to him. Maxwell kisses her quickly, then turns to Sarah and says, "It was a very beautiful reading." Sarah Kendall grabs his arm, squeezes it and smiles warmly. ■

Saturday Morning Sitting in a Café at 8:30 am Watching the Street Go By

Who on this street has woken up from a night of sex?
Who on this street has ever killed someone?
Who on this street is worried about a job?
Who on this street is late for an appointment?
Who on this street is enjoying the sun?
Who on this street wants a cup of coffee?
Who on this street is brooding about politics?
Who on this street has a bad leg?
Who on this street will be riding a bike?
Who on this street is angry at a dead mother?
Who on this street will hum a song?
Who on this street is tormented by a love gone wrong?
Who on this street will have trouble hailing a cab?
Who on this street drives a garbage truck?
Who on this street will enter a shop?
Who on this street will call a cop?
Who on this street knows that they're alive?
Who on this street harbors a burning rage?
Who on this street has hemorrhoids acting up?
Who on this street will seize a window of opportunity?
Who on this street thinks it's all an exercise in futility? ■

Street Smart

Jittery Joe is in the know
Slim Sam don't give a damn
Mad Maureen is a scream
Smiling Sally will never dally
Wicked Walter smashed his altar
Tired Tina ate her farina
Mad Minerva is here to serve ya
Mister Mac hit the sack
Caring Cora saved the torah
Jumping Jack took up the slack
Irritated Izzy is in a tizzy
Calculating Carl took on a snarl
Scheming Susan continues losin
Gangster Gina was never meana
Gang Green hit the scene
Killer Cohen heads for home
Stormin Sid put in his bid
Flatback Feingold is in the fold
Happy Helen carves watermelon
Rolling Rock put on a sock
World Weary is very teary
Tic Tac is finally back
Street Smart broke my heart ■

Random Thoughts on My Inability to Learn Languages

1.

I FIRST SAW ARNIE, my oldest and dearest friend, at a Free Speech rally at Queens College in New York City during a student strike. I think it was in 1962. This beautiful and intense figure moved from person to person, group to group, listening, speaking, engaged in the event with a seriousness much different than anyone else seemed to have. It was as if a spotlight followed him everywhere he went. Wherever he stood, it seemed as if something historic was at stake.

The next time I saw Arnie was in Spanish class. He looked spaced out, dazed, lost in some deep internal chaos. The only person more spaced out than me. Each day we would go around the room and have to translate a sentence from English to Spanish. Arnie was always the ninth person called on. I was always the twelfth. Neither of us ever got the answer right. One day I saw that the translations were in the back of the book. So I started memorizing answer 12. But Arnie never knew answer 9. So it really was answer 11 that I would have to give. Finally it dawned on me to memorize answer 11. Of course, that was the one time Arnie got the answer right. To this day we have never figured out how he did it.

2.

For nine years I went to Hebrew-speaking camp. Instead of learning Hebrew, I went off by myself shooting baskets. Even after nine years, I could say maybe 25 words. I couldn't say something as simple as "Please pass the sugar." I could read Hebrew to a degree, though I didn't know what most of the words meant. This is true of many Jews who pray. They can say and chant the prayers but don't know the literal meaning of the words. For three years running I was given the same primer to study from in camp. The only thing different was the technique of the teachers. The warm, embracing, encouraging technique of one of the teachers, while no more successful in helping me learn a word, has, as I write this, left me with a fond memory. And possibly some regrets for the frustration I must have caused.

3.

A friend from Japan entirely panicked at an anti-apartheid demonstration in Central Park. The sound system was awful. It was impossible to understand a word. She thought it was because her English was bad. Afterwards she just sat down in the street and started to cry. I've noticed that people when they are drunk or angry often speak a blue streak in a language they otherwise might have difficulty with. I suspect that a person in a strange country during a moment of heightened sexual arousal might get various languages all jumbled together.

4.

My father was a person not comfortable in any language. He came to the United States as a young boy from Hungary. He never really fully spoke Hungarian, though he was able to communicate okay in it. He never fully learned English, though he ran a business here. He was able to read newspapers and books in English. His problem was more in speaking and writing. And he could speak a smidgen of Yiddish. I often wonder what language his thoughts were in.

My father had to rely on his smarts. If he didn't know mathematical formulas, he could add and subtract and multiply and divide very quickly in his head. For his purposes, this was good enough. There was a point, of course, where this

71

wouldn't be sufficient. My cousin, a young and gifted mathematics professor, could not match my father in certain mathematical exercises. But by knowing the formulas, she could figure out certain problems that were way beyond the sheer force of my father's intelligence.

My mother was "better educated" than my father. She became an art historian. She writes English beautifully. And speaks fluently with a heavy Hungarian accent.

I think it is from my father, who by his wits could run circles around more "educated" people (I'm not talking about my mother here), that I developed some of my resistance to learning.

My resistance to language learning extends to computers, mathematics, physics, the social sciences, street slang, almost any and every language. Like my father, I can pick up things, just enough at times to get a sense of what is going on. But not enough to converse or move beyond the point where instinct and intuitive grasp can take me.

5.

My problems with English, my native language, are pretty acute. Only every so often can I write anything that makes any sense. Usually it is incoherent fragments written in a totally illegible scrawl that even I can't read. The scrawl translates itself into incomprehensible combinations of letters if I am attempting to write by typewriter. It is only very rarely that I am able to enter the space where I can communicate with written words. When I can, I can. It is almost as simple as that.

As I mentioned before, my father was never comfortable in any language. My friend Paula, on the other hand, seems more comfortable in Italian than her native English. It is as if she had been born into the wrong language. I remember seeing her, actually spying on her from a distance, speaking Italian to a friend. Her hand gestures, her facial gestures, her body language seemed so much more at home in Italian than in English. I spoke to her about what I had observed. She said yes, it was true. It is amazing to see people and the changes they go through with the language that they are speaking, how their gestures, the timbre of their voice, the depth of their laughter, their body language are affected by the language they are speaking. Sometimes these changes occur from one moment to the next.

6.

I was taught French in high school. I remember enjoying reciting a poem in class once.

Three years of Spanish in college. I visited Argentina a couple of years ago. Spanish made more sense there than in the classroom. In a limited way I was actually able to speak and understand it while I was there. I attend a poetry series in Brooklyn where a lot of the work is read in Spanish. While I don't understand much of what is read, I usually get real pleasure out of the event. This is also true of lectures and poetry readings in English, as well as various types of concerts. My mind rarely focuses in on what's in front of me. But often something important does enter my consciousness. This is why I'm never hurt if someone falls asleep at a reading I am giving.

I learned Hungarian from my cousin's mother as a child. My parents spoke English, not Hungarian, to each other at home. I think if I lived in Hungary for a year, Hungarian would be a language that I could learn to speak.

I can understand it when my relatives speak it. I have a much harder time when strangers speak it.

Hebrew? I still can't speak it. My ability to read it has diminished. But when I go to the synagogue to mourn my dead father, the sounds of prayer connect me deeply to him.

As for speaking English, it astounds me when I hear myself on tape to think that anyone can understand a word I say. Mostly sounds, a few expletives, a few key words, a bunch of you-knows, and that's about it. People have to work hard. Maybe that's the key. Or you know maybe they just I don't know. Anyway. ■

D. H. Melhem

MY MOTHER HAD JUST returned from three harrowing months of being in hospitals and rehab centers. She was half out of her mind, disoriented and frightened and angry. Nothing seemed to be able to pull her out of it.

She had a piece in the new issue of *And Then*, a magazine I co-create with some friends. D. H. sent me a very warm and insightful note about what my mother had written. D. H. was very kind to me during that time my mother was in the hospital. In all the years I knew her, she was always encouraging me and making me feel special and important.

I have turned everything upside down to try and find that note, but haven't yet been able to. Here though is an account of me showing the note to my mother.

"This is from one of the greatest poets in the country."

I read her the note. "This is a high compliment coming from her," I said.

"She's a very bright woman," my mother said.

The next day.
"What was it that your friend wrote about me?"

I read my mother the note. She repeated some of the words.

"I didn't tell you that she was Lebanese. And writes plays as well as poetry."

"And she likes my work?"

"Very much."

"What did she say about my work?" my mother asked me the next day.

I read her the note. "She knows what she is talking about," I said. "She is a great poet, one of the greatest in the whole country and she also writes literary criticism."

The next day.

"My friend, you know the Lebanese poet, is a big admirer of yours." I read her D. H.'s note again. My mother repeated the key phrases savoring them as she said them.

"She's very perceptive," my mother laughed. "It is wonderful you have such a great friend." ■

Two Faces of a Nazi Sympathizer

Written by Kato Laszlo Roth

IN 1948 WHEN FOR several weeks I visited my parents in Budapest, Hungary, I had one of the most interesting encounters and experiences of my life, when I met again my former German and Art History teacher, Dr. Ilona Hanvai. While I had a special aptitude for Art History, the German language was very hard for me and I never mastered it. The other Jewish girls in my class spoke German fluently.

I was frightened of Dr. Hanvai during my school years. Since I was not very good in the German language, she always drilled me in grammar while the other Jewish girls had the great privilege to be called upon to recite in German the great accomplishments of Hitler—like building good roads, creating jobs for everyone, stopping the inflation and others I can't recall. None of Hitler's brutality to non-Aryans was ever mentioned. The Jewish girls showed no emotions while reciting and I was fortunate that I was spared the experience. Actually, all of us Jewish girls were humiliated. I was tortured and put down by the constant drilling of grammar and being an example of stupidity, and others were forced to recite the great accomplishments of our enemy, in German.

In 1948 in Budapest, after not seeing her for 13 years, I happened to meet Dr. Hanvai by chance in the Hotel Gellert's indoor pool. I recognized her immediately and identified myself. I was still a little scared of her. She remembered the class and me and started to tell me how we students were her whole life, how she loved teaching and how she lost her job—I suspect because of her Nazi sympathies—was ill—had a mastectomy and that she was totally devastated and unhappy.

The fearful figure I remembered before the war became a pitiable figure as we talked on. She saw in me the elegant young woman who came back from America for a visit. Not the frightened Jewish girl of the past. As mentioned before, during our talk the old frightening image of Dr. Hanvai melted away and she became a sad human being who was happy to talk to me and even in a sort of way had admiration for me and was glad to remember old times.

As far as I was concerned, I felt no victory, only sympathy for her. Her cruelties during the German classes were not as important anymore and I was sad seeing her so destroyed.

Dr. Hanvai taught me between 1931-35 and in 1935 I matriculated in German literature among other subjects. In hindsight I believe—perhaps—her human side was revealed in the Art History classes where she inspired all of us—and after many years in America I finally became an Art Historian. Dr. Hanvai's cruelty and moments of humanity were living proofs of some of the many facets of a human being, in this case, two of the many faces of a Nazi sympathizer. ■

Elegy I

"I'M MORE CORPSE THAN person," Pete said one week before he died. His penis, his balls, his teeth, his ears, his nose were the only things that had not shrunk. His penis enormous in relationship to the rest of his body. His ass, once a source of great pride, was flopping skin. A gaping cavity when he bent over.

At the Gay Pride march a year after he had been brutally beaten, his head swollen beyond recognition, plastic surgery, a year of pain killers, Charles stood in a doorway as the throng of people walked by him. Gay Pride day. He stood in the doorway, wearing leather and chains, a look of timelessness, infinite patience. The look he wore when he stood in doorways, on street corners, looking for sex, waiting for sex, somewhere entering into a realm of pleasure and contact joined to everyone on the street. And here he stood looking and I don't know what he was feeling. He helped enormously to bring this day into being. How many of these thousands of people had he spoken to on the radio. Was he connected or separated from these people. The beating had been severe. Reconstructive surgery. And for years he would live in pain.

I remember at another Gay Pride march standing with Pete watching the AIDS quilt go by. We stood in absolute silence. It is one thing to stand and watch the extraordinary procession of quilts which individually and collectively pay homage to the dead. But to watch and wonder what your quilt will look like must be quite another.

My friend Mark had sex with any number of men when he was seven or eight or possibly nine. "It was like being in a candy store," he said with delight as we sat in his living room now 40 years later.

I flash on a short story I want to write. A protagonist from long ago returns. He is arguing with a friend, a former friend really:

"You'll never take that away from him," Maxwell thinks. "All your ugly theories won't take that spark out of his eyes." But in truth it is the deadness in his own eyes that frightens him.

His mind returns to the conversation at hand, which is about "dysfunctional" families, not childhood sexuality. His friend, really his former friend, is now on a riff about how unfortunate it is for a child's development when it has to be raised by a single mother. There is concern and compassion in his voice. What Maxwell hears is cruel reasonableness.

"Dysfunctional family means that there is such a thing as a functioning family," he says suddenly with a sharp, a very sharp edge to his voice. "Obviously certain situations are more painful than others and levels of abuse more profound." "Blah, blah," he thinks to himself. He feels he has marbles in his mouth. He feels he is betraying himself, making any concession at all to bad faith arguments. "No it's not 'dysfunctioning families' it's your functioning families that are the source of humiliation. You won't touch the structure. Functioning families are the structure of oppression. That's right they're the structure of oppression. The most 'functioning' family is a hideous monstrosity." The fury keeps coming and coming. It is far from hatred that Maxwell feels. It is a purging rage, that no longer purges. He is shaken. In fact he thinks with a delight that no longer delights him, "Every obedient child that murders their parent, every woman who murders her child makes the world a safer place from people like you." But the emotional truth of that statement no longer gives him satisfaction. The defeat of freedom seems so total.

"I'm more corpse than person." One week before his death. Only his balls and cock and ears and nose have not shrunken. And they are enormous in relation to the rest of his body. His ass just flopping skin. A huge cavity when he bends over. ■

Elegy II

CRACKS IN THE WALL and in the ceiling, stains on the window jump out at her as forms of life: goats, people, dogs with raging eyes. Currents of life energy run deep inside her. Her body at once alive and deadened. Her eyes on fire then freeze into a sternness as she hectors one lover after another for violations both small and profound.

Inside my imagination I embrace and heal. I excite and am excited. What comes out instead is jutting sensitivities that protect against contact.

When I was younger I felt I was some combination of a dashing prince and a kindly old Jewish uncle. Both images existed side by side. I had a calmness at times that created deep sexual trust and that allowed me to enter dangerous and profound places.

When I moved into this neighborhood it was totally alive. Gay celebration on every block. Out windows. On roof tops. Curtains on my windows. Half curtains. People could look in.

As years went by what might be seen by someone observing me: At 33 a sexy drag queen with a towel around my waist. At 39 an energetic young football coach still in very good shape.

Susan Wood writhing against the wall following my sexual instructions. Silhouetted against full curtains or in front of open windows.

The loud voice of a woman at various hours of the day and night. Orgasm ricocheting off the buildings in the courtyard.

Mostly it was pure pleasure to listen to. Occasionally an irritation. Then it stopped. ■

Shulamith Firestone

Contempt is always unjustified. Wait and see.
                              —Shulamith Firestone, And Then *#4, 1992*

AT THE FREE ASSOCIATION, an alternative school in the
'70s, a friend was leading a feminist workshop. I was the only
man in the room. My presence was interfering with the comfort
and flow of discussion. This led to its own long discussion. The
upshot was this would be the last time I would attend the group.
It didn't feel great to have to leave but understandable. At the
time I was in the beginnings of an extremely close friendship
with Shulamith. Our contact was heady and intense. I was one
of maybe three people in the world she was talking to. She was
withdrawing from political activity and was leaving it all behind.
Because of that, and because she was in fact paranoid, I couldn't
tell anyone I knew her. The women in the group were all read-
ing Shulamith's book. And there I was being asked to leave by a
group of women emboldened in part by the book. Her face on
the back of the book was staring at me from various directions.

The next day I told her the story. She understood why the
women did it. Essentially agreed with them. Also found it ironic.
We've been friends pretty much from then to the present. She
would disappear for long periods of time then reappear. Tear up
her Rolodex then reassemble the numbers. We haven't had con-
tact the last few years. She sent me a Rosh Hashanah card three
years ago, sending her warm wishes to Arnie and Mark. I was
the intermediary between her and a filmmaker who was referred
to in the *Times* obituary. She was a very close friend. She wrote
and did art work for *And Then.* Came to a lot of our parties. We
were in discussion groups and writing groups for many years.
Everything was kept low key. I loved her very much. She would
go crazy. Go on medication. Go off it. She wrote whole bunches
of wonderful things that didn't get published. Also did magnifi-
cent art work. She was close with Arnie and other people I know.

This is a very sad day.

I can't help feeling, I feel almost certain of it, that something similar happened to my friend Karen Cohen but I don't think there was a soul who had any idea how to reach me. One day to the next she stopped calling. Shulamith dead in her apartment; undiscovered for a number of days.

I first met her in the Paradox, a macrobiotic restaurant on the Lower East Side, later renamed the East Village for purposes of real estate marketing. Yoko Ono ate there before she was "Yoko Ono," though well on her way to being that. As well as Jerry Rubin. And I'm sure countless other similar people. George Dennison lived in an apartment above the restaurant.

Somehow Shulamith and I wound up at the same table. She was absolutely focused, and filled with ideas, theories and passion and categories. She was working on her book. Which was combining so many factors my head started spinning as she spoke. I just surrendered to what clearly was going to be a major accomplishment. I told her I wrote poetry. Just to say something. To her poetry existed in a much higher realm than the theoretical historical work that she was doing. So my status elevated in the blink of an eye. Saw her once on a TV show called *For Women Only* where she was a guest with Eleanor Holmes Norton. Two such very young women. Barbara Walters when she took over the show changed the name to *Not for Women Only*. An interesting change that instantaneously diminished whatever disruptive power the show had. Sadly and not surprisingly, I don't remember the name of the original host.

There was a period over a few years when I would periodically see Shulamith in the neighborhood. Her appearance changing each time. She would gain and lose weight. Her hair style different, her clothing different. It felt like more than just normal changes; they looked like disguises; she confirmed to me later that they were. But I always knew it was her. One day I approached her in the post office. And said something like I've seen you over the years and you always look different. But I know it is you. Always wanted to say hello. But hesitated. The contact was immediate, electric, thrilling, scary and deep.

I went to her apartment, a small pad on 2nd St. There was a medium-sized blackboard in the middle of the room. Plot outlines, timelines, history of the characters all laid out in detail. It was extremely impressive. She showed me sketches, small paintings, colored drawings. One was called "Asshole" and it was a colored drawing or watercolor of an asshole. Couldn't get the image out of my head for months. I was totally eroticized by it.

I invited her into a discussion group. She agreed but only if I introduced her as Kathy and did not tell anyone who she was. I agreed. It was not a great thing to agree to. At the end of the day it was worth it. Because our friendship blossomed. But I would never do it again except if someone was really in trouble. Because you are constantly making up things on the run, misdirecting, deceiving. It became very unpleasant.

And resulted in a few bruised feelings. A double deceit with a lover. Because Shulamith was someone whose work she admired. And "Kathy" was a woman I was clearly intoxicated by. They eventually became friends. Remember them both in a bar one night. Their auras intense. One a reddish orange, the other a bright yellow. Which was which I don't remember.

Shulamith wrote an extraordinary poem about her descent into hell. Step by step, stage by stage. It was not included in a feminist anthology about first person accounts of years in the movement and what happened afterward. Shulamith was hurt by the rejection. And as good as the anthology turned out to be, it felt very incomplete without it. During the time she described, I saw her sitting in the street looking deranged, a shopping bag lady surrounded by clothes and/or books. It scared me half to death. Didn't know what to do. Had to gather myself and essentially ran away.

Shulamith periodically called me from Boston where she lived for a couple of years. She was working at a company where she had a low paying, bottom of the totem pole job. Someone the firm wanted to do business with was visiting them. I think she was a very important scientist from a European country. Certainly "important" and from Europe. She somehow saw that Shulamith worked there and was beside herself with excitement and insisted on meeting her. The bosses had never heard of "Shulamith Firestone" and were barely aware that Shulamith was working there. But suddenly she became a major asset to them. So they had to go get her (I think she was working in the basement but here my mind might be embellishing) and she became an intricate part of the wooing of the scientist over the next few days, going out for lunch, dinner etc. She worked there a while longer. I don't think any of this affected her pay or the work she did. But it did affect how she was treated by the people running the place. How exactly I don't remember but it was decidedly mixed.

One characteristic not often commented on was that she was one part genuine screwball, a characteristic she shares with almost all my close friends. She had for example a rag mop and big bucket with a wringer for her tiny 2nd St. apartment. And she was very dramatic in how she described mopping the floor. With grand strokes and full involvement. She had a sense of absurdity about situations and about herself. One time she and I put our heads together to figure out a solution to some problem, maybe to move something from one place to another. We came up with the most convoluted ass backwards solution. But we got it done. I remember her standing on the top of the stairs and I was standing on the bottom and she flashed a big smile and said, "We're the wise men of Chelm."

She said this twenty times better than I'm going to. Anyway one time as we were watching people in the street she said that it was very important that mothers train boys to open doors for women. Because when a woman was burdened down with heavy packages, even if nothing else changes at least that would provide some minimal relief.

Loved quoting this to people. No one quite knew what to do with it.

One time I called Shulamith and she invited me to a demonstration in midtown outside a hotel where Bill Clinton was celebrating his 50th birthday. It was a demonstration protesting the assault on welfare. She was in real good spirits that day.

One pretty big concern of Shulamith's was that she would be thrown off SSI if she made too much money on *Airless Spaces* and then on the newly re-released *The Dialectic of Sex*. And of course not make nearly enough money to make it worthwhile. My blood boils whenever I think about it.

Fell in and out of Shulamith's life for decades (or maybe thrown out then re-embraced). Always loved her. A wonderful friend. Deep, compassionate, honest in ways few people can be. She suffered greatly often harrowingly. Even with that, knowing her brought me great joy and affirmation. In addition to *The Dialectic of Sex*, *Airless Spaces* is a magnificent book, as are many other things she wrote over the years, most of which haven't been published. She was also a wonderful painter and poet. And could be funny as hell. She helped change consciousness and paid a terrible price for it.

The crazed woman or man on the outskirts of a village wailing at the moon. Everyone keeping a watchful if distant eye out for them. Food supplied. Shelter provided. No one frightened by it. No one's sleep disturbed. Worrying only if the shouting stops.

Here you go mad in isolation. Screaming rages in small apartments disrupting the sleep or equilibrium of one's neighbors. People who themselves are often cut off and isolated. People who are in no way equipped to handle someone in such extreme pain. Particularly someone they barely know at all.

What happened to Shulamith. The immense responsibility falling on friends and family. They themselves probably teetering on the edges of emotional fragility. To let her die. Be injured. Not let her die. Become her jailer. Betraying her. Put a chemical lock on her emotions, on her creativity. Commit her to a hospital. Without community it is all so horrible.

One time she complained about a medication she felt was even more pernicious than the others. It masked the side effects. She spoke less slowly. Moved more quickly. She sounded and looked more "normal." "How I sound is not how I feel," she said.

Arnie and I would know early on when she went off her

medication. Weeks before the full effects surfaced. Suddenly very sharp, shimmering perceptions would flash out. No way we couldn't start laughing. They were so vivid and poetic. Like a sudden burst of light breaking through thick, dense clouds.

In speaking about someone, she would catch deep personality traits. The articulation of them so precise, maybe too precise. They were not exactly nasty but almost so. And other perceptions sudden and unexpected would stop you up short. That's when we knew trouble was ahead.

There was a period when she would speak about "bright normals," a pretty devastating category that I suspect included people like the editors of *The New Yorker* or those very bright policy makers in government. People that would constantly try to marginalize someone like Shulamith whose awareness and intelligence leaped across centuries. Who had a connection to the universe that was rare and profound. Who could tap into the deepest historical currents, who was not a part of the "real" world.

Of course no one is ever "normal." In that way Shulamith was unfair and like all such formulations it can freeze someone into something they are not. Still it was a kind of revenge category toward a smug oppressive arrogance unaware of its own extreme limitations.

One Final Memory. I was visiting Mark in Somerville. I thought it would be a nice idea to introduce Shulamith to my good friend Joseph who was a novelist and who wrote a semi-regular column for *The Real Paper*. (As an aside, Joseph and I at some point in summers past hawked both *The Real Paper* and *The Boston Phoenix* in the street.)

Anyway the meeting was a total dud. Joseph and Shulamith didn't connect in any way. There was no hostility. Just absolutely no chemistry of any kind.

Now I had a distinct relationship with each. And in some way was a different person with each. Certainly a different dimension of myself revealed to each. Interestingly enough the other day when I started writing this I was tutoring a student who was taking a sociology course. One of the terms she was learning was "impression management" that Erving Goffman used to describe just such a situation. It is that people present different impressions of themselves to different people in different circumstances. Never heard the term before, but here my impression management (as he described could happen) really went out of whack. Shulamith and Joseph each kept laying claim to the Robert they knew. Each never having seen parts of the Robert the other knew. I felt exposed and totally like a fraud (if you ratchet that word down a few notches).

Finally we wound up down by the Charles River. It was at night. There were no other people around. We sat on the bank of the river. Inches apart. The only people in the world at that spot. Each gazing out at the water. Three people who in certain significant ways were the same person. And there was probably not a thing we were seeing, an emotion we were feeling, a thought that was occurring to us that was remotely the same.

Periodically I have tried to write up that scene but I've never been able to.

I think they ran into each other sometime later and had a warm exchange. ∎

Out of the Ashes of the Warsaw Ghetto / Out of the Rubble of Jenin

Are the heroic Jewish fighters in the Warsaw ghetto the same Jews who have brutalized the Palestinians of the West Bank?

Are the brave Palestinian fighters who resisted the Israeli juggernaut in Jenin the same people who cut Daniel Pearl's throat after making him proclaim to the world that he was a Jew?

Are the tattooed survivors of Auschwitz also the Israeli pilots of Apache helicopters creating corpses throughout the Holy Land?

Is the ninety year old Palestinian woman clinging to her rescuers also the desperate 18 year old suicide bomber out to murder as many Jews as she can?

Why does a Palestinian child in a refugee camp think a Jew means soldier?

Why do some relatives of mine think every Palestinian is a potential Hitler?

Why do Jews want a state of their own?

Why do Palestinians want a state of their own?

Why is a colonial occupying army called the Israeli Defense Force?

Why are members of Hamas who want to subjugate Jews, humiliate women, murder homosexuals called freedom fighters?

What will a Palestinian state look like? I think, at best it would be a corporate controlled quasi-racist entity like Israel. At worst a secular monstrosity like Iraq. Or a theocratic nightmare like Iran.

What about a bi-national secular state? If it were to be brought into existence by armed struggle it would be an Arab controlled state with an oppressed Jewish minority.

What about two states side by side as a result of a brokered peace agreement? What would that look like? Israel's leaders want a Palestinian state that would not be a real state. It would be a weak state. A protectorate of Israel. Possibly of Jordan. Possibly of Saudi Arabia. Probably a Bantustan. For a state to be real it must have an army that can slaughter its neighbors and have a police force powerful enough to subjugate its own population. That is the state most people of good will want to be created. A state equal to Israel.

Thrown out of their land there are Palestinians who still have keys to their old homes. The keys the old Jews have on their shelves are the ones that opened the gates out of the crematoria.

For centuries Jews of the Diaspora have ended the Passover seder by saying, "Next year in Jerusalem." Each night Palestinians of the Diaspora say the same thing.

Two vulnerable, despised people. Both traumatized and often brutal. How will it all end?

One thing I know for sure, any Homeland worth its name is not a place any person should want to live. ■

2002

GAY MARRIAGE AND GAYS and women in the military are breathtaking victories and simultaneously enormous defeats. They represent the difference between social equality (far from being won) and the possibilities of liberation. Gay (LGBTQ…) and women's liberation challenged in deep and profound ways structures that perpetuate repression, oppression, militarism. These victories often reinforce those structures. ■

I LIVE IN GREENWICH Village. During the last election there was a fund raising benefit for Barack Obama in the home of a famous celebrity couple. Once the Village was the home of immigrant families and bohemian artists. Later the home of an insurgent lesbian and gay community. Now it is increasingly the home of movie stars and Wall Street executives. To some extent it felt good that the mild progressiveness of celebrity culture was actively opposing Romney. On the other hand to have Obama with his corporate smile and militaristic mindset feted just around the corner felt absolutely horrible. ■

DECADES AGO THE WOMEN'S House of Detention was located smack in the middle of Greenwich Village. It was an ugly building where women would scream out the window to lovers and friends and family. Or maybe just scream out in rage or madness. It disturbed the equilibrium of the neighborhood and the place was moved where it would be harder for visitors to come. A lush community garden was built there instead.

When you put people in cages or keep them poor and hungry better have them in a place where they cannot be seen or heard or smelled. ■

WHO CAN FORGET THAT video of Iraqi citizens shot down in the street from a U.S. helicopter? The initial frustration of the shooter at not getting the go ahead soon enough. And then his glee when the slaughter was complete. And then you had Secretary of Defense Robert Gates twisting and turning trying to put everything into some kind of monstrous context. And then there is Hillary Clinton expressing outrage at the damage done to the country because its cruelty could not remain hidden from view. End the scapegoating of the messenger! Free Chelsea Manning! ∎

END ALL JUSTIFICATIONS

(This is what I wrote for a placard I carried against the Israeli invasion of Gaza.) ∎

Locked In

AM MORE IMPATIENT WITH phone calls. Don't want any reverie interfered with, any TV show interrupted. I don't like to be jarred out of anything. Each person calling demanding that I fully enter their world the moment I hear their voice. This is compounded when I am not driven to talk, when my own pain or numbness or state of being is not pouring out of me. There is no consciousness that they are doing it. Occasionally yes which is fine. But mostly no, which isn't so fine. There are few perfunctory gestures at best. They ask almost to the person how my mother is doing. They immediately turn the conversation back to themselves. Finding some segue back no matter what I say. No matter the topic.

"My friend just died in a car crash."

"That's terrible." A split second pause. "I remember the time when I was about 12 I crashed into a friend in the school yard and badly scraped my knees..."

I don't want to fight for space. If I am compelled I will talk. And if I am insistent most of my friends will give me the attention that I need. But only if I keep ratcheting up my intensity. Otherwise you just feel their impatience to get back to what they want to say, have to say, can't stop not saying. Often I don't necessarily want to talk about anything in particular. Still I don't want the conversation totally controlled by the other person. And often enough I pull the phone away from my ear, utter a couple uhhuhs, and they keep talking without knowing the difference. And then there are the times that someone asks me a question about what I think and then gives me their answer after I say maybe five words. This one makes me absolutely crazy.

Other friends are pretty reciprocal. Which means that I can obsess at times and at other times they can. And of course there are times where there is real back and forth.

I think the frozen obsessive qualities of my friends have debilitated me. I dread hearing their voices except when I am totally ready for them. There is so little movement in their conversations. And I couldn't care less about what they are talking about. Because they don't care about me at those moments. There are others who care.

I know with Arnie I would use him as an indicator on what I should write about. Whenever he would fade out I knew I was onto something. Because I had freed myself from the iron clad grasp he would have on the conversation. My thoughts veered far enough away from his control that I felt that I had a liberated thought. This is funny because Arnie and I thought very much alike. And his focus helped him and in fact often helped me to think things through. But what to him might feel like a mutual conversation was me staying within the parameters set by him even if it was a place I would naturally be. It is only when I ventured outside them that he tried to exercise his control through what felt like manipulation—fading out, using rhetorical tricks that are clearly more unconscious than conscious, but very effectively absorbed from watching public figures control the flow, direction, topics and rhythm of conversation. With most other people I am much less caught up when they do this. So the experience is even more unpleasant. But it is never pleasant if this happens on a regular basis.

I often go on strike. I don't speak about what I'm thinking about or my life or really what is happening to me except in broad outlines. I save it for my writing. But the effect is more serious than I realize. It dampens my energy. My personality fades. My thoughts lose their vitality.

I am not sure why I'm not asserting myself more. It could be an expression of contempt. The contempt of the docile who in some way are contemptuous through their surrender. The patient probing listener. But too often it becomes exactly what it looks like. A kind of self-effacement laced with an illusion of superiority. And I can't continue.

This is all very different from exciting conversations where each might go off on their own riff but where you are igniting, inspiring each other. Parallel conversations. Off on your own solo riff but deeply in tune with each other. But most now are endless solos without much music. Just obsessive monologues where someone is just bombarding you with the pain of their lives. Or bragging to you about their importance. Strange line crossed where you become locked in the prison of their consciousness.

Generally it is hysteria and probably deep insecurity more than contempt. Maybe even a need to continually establish themselves with you. To show you how smart they are. But in a world where you are marginalized, dismissed and silenced it can feel like contempt or disinterest. And under any circumstances cumulatively it is very diminishing and unpleasant. And when I am in certain moods I dread hearing their voices.

I am also guilty of this but less so now than in the past. I used to be very forceful, aggressive, argue very powerfully, sure footed and in fact was very insightful and often dead on. I would steamroll or maybe in better times go off on powerful riffs. And see things very "clearly." One friend told me that she didn't want to join a discussion group Arnie and I were trying to set up. She said it wouldn't be a discussion group but rather a subtle, soft indoctrination group instead. That we wanted a group where we wouldn't really be listening to her, listening in the sense that we suspend the attachment to our own ideas and take in existentially what she wanted to say or where what she was saying was springing from. Not necessarily agree with it but not just waiting for the moment to step in and correct her. Or to use what she said as useful correctives to what we were thinking. She was right. Another time my old girlfriend Akemi angrily said to me as I completed a thought for her, "How I get there is as important as you knowing where I am going." Some friends at times felt bullied by me in conversation. Trumped by me. They felt I would try to outflank them and undercut them in every conversation. They often felt hurt and angry about this. I took a big step back. At times this led to better communication. But other times someone would just fill the aggression void, becoming impatient and dismissive with what I had to say. It would now be them doing the steamrolling. I have a lot to offer on certain subjects. And it shocks me how little curiosity there is. Mostly this is true in private conversation. Generally though my friends are very attentive and respectful of my written work. And more often than not pay real close attention when I speak in public.

For reasons I don't fully understand, the dynamic between the friends I am complaining about and myself shifts dramatically if there are one or two other people around. In those situations the conversation is usually pretty fantastic. Everyone listening, learning and enjoying each other. Why? I don't know why. But I feel good when it happens.

You tell a joke and I laugh
You tell a joke and I laugh
You tell a joke and I laugh
You tell a joke and I laugh
I tell a joke and you don't laugh
You tell a joke and I laugh

You tell a joke and I laugh
You tell a joke and I laugh
I tell a joke and you don't laugh
You tell a joke and I laugh
You tell a joke and I laugh

You tell a joke and I laugh
You tell a joke and I laugh
You tell a joke and I laugh

I tell a joke and you don't laugh
You tell a joke and I don't laugh
You wonder why I didn't laugh ∎

FRANK CASTRONOVA WHO I delivered newspapers with was a prognosticator of unparalleled accuracy. His indicators were very much his own. If the third street light in a certain neighborhood in Manhattan was out, he would use that as data and tell me who would win an election in Trenton, New Jersey three months in the future. He was almost always right. When the first Persian Gulf war was about to be fought he predicted its trajectory—when it would start, when the ground war would begin, when victory would be declared, what public pronouncements would be made and when. He was off by one day in his prediction of when it would end. And so on and so forth until he died.

Whenever I would tell my political scientist friends things that Frank said they were too polite to scoff, but too foolish to actually listen. ■

A FRIEND OF MINE who worked in a hospital had a very serious ongoing reaction to the latex gloves she had to wear. We went to a lawyer who was involved in a class action suit of people who had similar reactions. Each time my friend related something very negative the lawyer seemed pleased. Each time my friend had been spared a negative reaction others had had, the lawyer's voice dropped in disappointment. At some point my friend and I broke out laughing. The lawyer kind of joined in. ■

Death Watch

I DON'T WANT YOU to make a claim on me at the end of my life. I don't want you to appropriate my life. I don't want you to be in the hospital and sit with me when I'm dying. I don't want you to steal my last days. I don't want you here holding my hand. I don't want you to be the last person I see. I don't want you defining my last moments for me. I don't want you here. I don't want you to be in my good graces. I don't dislike you enough for that to be a problem. I don't dislike you at all. I don't want you assuming an intimacy I never wanted. I don't want you to be my best friend. I don't want your presence hanging heavily in the other room. I don't want to think of having to ask you to leave. I don't want someone coming to visit me see you in my room and not want to disturb us. ■

Entrance Exam

WHEN I TOOK the entrance exam for Stuyvesant, a math and science New York City high school, I could barely answer any of the multiple-choice questions that made up the test. A thought flashed in my brain. Maybe the computer had some pattern in how it set out the answers. I shut my eyes for thirty seconds and tried to enter the rhythms of the computer. Then with my eyes maybe half-opened, I let my hand answer questions I didn't even bother to read. I passed the test and spent the next three years in misery. ■

Hall of Fame

I JUST READ THAT Richie Guerin was elected to the Basketball Hall of Fame. I let out a yell. When I was a kid I met him outside Madison Square Garden where I would wait after Knick games to collect autographs. In addition to being a great player, he was an exceptionally warm person. Members of his family used to wait out there for him too. They all looked so much alike that I would break out into a smile whenever I saw them. I remember someone—I'm almost sure it was his mother—who had this engaging contagious embracing appreciative encouraging fun filled smile.

Richie gave me his home phone number when I asked him if he could come and give a clinic to our junior high school team. There was no team. So I tried to create one out of scratch. But sadly to no avail. That notwithstanding, Richie Guerin has been in my personal Hall of Fame ever since. ■

On My Window Sill

Two green tomatoes
from Arlene's urban garden
One turning red
the other still green
What does that mean in the scheme of things ∎

The City of Florence

WHEN PATTY AND CHARLOTTE would get rip roaring drunk they would belt out Christian songs from their childhoods, songs I never heard, songs that brought you to the gates of heaven or into the darkest corners of a guilt laden hell. And they would sing and they would laugh and they would drink and cry and then turn on each other with fury. Bitter with class resentment and class rage, it was mostly Charlotte who would go on the attack. And the next day both would have hangovers. I remember Patty best, holding an ice pack on her head while downing aspirins. I was totally in another consciousness. Never drunk, I was hanging with people who drank. And so I was always out of the loop.

When I walked through Florence it was only after I drank wine that the city made any sense. I realized it was designed, built and inhabited by people who drank wine. ∎

Meditation on Race

YOU CAN PROJECT ONTO someone deep racial rage when they just might be worried about the corns on their feet. ∎

Reasons Why Someone Might Not Want
To Be Lovers With Me

I'M ANTSY, GUARDED, COMPULSIVE, don't believe in relationships, I'm scruffy, hysterical, half-focused, too scrutinizing, distant, I'm highly emotional, somewhat too controlled, too intense, too attentive, I can touch deep emotions, I'm outside the swim, I'm too tentative, I'm too bold, I'm passive, my mind is always elsewhere, I'm too fearful, I send out mixed messages, I stop at too many red lights, I don't flirt, I'm too ideological, I don't initiate activities, I don't want to live with anyone, I hate conversations about relationships, I have a tendency to go round and round, no one knows where they stand with me, I can be too negative

Reasons Why Someone Might Want
To Be Lovers With Me

I'M AT TIMES VERY attractive, I have charisma, I'm passionate, I'm intense, I'm insightful, I'm loyal, I'm understanding, I can zone very deeply into someone's sexual needs, I'm attentive, I'm accepting, I can bring people together, I'm empathetic, I can stay the distance, I can step outside daily life, I have a funny sense of humor, I'm playful, I'm flirtatious, I'm hopeful ■

A June Wedding

ONE HUNDRED AND FIFTY couples of politically and cul-
turally progressive orientation are getting married in the gym-
nasium of Barnard College. Most of the people getting married
happen to be Jewish, so it has been agreed that a rabbi will
oversee the ceremony. He is a nice man with a delicate touch
and a sensitivity for feeling. The ceremony in fact will be non-
denominational.

The relatives have come. They are happy it is a wedding.
Yet it is something even more than that. For the first time they
feel they can fully join the rebel spirit of their children, who now
have come to the fringes of middle age.

Almost half the brides and grooms were previously mar-
ried to other persons and divorced. But whatever unease the
parents may feel, they are comforted and indeed excited by the
moving and tasteful promise of modern consciousness joining
ancient tradition.

Notes and papers are passed back and forth among the older
men; occasionally an older man will furtively hand a younger
man an envelope and the younger man will quickly place it in
the inside pocket of his sport jacket.

"A real Wed-In," one of the older men says with a slight
ironic laugh. And he repeats the same observation again to a
number of people, not in an ugly or cynical mood, but more
in the mood of a person who has seen it all, will move with the
times, but never lose his equilibrium.

The older women gather relatives and friends together,
then call one of the five hardworking photographers roaming
the auditorium to take pictures of the people they have just
assembled. The older women are all beautifully dressed, ani-
mated and warm. The mothers are a little more anxious than the
rest, hoping that this time their sons and daughters will finally
find some real peace and that this love will, unlike the previous
relationships or marriages, not send their children into those
awful and terrifying depressions.

Some of the younger women who are getting married, cruelly disappointed in their previous relationships with men, have had lesbian affairs. Although they sincerely feel these affairs were important for their development, they concluded that the same problems inevitably develop in both gay and straight relations. The men, sensing this all along, have related exclusively to women.

The grooms are gracious to the various guests, particularly attentive to the relatives of the brides. Most are dressed informally; the few dressed in tuxedos seem especially jaunty. The best men all are wearing beards. All are drinking scotch and though they do not look exactly alike, all seem equally delighted at the role they will play in the events of the day.

Some of the brides move from guest to guest, speaking briefly but intimately with each person. Others look anxious, wringing their hands and flashing smiles at friends.

The air conditioning in the gymnasium and the warmth of the large number of people keep the room temperature very pleasant. A guest list is placed by the entrance of the gym. There is a constant short line of people waiting their turn to sign it. Within three weeks the guest list will be mailed to the couples and their immediate families.

A best man leaning against the folded-up chairs looks up at the ceiling and then at the basket. Another best man greets an old friend and they catch up very quickly on the present state of their lives, not dwelling on former or present conflicts of politics.

Sons and daughters, younger brothers and younger sisters, nieces and nephews roam throughout the gym, finding each other and playing together. Two young women of about sixteen are carrying a flute and a violin. They will perform together at the reception afterwards. One is the youngest sister of a groom, the other is her best friend. They have played many duets together, but this one will be special. Their faces are serious; they touch each other's arm with anticipation.

The oldest son of a groom adjusts the cuffs of his shirt. He sees his aunt and runs over to her and gives her a kiss. His aunt's hair is dry and she smells of cigarettes. She is his favorite aunt.

The aunt feels as if she herself is still a kid, and the touch of the tender cheek of her almost grown-up nephew frightens her.

The sister of a bride has just come in from California. She is laughing as she signs her name on the guest list. She recognizes many of the names. She picks up a program, grows uneasy with the names of some of the people getting married. Long, complicated stories and associations flash through her mind. But her sister had seen her enter and is standing just a few steps away looking longingly at her, with a smile so thoroughly joyous that the memories of past entanglements simply disappear and she runs to her sister, and they embrace laughing with almost total abandon.

The various wedding parties have brought flowers and plants and have placed them throughout the room.

A little boy grows uncomfortable. He sticks his hands into his pants to straighten the underpants that are irritating him.

There is an impatient clapping of hands. Finally the brides and grooms are called forward. Music is played. The massed brides and grooms shift slightly as they wait for the ceremony to begin. The room has not yet grown quiet. Not everyone is aware that the wedding is about to start.

Finally everyone is at their place. The various wedding parties seem both to blend with yet stay apart from each other. Loyalty, autonomy, solidarity, and finally community. The ceremony begins.

The rabbi gives a warm greeting, speaks generously of the gathering, speaks painfully about the economy, speaks forcefully about the importance of changing sex roles, the psychic, spiritual and economic independence of women, and the need for men to learn to develop their nurturing selves.

The room is silent, actually silent. There is rapt attention; no jokes or wisecracks, no uneasy glances. The couples now gaze into each other's eyes; the men are like dutiful boys, earnest, considerate, loving; the women's faces are free of pain, flushed and romantic. For these few minutes there is no feeling of cynicism or irony. No one will steal this moment from them. ■

My Penis

Overview

EXCEPT FOR AN OCCASIONAL check-up by a doctor and one or two very notable exceptions, my beautiful but lonesome penis has had no one but me pay much attention to it in recent years. Once the object of much interest, speculation, wide-ranging excitement, desire and affection, it seems not to arouse even the faintest curiosity in anyone. It is hard to imagine a whole world full of people—billions of them—and there being not a soul who has any sexual interest in it.

The one or two exceptions when it was noticed and appreciated resulted in chaos. Its basic role in recent years however has been in the occasional jealousy it provokes in suspicious lovers of friends who project onto it powers that may or may not exist.

My profound disappointment in radical movements and in what for me was once the beginning of a powerful sexual counter-culture has probably played the most critical role in denying my cock the pleasures that are its birthright.

I often feel I'm doomed to a life of sexual loneliness. And the pain of that thought is immense and frightening. In almost any sexual encounter one almost immediately comes up against a bedrock of pain and terror and bitterness. Without a community to help me understand what is going on as well as provide solace and support, it often feels all just too much for me. Just the other day I received a letter from a close friend who said that she felt "devalued" by men because she wasn't married. Immediately I had one thousand things to say. But the truth is that I don't feel that we have collectively come up with much to help her heal her wounds.

The Institution of Marriage and its at times slightly less pernicious cousin the Institution of Relationships are treacherous structures designed to prevent deep human contact.

Sexual freedom was and is a basic cornerstone of my political and social vision. Almost from my very first moment of political consciousness I fought against deep forms of puritanism and bigotry both within the general society and within radical social movements.

In recent years too many people I've worked with have made their peace with the social order. Nowadays if two lesbians say that Harvard is a good school or a sex radical says that there should be a strong police presence in Crown Heights I can be de-eroticized for a week.

Herpes

I've had herpes since my early twenties. At first no one knew what it was. Small blisters on my cock. Appearing then disappearing. I'd get them fairly frequently. I had sex even when the blisters were open. No one seemed to worry much about it. And fortunately, I'm almost certain about this, no one ever caught it from me. I went to a VD clinic to check it out. A very old man, red faced and bleary eyed and totally drunk, took my blood. His eyes focused in on the veins of my arm. The only thing that reassured me was that he was drunk and that he was old and that he must have been taking blood in this condition for many, many years. I was then sent to a young crew cut doctor who had a midwest accent and had the air about him of a NASA technocrat. He said officiously, "Drop your drawers," examined my blisters, said he didn't know what they were and sent me to an older Eastern European doctor who in an unbearably reassuring voice told me not to worry as he took a scalpel and started to scrape away at one of the blisters. The more reassuring he got the more terrified I became. He was reassuring himself, not me. It was absolutely clear to me that the deepest part of him wanted to cut my penis right off. I broke into a cold sweat and had a glimpse of a deep terror. At one point the blisters started to bleed. He took a sample. Within fifteen minutes it was determined that I didn't have VD.

During periods of stress, usually periods of sexual stress, my herpes would flare up. If a lover went on vacation it would inevitably appear, functioning as a kind of chastity belt. Even now in a sexually tense situation I might get it. Once when I was about to visit a lover in Georgia, a visit that was months in the planning, it flared up just as I was about to go. I brought condoms with me. She didn't want me to use them. One basic function—the avoidance of sex—thus neutralized it was years before I got another attack.

In the early eighties a herpes hysteria swept the country. In bars, at parties, at Writers Union meetings, at my parents' synagogue everyone was telling the very same ugly herpes jokes. Conversations were thick with a sex-negative rage. Friends wrote puritanical and guilt producing pieces about personal and social responsibility. And through it all no one ever thought that the person they were talking to, or that the person sitting next to them, namely me, might have it. I decided I would never, ever, let a comment pass without saying something in return, without saying that I was one of those people that they were talking about.

For five months I felt contaminated, stigmatized. I felt no one would ever touch me again. The bigotry was that thick. Tragically it was the AIDS epidemic and the hatred and ignorance that it unleashed that shifted public focus and allowed me some room to breathe again.

As a result of all this I can understand very well how someone can be driven into a closet. I also understand why someone might lie about having something that is both contagious and life threatening. Even if it means putting someone else in terrible jeopardy.

Urinating

A deep yellow. Sometimes it's just the color of water. Usually some color in between. When I was a boy my father would show me how to piss in the toilet. We would do it together, our two streams criss-crossing. His flow was very powerful, making foam like bubbles. My father's cock was thick. Mine was small and fun to play with. Even today when I urinate I don't usually make bubbles as big as my father did. But like the color it goes through many changes.

When I was a boy I visited Hungary with my parents. While there they sent me to a camp for a few weeks. One night I had to go to the toilet. It was dark, cold and frightening. I vividly remember making my way through the cold darkness. I remember this experience often. I usually have to urinate once or twice a night.

I don't ever recall pissing in my bed as a kid. I did have wet dreams as a teenager which was a source of embarrassment and pride and something that would inhibit me from sleeping over at other people's homes. Sometime in my early twenties I developed a mild anxiety, which I still have to a degree, about pissing in my sleep. I think I might have developed this while smoking grass. To overcome this anxiety I would try to sleep through the need to go to the toilet. I never did piss in my bed. But at one point it made more sense just to go to the toilet. So for whoever is interested that's what I do.

On occasion, while pissing, one woman or another has grabbed my penis and started guiding the flow of urine. This has always been done with extreme giddiness. My penis has been moved in various directions and at various speeds. Things have been done with it that I never had dared to do. And things have been done with it that I would never have thought were even possible.

Circumcision

A few years ago I was at a neighbor's apartment. He told me of a book that a friend of his had written. The author was a Jew who had worked as a spy for the French Resistance during the Nazi occupation of France. He and his wife, also a spy, had successfully befriended the Nazi commandant of the entire region and as a result were able to steal some very important documents.

In order to keep their identity as Jews hidden they did not have their newborn son circumcised. I asked one or two questions and it turned out that their son was someone I had gone to camp with. I remember the fascination with which I watched him urinate in the woods. A meeting was set up where by the tiniest of foreskins we were reunited after thirty-five years.

• • •

Reason number eight or nine why I never wanted to have children was that if it were a boy I didn't want to be a part of a decision whether or not to have him circumcised. Some friends of mine are very bitter about having been circumcised. I try not to think too much about it. The act on the face of it must be traumatizing. Arguments about health seem to go both ways. The friends who are bitter feel that it has diminished their capacity for sexual pleasure. My strong feeling is that if I had a son I would not want to have him circumcised. Weighing heavily against this is the feeling that as a Jew I would be making a major capitulation to a hostile Christian world. Fortunately this is a decision I doubt I'll ever have to make.

• • •

I've gone to two brisses in my life. Both times, almost as a reflex, I grabbed my genitals just as the circumcision was being performed. I wondered each time how the other men were feeling. I thought I saw something like suppressed glee on the faces of some of the women. Whether that was true or not I have no idea.

Observation

1

At twelve I see my friend's black pubic hair. He is a half year older than me. I haven't yet grown any pubic hair myself. This thick new growth separates us completely. I am drawn to it. I am scared of what I see. I'm in a rage.

Was it desire I was feeling? Possibly. Was it envy? Certainly. I felt he had a certain sexual power over me. I know it looked pretty. And I know I looked away. And I know for years afterwards I tried to obliterate him for it.

2

When I was a kid I would hang out with professional athletes. Mostly basketball players and wrestlers. After wrestling matches I would wander through Times Square with Johnny Valentine who at the time was a Villain. Later they made him into a Hero. Other times I would wait in the corridors of Madison Sq. Garden hoping to get the autographs of basketball players. On occasion I would talk myself into NY Knick practice sessions and if I was lucky wind up in their locker room afterwards.

I had a crush on a girl who reminded me of the very thin, powdery white, smooth as silk, blond starting forward for the Knicks. And I remember sitting in the upper balcony of the Garden and having powerful sensations run through me whenever the delicate shot of the other starting forward, a graceful, powerful black man, would swish through the net. The feeling was not that different from the love I would feel for the nurse in camp whenever she would take my temperature. A strangely beautiful world would open up for me for the two or three minutes the thermometer was in my rectum. I remember wondering to myself how I could have such powerful feelings of love for such an old woman and then wondering how those feelings could disappear so completely from one second to the next.

Back now to the Knick locker room and to the time I looked at the penises of the various players as they emerged from their showers. Some were circumcised. Some were not. All the penises of course were bigger than mine. Still they looked very much like mine. Certainly how I thought mine would look when I grew older. The only exception was the player with the delicate shot. His penis was very big and very gray. And it had a hole the size of a pencil. A friend I was with could not keep his eyes off of it and started to giggle.

Years later, years after the player retired, I saw him being interviewed during halftime of a basketball game. From a very gracious, pleasant sexy young man he had become this slick and arrogant multi-millionaire real estate magnate. A shiny manicured fullness stood now in the place of a once beautiful athlete. And the heart of the early adolescent still in me broke into a thousand pieces.

Sexual Politics

At seven I remember how big and strong and smart and intimidating girls my age seemed to me. One night in the country I was standing outside in a field and like a bolt from heaven was filled with wild excitement. "Yes, but at thirty-five," I thought to myself, "I can have children but they can't."

Sensations

My sex seems stuck in a corner of my brain. Locked there by fear, despair, disappointment. All sensations at times seem stuck in that place. I often feel like I'm talking out of the side of my face.

• • •

Once when I was deeply in love and filled with almost constant desire I felt something like a thin silk cord stretching from my heart to my groin. It was one of the loveliest feelings imaginable. It stayed there inside me for maybe three months. One day it just disappeared. It has never returned. During that period my penis felt totally alive, also much thicker than it has ever been.

• • •

Once after sex with a woman I had just recently met a thin strand of semen covering an entire bed connected our genitals. It was quite beautiful. Taking a chance at being misunderstood

I said, "See, look, look how we're connected." My comment as I suspected it might made her a little nervous. Trying to quickly reassure her I said, "Connected. I mean connected just for this moment."

• • •

"Licking my semen from my fingers," a character in a short story of mine thinks to himself in a Yoga class, "I relax, completely relax." I myself am rarely that relaxed. The few times I have been I have experienced a pleasure similar to his.

• • •

Tuesday, 1988

Teeth hurt
Joints swollen
Eyes out of focus
Hands slightly trembling
Rash on the forehead
Balls feeling strained
Heart aching

This poem was most popular among older women who to a person said except for one line they felt exactly like I did.

• • •

I remember my aunt in the hospital shortly before she died. Her arms and legs were shriveled. At one point the sheets fell off of her. I felt a slight tingling in my balls. It was not a very comfortable feeling. I don't really know how to describe it. Or what it means. But often I experience the same sensation when I see the flesh of someone in an extreme state of physical deterioration.

• • •

Twice as a kid I remember while I was watching TV my mother came over to my father and sat on his lap. They were very rarely physically affectionate in front of me. Both times strong uncontrollable sensations surged through my body. Each time I turned on my stomach and pressed hard as I could against the floor until the feelings disappeared.

• • •

Once when I was a kid I was sitting in a movie theater and a boy and a girl, a few years older than me—teenagers—were sitting in front of me making out. I had just read a book about sex that my parents had given me. One chapter had been about teenage sexuality. Flooded with desire, rage, confusion, jealousy I repeated to myself what I had read in the book. "Teenage boys and girls often engage in forms of sexual experimentation. Teenage boys and girls often engage in forms of sexual experimentation. This is an example of a boy and girl engaging in a form of sexual experimentation. This is an example of a boy and girl engaging in a form of sexual experimentation." I kept repeating and repeating this. Hard as I tried I could not make the feelings fully disappear.

• • •

About nine years ago I was falling in love with a woman from Japan. She had just returned from a visit home and was staying in my apartment for a few days. One evening a couple of friends came over for a visit. Though a powerful radical figure in Japan she was also painfully shy, insecure about her English, frightened of new people and suffering from jet lag. Just as my friends arrived she went into my bedroom. At one point I went into the room to see how she was doing. She was asleep, her body pressed against the wall, the covers up over her head. All I could see was the top of her head. Her hair thick and black. I stood there looking at her. I was overcome by feelings of tenderness and love.

Suddenly wild racist, misogynist images flashed through my brain. Ugly jokes, bizarre stereotypes, fragments of conversations I didn't even know I had overheard had become a part of me. I felt in the grip of a hideous sexual/racial history that spread across centuries. There is no way to avoid or escape the implications of those feelings.

How to handle all of this or any of this is far from clear to me. And it doesn't help when the air is filled with punitive sex-negative mantras that make deep explorations of desire almost impossible.

Dreams

In the last year or so I've had a number of dreams about being in a public toilet. The floors are wet from overflowing toilets, leaking sinks or possibly urine. There are wet brown paper towels on the floor, on the toilet seats or in the toilets themselves clogging them up. I need a place to piss. If in the dream I've found a place clean enough I'm relieved to discover when I wake up that I haven't pissed in my bed.

Sex with women occurs rarely in my dreams. And it rarely involves sexual intercourse. Usually one or both of us are wearing clothes. Sometimes the dreams are very hot. Sometimes not. A dream about someone I know might offer me clues about their sexuality. Very rarely are my dreams unpleasant. But very rarely have they been wildly orgiastic.

Twice in my life I've had sexual dreams involving men. Both times just as we were about to fuck the man's penis turned into a vagina.

Conclusion

Three weeks before my 50th birthday I was lying on my couch in the living room thinking about the sexual wilderness I inhabit. I felt almost beyond pain. There was a certain comfort that I was feeling. A big birthday party had been planned. And for that day at least everything sexual seemed to be settled.

At my 40th birthday party two lovers of mine, totally unknown to each other, stayed on opposite sides of a room for the entire party. They were almost like dancers. If one would move then so would the other. The distance between them always remained constant. As for me I was just hugging and kissing everyone in sight. This was done out of celebration and joy. But I have to admit that it did provide me with a cover. In the meantime friends who did not know of my relationship with either of my lovers would flirt like crazy with one or the other. The whole thing was more comical than anything else. Still there was a degree of tension I could have done without.

Three weeks before my 50th birthday—no sex in sight— why not let things be. Three weeks before my 50th birthday, my defenses way down, deep patterns of inertia slightly jarred, why not take advantage of this. Let something happen for a change. No fuck it. Who needs it.

"Well, I need it."

"Who are you?" I asked. The woman smiled. She was a black woman with full lips and big breasts. And she had entered my mind just like that—totally without an invitation. We had never met. I had never even seen her before.

This was more than a sexual fantasy, more even than a sexual daydream. It was something like a visitation. And she was going to stay as long as she liked.

"It is only three weeks before my 50th birthday. Everything about me and my friends concerning sex has been settled. Okay, at least for the short run. I don't need someone coming in now and unsettling this balance. Let me have my party. No jealousies, no guilts, no confusions, no sneaking glances. Everything is settled."

"Who you kidding. Nothing is ever settled."

"Why now?" I asked.

"And if not now, when?" she replied.

And it was clear as clear could be that I would meet this woman for real.

So I left my house that night wearing a brand new shirt. My mood was some combination of resignation, acceptance, anticipation and hysteria. There were two events to go to. First there was an open reading in Brooklyn. Then a party in Manhattan. I was sure it was at the birthday party that we would meet.

The reading took place at a karate school. I entered a dressing room where a friend was tuning his guitar. Right near by, kneeling on the floor, a huge tote bag by her side—there she was for real with a beauty more breathtaking even than the deepest part of my imagination had been able to conjure up.

"My God, not so soon. I was expecting to meet you later," I thought to myself. My friend Sohnya Sayres once described a woman in her dance class who she later found out was Madonna: "I had seen her in the dressing room of the school appraising her body in the mirror with a concentration or something like it that I never caught in a woman before. I couldn't take my eyes away. This woman short, plump, variously arranging her breasts was... words are hard to find, 'complete.' She dressed slowly in an extraordinary costume, never taking her eyes from the image."

The woman in front of me was remarkably similar. But she had a mystique very much her own. She arranged her breasts so they flowed out of her almost totally unbuttoned white cardigan sweater. She rummaged through her tote bag filled with books, clothing, tape cassettes, cosmetics and a huge comb. She looked up, reached out her hand and introduced herself. Shaking her hand I said, "Hello."

I started to say more but caught myself. "Robert be quiet. Just shut up. Don't talk. You'll scare her away. Keep cool. Talk to her later." I quickly left the room and went to the area where the reading was to take place. I had decided to read three short poems. "Read something sexy. Something with real energy. Something that will impress her. No, stick to what you planned on reading. You never know what anyone likes." I read my three poems. She smiled at me. Throughout the evening our eyes would catch. Her gaze was steady. I would turn away.

At one point a deep sound of appreciation came from her when one of the poets used the word pussy. I looked over at her. Something about her cheekbones. Maybe it was her eyes. Maybe the way her face was set. "Oh my," I thought to myself, "this most beautiful of women might just be the most beautiful of men." Certainly I had seen men in drag with breasts that big before. I really could not tell.

The hour was getting late. As I started to gather my stuff:

"You're not going to leave before you see me perform. Are you?"

"No. Never. Of course not." And without skipping a beat, "Want to come with me to a party later."

"Yes!"

The performance was electric. Different personas emerging from one second to the next. Ambiguity upon ambiguity. A powerful sexual energy flowed from every movement, every gesture. And at the end the audience just erupted with delight.

Later at the party in a dark corner of a crowded room:

"Do you know the people here well?"

"I can't talk. I'm too nervous. I'm almost hysterical. You're too beautiful. I can't breathe."

She? He?—Certainly someone deep within their own mystique—But for the moment she She kissed me. We drank in each other's flesh, each other's heat. Near us old romance movies played silently on the TV screen. At one point Happy Birthday was sung in another part of the room. Twice I went to get a drink. Everyone wanted to touch me. Touch my arms, my hands, my face, my back.

My body was on fire. We would moan loudly, then catch ourselves. Other times total confusion. Had I stepped into someone's performance piece or had someone stepped into my fantasy? And then. "Let me show you how you make me feel." A throbbing hard on? A wet pussy? I didn't know what it was that I would find. It was a moment of absolute freedom. And absolute joy. I knew that whatever I would find would bring me/us that much deeper into paradise.

So much for now about penises and/or possibly vaginas.

My next piece will be about my biceps. ■

Cities

Sex and the City

IN AN EPISODE OF *Sex and the City* one of the main characters, a woman in her early thirties, had a "what the hell" attitude toward an older, an actually older, man, maybe someone in his seventies, and thought why not go for it. She was actually attracted to the man. They went into her bedroom and she let out a scream as she saw his flapping ass. And this was supposed to be funny, a shared joke that everyone in the audience was supposed to understand. Certainly the women. Most of whose asses like mine if we live long enough will probably look like that. Mine I suspect much sooner than most. At times something really ugly surfaces in these shows. An attitude usually hidden under veneers of pseudo-sophistication starkly reveals itself. Here as an ugly joke, a painful joke. The cultural paradigm reinforced with a vengeance. If it is the squeamishness of the character or her inability to run with the impulse of her desire it is one thing. A very interesting thing in fact. Or if she was repelled okay that also is interesting. Or if it was just a frightening turn-off, why not? Or simply a turn-off. It happens. We're attracted to whom we are attracted to. If someone isn't attracted to me let's say because they are attracted to firm young bodies I don't love it and it can be painful, but what can you do but be miserable and disappointed and do your best not to internalize it. But if the person somehow assumes no one can, or in this case no young woman can and they share this assumption with friends, assuming no one in their right mind could or are perplexed (not curiously perplexed but disdainfully perplexed) by it in the sense of "how could she/he?" then it would really be very hard for me to be friends with them. They help poison the environment, making contact that much more difficult and that much more fraught with stigma. In truth social bigotry and programmed assumptions are so deep I probably could remain friends. Certainly I'm far from immune myself to attitudes and assumptions I'm not proud of having. But I couldn't let it pass without saying something. I would have to talk about it. If our desire conforms to the standard norms so be it. Might be something to examine or just accept it and go with it. No big deal. However, if it is assumed that someone is self-evidently beautiful and someone else isn't, that is very dangerous and treacherous and can be searing in its impact. It was the assumption of the show that anyone would be turned off and no one could stay in that room; that was ugly, very ugly. Anyone or everyone would run out of the room. Certainly any sexy, sexually active young woman. Maybe another older person whose own ass is flapping would stay. Aren't they so cute together. In fact they might be.

Had caught the show just as they were going to the bedroom. It was an actually surprising, hopeful and exciting moment. Didn't know what brought them to that point. Curiosity? Desire? Liking someone and wanting to be close. A wish to try something new.

Then the raw humiliation of the man. Well what can an old man who feels desire be other than a gag line. Or for that matter can a young woman entering difficult, stigmatized territory not be made to appear absurd and ridiculous for doing so. This is a comedy after all. Never pleasant to disengage from a sexual situation. Very hard thing to do. Have done it. Have had it happen to me.

So there it is. One moment of real abandon, one real break from the cultural narrative and look what happens. You run out of the room screaming. Don't know much about the show. I know that students I tutored used to watch it to add words and sentences to their vocabulary. Also obviously a turn-on. *Desperate Housewives* another favorite. Relationships, sex, intrigue and the seeking of pleasure. Chaos humor pain. Explored, unexplored. Here presented as the propaganda patter for normalcy laced with the ugliness of age hatred.

Katrina—Voices of the Lost

How else but through music and song can the tragedy of New Orleans be told.

From the very first chord of *Katrina—Voices of the Lost*, you're thrust into the center of a nightmare. Whirling winds and torrential rains surround you. Death is everywhere. You hear the pleading and the desperation. You feel the impotent rage.

This magnificent cantata is driven by concern and indignation, and a very profound love. New Orleans was not one monolithic city. Through the subtlety of the music and beautiful poetry of the words the psychological vulnerability of very different types of people is revealed. We see them as they try to make sense of forces larger than themselves, as they try to cope with the tragedy that they are confronted with.

Waking up when others have not yet gone to sleep, the fisherman begins his days of toil. But on this day the water is rising. The horror mounting. He pleads with God about the injustice of it all. He has nothing to do with the tourist city of sin. Why is he being punished so. His church is decimated. And in this city, which has music at its core, even the banjo and horn he plays in church are washed away.

Down by the river where the fisherman works, others in states of tender, sweet, maybe romantic longing take in the magic of the night.

> down by the river
> sun soon coming up
> café café café
>
> in between moondown and sunrise
> limbo space between the dark and the light
> café café café

Elsewhere the city rocks. What the fisherman thinks of as the tourist city of sin comes magnificently alive. Breaking free from the hefta do hefta do life, they proclaim a hefta dance hefta dance life. But joyous, unhinged, glorious defiance suddenly morphs into manic, tragic denial.

> Oh Mr. Rain Mr. Rain won't you go away
> And don't you please come back til Election Day
> 'cause we want to party and we want to play
> and let the good times roll!

But the rain doesn't go away. The fisherman's God does not relent. And when Election Day comes, it will bring a kind of cynicism and neglect that no one can escape from.

Margaret Yard and Michael Sahl have a deep grasp of social and political realities. The final part of the cantata takes a long, hard look at a nation and social system driven by greed and criminal arrogance.

> Oil-dependent we forget who governs us
> Oil rich and oil friendly
> We are beginning to glide and slide
> On our greasy oil base

I think of Condoleezza Rice, an oil tanker named after her, on an afternoon respite from her job of destroying nations, trying on shoes in an expensive boutique while the rages of Katrina were devastating New Orleans. I imagine her now sitting in as a guest pianist at the next performance of the cantata. The Voices of the Lost have entered her and they help her find her way.

Can America also find its way? Maybe. Maybe not. But the mournful, angry Voices of the Lost are everywhere. And they won't go away until they are heard. ■

On the Rape of Abner Louima in a Brooklyn Precinct House

THIRTY YEARS AGO I was sitting in my friend Lennox Raphael's apartment smoking extremely strong grass. Grass stronger than I was used to. My girlfriend Lisa Howell was there. As well as another man. Lennox was from Trinidad. He was a poet, a playwright and a very good cook. It was at his house that I first ate curry, tasted chutney and ate really extraordinary vegetarian dishes. There was always a nice flow of energy between us. He was someone I really, really liked. The other man in the room was someone I had never met before. Like Lennox he was very dark and he was also quite big. He had a real softness to his face. We passed a joint back and forth. The man was lost in his thoughts, doodling intently—I thought nervously—on a piece of paper a little to the side of him. Suddenly I fixated on the pen. I saw the pen as a weapon. He is going to stab me with it. Come on he's just lost in his thoughts. He was lost in his thoughts. Just lost in his thoughts. He's going to stab me. His face was soft. He was going to stab me. Absolutely no hostility was coming towards me. He's going to stab me. My fear and panic were acute. I settled myself down. When he left the room for a few minutes I told Lisa, who like me was white, who had grown up poor and on welfare, about what had happened. She answered in a voice laced with contempt "Why don't you just fight him already and get it over with." What I heard her say was "Why don't you just fuck him already and get it over with." Which was, of course, even more to the point. ∎

—*Read June 14, 2000 at an event at City Hall protesting the police killing of Amadou Diallo.*

"You're Now the Adult"

MY MOTHER FELL a couple days ago, the second time in a couple of weeks. She falls a lot and it is getting more and more frightening. This time she fell in the elevator. Leaning forward she fell backwards hitting her head on the floor. She had to crawl out of the elevator on her back. I am more than a little concerned. There is not much I can do. Somehow I have to convince her to get someone to live with her. She had a couple of different women live with her over the years. She is of two minds about it. But having someone there reduces the chances of an avoidable catastrophe. Had a dream about her last night. It was not a nightmare but a very painful one nonetheless. My friend Freddy who I haven't seen for years had brought my mother and me and possibly some other people together for dinner. There was a warmth I was feeling for my mother. Freddy said why don't you kiss her. I resisted. A bit later I saw my mother had dyed her hair blond. There was a slight greenish yellow tone to the blond and it had not been fully applied. She was a little younger than she is now. And it was clear she wanted to look beautiful for the occasion. And she did.

I went over to her and kissed her a bit to the side of her lips, just barely touching them. And I woke up.

Skin draped over bones. A feathery physical presence. Lying in bed, her head cocked a bit to the right, she stares at the ceiling. Her fingers anxiously intertwined. Her 90th birthday just two months away.

My mother stubborn. Each fall more scary than the one before. I was very frightened, thought she was going to die. What to do? "You're now the adult, she's the child." People started drumming that into my head. It felt wrong. But I didn't know what to do. Everybody is so fucking definitive. Always definitive, as they say exactly opposite things from one minute to the next.

Act decisively. Bullshit. It was uncharted territory for me. I did let what they told me affect how I acted. The alternative to me was a kind of passivity. And that also was about as bad.

But the truth is we are both adults. Some of her decision making abilities are seriously impaired. Still you're involved with an adult who has lived a life, who has survived inside that life and even if something is scrambled it is the elements of their consciousness and experience that are scrambled. And they are not children. And as Carletta once wrote about animals, children shouldn't be treated like children. Certainly not the way an old frail woman thrown into an unbearable situation should be treated. ■

ER Horror

LAST NIGHT MY MOTHER was still in the emergency room after over 36 hours there. When I had left her the night before they said that she would be in a room of her own in a couple of hours. She was moved from place to place inside the emergency room and for a while in a holding room. When Marlene and I got there last night she had been misplaced, then found in a dirty room off from the other patients. Her door was kept open by a bin filled with dirty laundry. They had a huge security guard by her door and she had been held down with cloth restraints. She thought she had been kidnapped and held in a private house in Queens by a mother who had complete control over her son. And she was being tortured. She did not understand how a Jewish woman could do such a thing.

When we got there the restraints had been removed because two friends of hers, Marta and Nellie, raised hell. She had big bruises on her wrists. I brought her to the hospital because she was hallucinating that she was hearing music.

One ambulance driver tried to convince us (after the fact) we should never have called him. He said all she had was "music in the ear" something older people who are alone often get. It is now more than two years later. In retrospect he was right.

On the way to the hospital my mother realized that the music she had heard was really in her mind because she was hearing it in the ambulance in a much softer way. She was totally intrigued by the beauty of the music knowing it was not real and yet enjoying it nonetheless. The emergency room was harrowing. It took hours before she was seen.

After endless hours of hell Marlene and I got her moved to a very nice room on a clean floor with people who were very kind and attentive. No restraints, and instead of a security guard the person she was with when we left was someone engaged in an interesting conversation with her. And so there she is now. Will learn more today what they are going to do next. I won't even go into the horrors of the first day. I will probably need some help in figuring out what to do when hopefully she gets out.

Marta and Nellie two sentries standing by her bed. They asked the person in charge of the ER, "What have you done to her? Just hours ago she could speak brilliantly about anything."

The ER a dungeon of neglect and horror. A great investigative reporter in her early writing career, Marlene Nadle has the same focus, determination and smarts she had then. She had the almost legendary ability to track a naked general sitting in a sauna in the most inner secret sanctums of the Pentagon and get him to reveal whatever information she was looking for. And here she was putting all her amazing talents to use as she organized the entire ER to get my mother moved to another floor. She even spun around those whose job it was to create the obstacles, recruiting them into an army up against a heartless almost criminally negligent hospital bureaucracy that they temporarily forgot they were the mainstays of.

A young woman wearing a white uniform with playful tumbling colorful animals on it came and rolled my mother on a gurney out of the ER into the elevator up to the 6th floor.

A stunning, very pregnant Indian nurse greeted her with attention and kindness. My mother thinking we were at a book party asked her whether she was a writer or a publisher. A very sweet man, Marlene thinks a nurse, I think a nurse's aide, sat with her afterwards talking with her as we left. This changed later into an alternative memory about being brought to the backroom of a bookstore to be examined by a doctor and his beautiful pregnant wife. My mother even now perplexed about why they would have an examining room in the back of a bookstore. ∎

Seduced and Abandoned?

WHEN MY MOTHER WAS gravely ill, the two doctors who were the most forthcoming, who seemed the most empathetic and the most engaged, were also the two who at the end of the conversation said that this would be the last time we would meet. Each gave the impression during the conversation that they would see me again. One was a Hispanic woman, colorful extensions in her hair, with a smile on her face, almost singing to herself while doing paperwork behind the desk at the nurse's station. The other was a man who I think was both Jewish and gay. Each was psychologically insightful and unusually astute. Each had a senior position. Each gave the impression that they would be there for you. The thing that struck me is that it happened twice.

I think each of the two doctors could allow themselves a certain openness and vulnerability because they knew they would likely not be seeing us again. It is hard to know if the promise came from the intensity of the conversation and the clear emotional need I had. A subtle guilt on their part that this would essentially be the sum total of our contact. They were caught up in the flow of the moment, did not want to break the momentum of the conversation.

I could open up to them. When speaking with Dr. Hernandez I almost wept. To be able to draw me out in such a reassuring manner would very likely be part of their training. But to make a promise, even an unstated promise, that you know you won't keep would not be.

I can see how someone could be very distraught by what could feel like being abandoned after a need was stimulated. With me that feeling was fleeting and not terribly deep. Gratitude being far more what I felt. Still it did create an unnecessary expectation. And after all this time the experience continues to gnaw at me.

On the phone during a long and very helpful conversation with Dr. Hernandez I spoke of the remarkable transformation my mother had undergone, the brilliance of her observations and the profound state she was in. "I'm looking forward to the possibility of having that experience with her." Only to tell me the next day she was going on a three-week vacation. And telling me that when we had originally spoken she didn't think my mother would survive the night.

Dr. Hernandez had been trying to prepare me for the real possibility of my mother's death. She was almost sure that my mother was at death's door. When I saw her the next day, she was surprised at how my mother had rallied.

At the Comprehensive Care Plan meeting a couple of months later I said, "My mother seems to be preparing herself to die. She is in a profound state." "I don't doubt it," Dr. Silver, a doctor in the geriatrics division answered. "But that doesn't mean that she will die."

He brought me up short. I was caught up with the magnitude of my mother's journey and locked into my own sense of things. I didn't realize just how locked in I was until that moment. I greatly appreciated him telling me that. And she in fact lived four more years.

At that meeting though, it happened again. Dr. Silver giving us the impression that he would be there for the long haul or as long as the haul would be. Not someone just attending this one meeting. I don't remember his words, but when the shift happened there was a slight change in his voice. It was very similar to how Dr. Hernandez sounded when she told us about her vacation. That it happened a second time underscored the first. Otherwise I probably would have forgotten about it.

I don't think the unstated promise in any way was necessary to the comfort they gave me. For it came well into the conversation. The expression of concern and emotion maybe would have been more difficult for them if they knew they would have to see me again. Possibly if a certain barrier or speed bump had been placed up earlier the flow of the conversation might have been somewhat interfered with. They certainly were more intimate and personally attentive than the other doctors I dealt with.

Now it could be that I associated understanding and awareness and attributed a particular consciousness to them because one was Hispanic and colorful, and the other gay and Jewish. I remember once being chastised by a rabbi for speaking at what she considered an inappropriate time. I was surprised that she took the institution she was part of as seriously as she did. I didn't think as a woman she would. But clearly I was wrong. And here I was wrong again. Because in the crunch the identification, certainly the attachment to the job and institution was paramount. Great insight there, I know. But I still get fooled each time. Emotionally fooled, at least.

Even with (or possibly because of) all that's going on, the attention is flattering. You are "seen," taken seriously. Obviously what is said is significantly scripted. How could it not be. But it still feels attentive and personal. Yet almost on cue, the door clamps down hard. Your time is up. It was a significant time. The parameters set up seem loose with a lot of give. But not as loose as it can feel.

What can you do? They need to disengage, other patients to see. And you know they have to protect themselves from someone's extreme need or from any attachment you might want to form. As well as the possible multiple, endless calls you might make.

One time there was a change in plans about what was going to happen with my mother. She was going to go to rehab rather than to a hospice. The change in plans happened so quickly I called Dr. Silver to check on something about the change. He said with real impatience, "I already told your brother this." How was I supposed to know? Hadn't yet spoken to my brother. And if my brother in fact had told me, there was no reason that the doctor couldn't tell me also, just to make sure my brother got it right. Or if I had a question he could explain it. In fact, if you want to get technical, I was the one designated as the person information was first supposed to be told to. Then again maybe he had to run to the toilet. ∎

Charisma

SAW MY MOTHER YESTERDAY in the hospital. A visitor came by. Someone whom she has spoken to for years on the phone. Ruth, a woman younger than myself, the daughter of a friend of my mother's who had a four-year ending badly painful affair with a psychoanalyst, a "brilliant charismatic" man who touched her in deep and profound places. Places, she said, that her husband could never reach. At the time she told her husband straight out about what was happening; he still wanted to be with her but she told him that she had to leave him. After her break-up with the psychoanalyst she returned to her husband. From time to time, she still sees the ex-lover who has grown very old and frail and helps take care of him.

My mother suddenly very alert waded headlong into the conversation, constantly referring to the ex-lover as "That son of a bitch." In truth her words seemed to grow more out of loyalty than real conviction. But when Ruth insisted that she wasn't a passive victim in the affair, that it was something that she chose to do, my mother answered that charisma was a powerful allure and people with it have some responsibility for its power. Back and forth. Great discussion about love, life and desire. ∎

Routine Car Stop

ONE NIGHT MANY, VERY many years ago I was standing on St. Mark's Place, watching a group of cops making "routine" car stops. I saw one cop motion to a driver to pull over. At first the driver—a young black man in the car with his girlfriend, a young black woman—didn't see him. The cop, who was white, thought he was being ignored. So he jumped in front of the car, which was inching along, and yelled that the driver should turn right. The driver—his eyes darting back and forth—looked totally confused and panicky. Whose right? His or the cop's? He turned in one direction to pull over and almost hit the cop. The cop became incensed and looked genuinely scared. He grabbed the driver out of the car, threw him against the door and put a gun to his head and screamed, "You tried to run me over. You tried to run me over."

It was a near tragedy. The driver had done absolutely nothing wrong. But even short of a tragedy, it was a three-day weekend, so the driver had to spend four nights and three days in the Tombs. His car was towed and he had to pay for that. His girlfriend was beside herself with worry. She didn't know what was going to happen to him. They were here from Philadelphia and she had nowhere to stay and knew no one. A couple of my friends agreed to put her up and all of us spent the next number of hours trying to find any organization that could be of help. This on a late Friday night of a three-day weekend. Months later she called and said I didn't need to be a witness, that the charges had been dropped. ∎

Chased

ONE NIGHT MANY, VERY many years ago I was walking down Waverly Pl., on a dark street adjacent to Washington Sq. Park. The street was deserted except for two short tough looking white men walking in front of me. I'm also white and had long hair and had $80 in my pocket—a full week's pay I had gotten earlier that day. The two men made me nervous so I walked quickly around them, making a wide berth and continued walking down the block. I had gotten about half a block ahead when one screamed at me. I turned around, didn't know what he was saying and continued to walk. He screamed at me to stop. I looked back again, stopped. They then started walking quickly towards me, shouting all the while. I started running as fast as I could, looked back and saw them chasing me. I turned a corner to 8th St. and ran into a shop for protection. They followed me into the shop scaring me half to death. They had walkie talkies and were some type of civilian street patrol. "Why did you run?" "I thought you were going to mug me." "No! You were going to mug us." "How can I mug you? I'm half a block away and walking in the other direction." "You were behind us and you'd better not forget it."

Once in the street we were surrounded by a growing number of people who started shouting and cursing at them. The two guys frantically called the local police precinct on their walkie talkies. One of the people in the street said, "Walk away; they can't touch you." Others said the same thing. So I walked away. Two minutes and a couple of blocks later I heard sirens coming from various directions all converging on that spot.

A chilling thought I've never been able to shake. What if I ran to a cop and said, "Help! Two men are chasing me." ■

Robert at 80

What a Pathetic Life I Lead

A German filmmaker in her 70s
A Zimbabwean woman in her 20s
Love them both
Wildly attracted to each
Have no chance with either

"I'm a very good lover, a terrific friend and a lousy boyfriend." I would say this to women and it worked like a charm and more often than not we would have sex. An anarchist poet living in the Village. Sometimes that's what it would be. We would keep it that way. A bit impersonal, more impersonal maybe than it should have been. It created a space of excitement and had an allure of freedom. Sometimes my actual talent would disrupt the fantasy. "Hey, you write beautifully" with a slight surprise that was always a bit hurtful. But still I enjoyed it. It moved from a kind of cool "impersonality" in playing out a fantasy, to a subtle but real distancing which while at times disorientating was not the worst thing. Because I thought it was still mostly play acting and not all that impersonal. And I said what I said with conviction because I thought it was true. But unfortunately emotions crept in. Jealousy. Possessiveness, expectations etc. One lover said, "I have the worst of both situations. I'm too caught up with you to have other lovers. And I don't have the security that a commitment would give me." And that was it in a nutshell. Not exactly a nutshell. Because it doesn't include my own insecurities and jealousy. Once I understood that I really couldn't follow through I could not say it again. It would have just been a line, a lie to get sex. And without conviction it wouldn't have worked anyway. So I stopped saying it. Have not really been able to figure out what to say or do since.

My downstairs neighbor. A very thin dark brown woman always spectacularly dressed. A Mohawk haircut and an aura so bright it lights up the stairs or the street, always bringing a big smile to my face. Before we actually met I saw her talking to a tender, muscular man who works in the restaurant on the ground floor of my building. His father had recently died and he had been away for quite a while to be with his family. They stood in the vestibule, her empathetic face filled with emotion, her heart wide open and present. A couple of months later we spoke. A fashion designer from Zimbabwe with magic, soulfulness, tenderness and wild, brilliant perceptions. My head spins whenever we are together. What can I have with her, a woman in her 20s maybe early 30s, who wants to get married and have children. And who doesn't want anything interfering with the plan.

There is nothing I can say at 64. If I were 28 or 33 or 42 I wouldn't have wanted children any more than I do now. And I certainly never wanted to get married. A younger me now would probably be different than the younger me then. Who knows how and in what way. But for better or worse it is this older me that's at issue. What would I need to change in myself to have even a remote chance of being lovers with her?

Friends with benefits? My feelings for Aziza too intense and complicated for that. Fuck buddies? There is I guess a difference between fuck buddies and friends with benefits. Fuck buddies might in fact be easier. More straightforward. More direct. Why? I don't know why. Just felt like saying it. Though haven't heard that term for a while. Francesca's fuck buddy moved into her apartment after 9/11. He came over the night before and it was two years before he left. What starts out as friends with benefits often winds up on court TV. At 65 being Aziza's "boy toy" is probably out of the question. But then again stranger things have happened.

I think again of my beautiful downstairs neighbor. For the first time age really comes in on me. I think of myself at 80. That is just 15 years away. Though 50 was a while ago. And what does she need with that? And how then can this intimacy be expressed without committing her to the possibility of tending to an old man. Obviously anything can happen to anyone at any time. But here there is an almost certain future if I live that long. A commitment to each other would take that into account. Eighty though is still potentially very vibrant and very sexual. Another reason monogamy as an ideal is shit. With some real fluidity between us whatever sexual connection we had would not limit her to it. Me neither I guess. But in this case it would be her I would be most concerned about. Why am I obsessing and fretting about something that is very unlikely to happen? I guess because it's fun to do.

Months later. We speak about one weekend before we became good friends, when she was still living downstairs, when she cut herself off from everyone and everything. No e-mail. No phone. A four day urban retreat, looking deep into herself, trying to find a "purpose," a direction, a deeper meaning, a deeper pursuit. I tell her about a small cottage on the top of a hill somewhere in Zimbabwe where I imagine living when I'm 80. In my fantasy Aziza has created some space for me on a large plot of land that is dedicated to some very significant pursuit. Maybe a place for children. Maybe something entirely different.

"What will you do there?" she asks. "Well, I'm there. That should be enough," I answer. "You have to do some work," she laughs. "You can't just live there." "I'll be a presence. What more do I have to do?" "A presence *is* more than enough," she answers, yielding to the power of my argument. And so there it is. My future. A cottage on a hill in Zimbabwe. The destination a certainty. The route getting there very much a mystery.

Walking toward the East Side I come to Greenwich and 10th where there is a fork in the road. Totally forgot where I am going, who I am visiting. A total absolute blank. This has happened a few other times recently. Two times at that very spot. Scary feeling. Tried to relax. The destination returned and I continued. At 80. Hot muggy Zimbabwe summer. Wild committed energy everywhere. Up and down the hill. Not knowing where I am. Which direction I am going. Maybe this is something that will happen from time to time. Hopefully no more than that.

The total blank was very scary. Maybe try to surrender to it next time.

My father at 76 had sold his business, but still tried making deals, still overflowing with energy. "You're still wheeling and dealing," I said. "I'm doing more wheeling than dealing," he replied. ∎

July 16th

MY FATHER AND TWO of his sisters all died July 16th. Each in a different year. I just noticed that the piece Steve Sprung mailed me was printed on July 16th. July 16th just came and went. I didn't even notice it was there.

I mourn my father on the Jewish calendar which comes out on a different date each year on the Gregorian calendar. So it is interesting to me how I don't even know it is the 16th unless I need to know it for some other reason. Even then, if it registers, it does so only briefly.

To have one brother and two sisters all die on the same date is pretty astounding. Another of my father's sisters died July 8th, only eight days before my father died. Almost at the precise moment she died my father called out her name as he himself slipped back into a coma. We buried my aunt Margaret between visits to the hospital. The oldest of eight children, she subordinated herself to everyone else in the family. My God! and here too. Just the briefest service in the midst of a vigil over my father.

I kissed my Aunt Margaret once on the lips near the end of her life. She said something about being kissed by a man. She had never had sex (I don't think) in her entire life. Her lips were hungry for my lips.

On my father's 75th birthday, the same week as Margaret's 83rd, we went to a Japanese kosher restaurant Shalom Japan run by a Japanese Jewish woman. It was a great night. Japanese Jewish food—kreplach in miso soup. Loud boisterous tables all falling over each other. The kitchen was in disarray, the waiters unorganized. Food coming late, wrong food coming, etc. A total scream riot. Orthodox Jewish families having a chance to eat Japanese food. The Japanese Jewish woman was also a performer—a comedian and a singer. At one point she said that she was the original JAP. My aunt Adele thought it was a silly and sexist joke. I thought it was very funny.

Diners were invited to come up to the mic and perform. As

is often the case I was asked—this time by the people working in the restaurant—if I were a celebrity.

What I remember most about that night, the night as a whole is still quite vivid, is a singer, a man, a paid performer not a customer, singing a love song, and directing a whole stanza towards my aunt Margaret. Shortly thereafter she took out her lipstick and applied it quickly, almost furtively. My aunt Claire understood immediately that she had done this for the singer. I had noticed it but had no idea as to why. As Claire spoke to me I felt both the beauty as well as the deep, unfulfilled, and to a significant degree self-betrayed, longing of Margaret's life.

At times Claire had spoken to me with real bitterness about Margaret as a young woman. She called her a traitor both to her gender and to her generation. Margaret informed on Claire to their parents about Claire having had sex. For her entire life she was too good, too self-sacrificing, too frozen by the heat and fury of repressed desire. The oldest of her brothers and sisters, she was the one who never fully went out into the world.

Her brothers and sisters each in their own way were quite astounding. Uncle Alex fought in Spain and ran for Governor of Ohio on the Communist party ticket. He was a playwright and furrier. Near the end of his life we took a walk on a road near his home in Vineland, New Jersey. He told me how, in Spain, he ordered the execution of a comrade, and now, years later, he was pretty sure the man was innocent of the charges. He said it with a certain degree of sadness, maybe even with a certain degree of remorse. But it felt more like a kind of acceptance that in horrible circumstances horrible things will happen. Or maybe it was something to this effect: He died then and I'm going to die now; in the scheme of things what does it matter.

Another uncle, Uncle Phillip, invented diet bread. A huge bread company stole his recipe. There was a small, out-of-court settlement. As a young man he toured the country, as a mind-reader, with Will Rogers.

A young black man—shaved head, earrings, glasses—is poring over long yellow legal pads, writing intently. I look over at his pads, small neat handwriting filling up page after page. He is wearing a white shirt. His back is facing me. I have an overwhelming desire to put my hand between his shoulder blades and have his powerful creative energy infuse me with even a fraction of its power.

As a teenager my aunt Claire would make impassioned political speeches in Union Square. Later she edited the Transport Workers Union newspaper. Mike Quill was the leader of the union. Mike Quill was flamboyant, dramatic, and had a thick Irish brogue. He talked a good line or at least a quasi-militant one. But always at the 11th hour he would capitulate with very little to show for it all. It was only as he was nearing death that he called the strike he had always threatened to do. And for a few glorious days he made his dramatic declarations out of a jail cell.

There are two things that Claire told me about Mike Quill and the Transport Workers Union that have stayed with me to this day. One was that Quill and his friends felt almost total contempt for anyone operating with any degree of morality. They felt that such a person was incredibly stupid and weak. The other thing she told me was that if a person defied him in the union, if that person was very crucial to him, defied him on a matter of principle, defied him to the point of quitting or being fired, Quill, after a few months, would call and apologize, saying that the person had been right and beseech the person to come back. Almost inevitably the person would come back and never, ever again be a problem.

Once when I was in a room with Stanley Aronowitz and Cornel West I made a comment from the floor that was pointed and bitter and deep. I spoke of various ways that I thought social resistance was being turned into a cash crop. Stanley and Cornel became enraged. Cornel his face getting darker and darker responded with uncharacteristic harshness. He tried playing to the audience but it didn't work. I had touched a real nerve. And the audience was very emotionally torn between their respect for Cornel and the truth of my comments. I was not that upset with the harshness of his comments for I understood they sprang not from meanness, but from a place of knowing and not wanting to know that what I had said was true. Sadly given the actual trajectory of his public life even more true now than then.

Once when I was arrested by a cop for interfering with the questioning of a person on the corner of St. Mark's Place and Second Avenue, as we sat in a cab he had commandeered to bring us to the station house, he started jabbing his finger into my chest, his face getting redder and redder. "You see those things," he said pointing to the handcuffs holding my hands behind my back, "that's what you're trying to do to us. I don't understand this. You seem like a nice person. You're not supposed to be here. The other guy is supposed to be here." The other guy had slipped away during all the commotion. The harder he jabbed me the safer I felt. He seemed confused and frustrated not punitive or violent. He told me a minute or two later he needed to calm down and wanted to talk.

The next several hours we talked and we talked, he moving me from place to place inside the station house so that we could continue our conversation. At one point he said, "Well you're entitled to your opinion and I'm entitled to mine." "Yes, but your opinion is why I'm in here," I replied. A light went on in his head. He started making connections upon connections. His life endangered every day, his emotions had a kind of electricity, a kind of existential weight mine never had. The connections he was making about his life, his job, the society were deep and profound and dizzying in their power. At that moment he understood the world in ways that I never had.

The next day we negotiated. He dropped the arrest charge. I dropped a false arrest claim. Afterwards while standing with my friends who had come to the court for support he came over to me and in front of everyone said, "I learned a lot talking to you last night."

After my encounter with Cornel, he called me over and

apologized. He said he didn't know what had gotten into him. We talked a bit about the issues I had raised. Power yielded to me. A part of me felt so incredibly flattered by it. I also understood how difficult it would be to challenge him at such a basic level again.

When Claire spoke so tenderly about Margaret putting on her lipstick I was deeply moved. Also I was fairly shaken about how little of the world I actually knew. Now I don't think I have to understand everything. But not to understand that! I must have been protecting myself from some place of empathy/understanding. Gender. Age. Loneliness. Vulnerability. Desire. Who the fuck knows what. There is so much I don't understand. ■

Oliver Stone

DURING AN OPEN READING in East Harlem, someone read a poem with a few anti-Semitic lines. It was a long poem with much power and beauty in it. Yet it was ugly and stupid. Written by a poet all filled up with himself. A mosque in Cairo. A church in Kansas. A nationalist meeting in Russia. A communist cell in Thailand. A gathering of black radicals in Brooklyn. A neo-Nazi gathering in Austria. Today it was Oliver Stone's turn to say something about Jews.

"Hitler did far more damage to the Russians than [to] the Jewish people, 25 or 30 [million killed]."

The reason few people know this, according to Stone?

"The Jewish domination of the media," he said. "There's a major lobby in the United States. They are hard workers. They stay on top of every comment, the most powerful lobby in Washington. Israel has f***** up United States foreign policy for years."

Then getting himself deeper and deeper in a hole with each attempt to extricate himself from it. "The fact that the Holocaust is still a very important, vivid and current matter today is, in fact, a great credit to the very hard work of a broad coalition of people committed to the remembrance of this atrocity—and it was an atrocity." Very nice of him to acknowledge that.

I know what it is when I try extricating myself from a hole of my own creation. And how each explanation creates a bigger problem. So I think I should cut him some slack. But clearly it is not out of nowhere this shit is coming from.

These "essential truths" are rooted so deeply in paranoid projections. Smug in his ability of stripping away liberal pieties that are often used to hide and mystify oppression, Stone reached into a grab bag of instantly available prejudices and pulled out what I am sure felt to him like nuggets of courageous truth telling. This stuff is just out there. He had recently finished his movie *Mi Amigo Hugo,* a tribute to Hugo Chavez, leader of

Venezuela. Over the years Chavez has said suspect things about Jews. Nothing too horrible. Nothing too good either. So it is not hard to imagine a nod and a wink between Chavez and Stone as he made the movie. Of course that doesn't mean that it happened. And if it did happen doesn't mean it would spin out into anything more serious than just the self-assured arrogance of two know-it-alls pontificating in a poisonous environment. ∎

Next in Line

A BELLIGERENT NUCLEAR SUPERPOWER, greatly humiliated and to a degree thwarted, is constantly looking for enemies to conquer. Any nation or movement that resists instantly becomes the most monstrous thing on earth. This time it is Iran. So the abuse of women, to a lesser degree the humiliation and murder of homosexuals, and the ugly holocaust agnostic pronouncements of its President—Mahmoud Ahmadinejad—are the things highlighted. Yet, with just the faintest traces of embarrassment, the same U.S. government aligns itself with Turkey, a country that not only denies a holocaust, that of the Armenians, but also was responsible for the holocaust it is denying. And the President and Secretary of State succeed in silencing the Congress, a congress that at best is docile and passive about the crimes of its own nation, from condemning it. Similarly, the U.S. attempts to put a veil around other countries, such as Saudi Arabia, where human rights abuses are at least equal to, if not greater than, those of Iran. And if at any point Israel becomes a liability to its global designs, the oppression of Palestinians, rather than being apologized for and facilitated, would be the subject of multiple sanctimonious pronouncements by U.S. officials. Such is the nature of governments and their apologists. ∎

Sometime in 2010

March on the Pentagon

I WAS ON A BUS going from San Francisco to Washington for the 1967 March on the Pentagon. The bus was divided into two parts. Those who called themselves politicos. Those who called themselves hippies. The distinction made no sense to me since I thought of myself as some combination of both. What slogans to write on the side of the bus? A compromise was reached. One side of the bus said "Make Love Not War." The other side said "Up the Ass of the Ruling Class." In my mind that confirmed my point. Because under the right circumstances both slogans would be saying the same thing. ∎

Argentine Journal

These are unconnected excerpts of a journal I kept in August, 1992 while in Argentina on the occasion of my aunt and uncle's fiftieth wedding anniversary.

1

AS WOULD BE EXPECTED, I arrived at the Sheraton Hotel in Buenos Aires and the first thing the man behind the desk asked me was whether I was a movie actor. Since January I have been stopped at least thirteen times and asked if I was an actor. No one quite knows the actor's name—it might be more than one person—it is always someone just on the tip of the tongue—there's usually a snapping of the fingers as the person tries to figure out who I am—though sometimes they do identify me by movie if not by name. New Year's Eve at Judith Malina's party a woman drunk and somewhat obnoxious

A digression: They have chocolates and drinks in a cabinet in my room. I thought they were gratis. But in fact it was $3.25 for potato chips. $7 for a small box of chocolate. $11 for cashew nuts, etc. My brother is upset because he ate the cashews! Just stumbling out of bed could cost a bundle.

The woman at the party said to me that the movie I was in was lousy, but that I was pretty good. I felt insulted that someone would be that cavalier with my work so I made some comment back. A man then asked me if I had really been in a movie and if so what was my name. I told him that the movie had generated such hostility that I didn't want to talk about it any more. A few weeks later at a restaurant a waitress asked in a most respectful way if a couple at another table could have my autograph. Another time—here I'm only giving the most notable encounters—three young black women saw me and immediately huddled together. I was delivering newspapers into a building and one of the women followed me to the building. But as she was about to enter I was just about to leave. I was standing one step above her—she looked startled—I made a playfully menacing face at her and she ran to her friends screaming—all three huddled together shrieking as if they were in a horror movie. I went over and said something. They shrieked louder combining horror with the giddiness of being approached by a celebrity. They mumbled "ghost" and dashed by me in a screaming clump and ran into the building. Just a couple of days before I left New York a man came over to me and said he admired my work and shook my hand. I was deep into my own head and somewhat unnerved when his hand entered through some protective field I had placed around me. At first I thought he might have seen me give a reading or somehow knew of the magazine or had read something that I had written. But in truth he had just seen me on a VCR the night before while watching *Ghost*. He had seen me walking on Twelfth Street just a few days before and had decided to approach me the next time he saw me. He said I was also very good in *Taxi Driver*. The man at the desk in the hotel said I was terrific in *One Flew Over the Cuckoo's Nest* with Jack Nicholson. Ghosts and lunatics all. My charisma is pretty intense.

2

We finally arrived in Buenos Aires at 1:30 PM, a good seven hours after we were supposed to. My aunt and uncle had been at the airport since 5:30 in the morning. It was a real pleasure to see them. My uncle had lost some weight. I thought he looked well. My mother thought he looked terrible. He had a real playfulness about him. But also a dark cloud hangs over him. A depression. A storm. There is a generosity and a lurking anger. You have to know your place. Where that place is is hard to define. But it is there. He gives you tremendous latitude but there is a very definite and dangerous line you better not cross. He makes me a little worried. My aunt and uncle will take us out later for dinner.

If you don't look left for just ten seconds the poverty barely visible from the highway can be missed. As we drove into the heart of the city from the airport, the vast shantytown could not be fully hidden from view. The outer edges could be seen in that one instant. Getting to the restaurant late last night by cab— a group of men were huddled in the back of a battered pickup truck. They looked worn out, tired, darker than most people I have so far seen. For a day and a half poverty has almost totally been hidden from my sight. But there are warnings in the hotel to be careful about everything. This my brother saw immediately. Protect your valuables. Don't open the door for anyone. Driving from the airport, with almost an act of will my uncle seemed to obliterate the poverty around him. Nothing unpleasant could divert his attention. My uncle's robust gusto can hide from view what might be just below the surface.

It is possible, I suspect, except for the fear or for some sudden unexpected intrusion, not to see the misery and poverty lurking somewhere near and around you if you are wealthy enough to shield yourself from it. My uncle, now the president of a multinational corporation, has the energy to burst through unpleasantness or even horror. My aunt and uncle have suffered enormously in their lives. Concentration camps, slave labor camps. Family members murdered. Their son, four years ago, dying in his thirties.

While in Auschwitz my aunt established a routine. She did this to preserve her dignity and to help keep herself alive. Each morning she would go into the courtyard outside her barracks and wash herself and comb her hair. She did this even in the coldest of winter. Once while standing in the snow she forgot where she was and for a moment before crashing back into despair, the beauty of the day sent her into a reverie.

A Nazi, a particularly brutal Nazi, took a liking to my aunt.

He told her that she reminded him of his sister and that he would protect her in any way he could. No sex was required. Her staying alive provided him some sense of his own decency.

About five years ago I went with my mother and brother to a glatt kosher super orthodox hotel in Staten Island for Passover. So kosher was the hotel that even matzo balls couldn't be served for fear that the hot soup would leaven the flour. They had an elevator that ran by itself, stopping at each floor, opening up by itself so that no buttons needed to be pushed and so no electricity would need to be turned on. The place was filled with ultra-orthodox families. Many rabbis and many wives and children. There were some single orthodox men and women looking to get married. And then there were people like myself who were not of the community but had come with relatives. Whatever our differences with each other might have been, being separate was what joined us.

The hotel was on its last legs. It had been sold to the city to be turned into a welfare hotel. One last month was being squeezed out of it by its owners. Traps for rodents were placed throughout the hotel. The traps were quite visible and not very comforting. Our rooms were a mess—holes in the ceiling, showers not working, etc. A mattress in my brother's and my room was soaking from a leak in the ceiling. Clearly the management of the hotel was not going to put money into a place they had already sold. The food, to be fair, was plentiful and delicious.

Back now to those of us not part of the ultra-orthodox community. Outside the hotel we might want nothing to do with each other. More probably there would be no reason for us to meet. Our interests, our preoccupations, would more than likely have kept us apart. But here we were all "outsiders." We were connected in our estrangement from what to us (independent of what might be genuinely appealing about it) (and maybe for very different reasons) was the rigidity and confinement and oppressiveness of this ultra-orthodox community that for reasons of family obligations we had been cast into.

It was there that I met a man who had been in the foreign service who had worked in Chile before, during and after the

Pinochet coup. Pulled together as "outsiders" we began to talk. When he mentioned what his job had been I asked him if he minded me asking him some questions.

I told him up front what my politics were. I told him I was asking my questions to find out information and not to bait him into an argument. He was eager to talk. He wanted, it seemed, to unburden himself. I asked him if he felt remorse about what had happened, did he feel what had been done had to be done, etc. He told me it was a painful and difficult question. That he felt some guilt in being a part of what happened. He thought, however, that Allende had helped bring it on himself by not being able to control the ultra left wing forces in the society. He didn't think a fascist response had been inevitable, and he thought that the vital interests of the United States could have been protected differently. And yes, he did feel remorse. I asked him what his specific job had been. I don't remember his answer. I asked him what his role in the destabilizing of the Allende government had been and whether or not he had a sense of what his role was in the larger design. He said the higher up you are in the planning the more clear is each part of the whole. So someone can help in the building of a school and not have even a vague notion of why they were being sent to that particular village at that particular time. So while he knew that his job was to protect U.S. interests and that Allende was viewed with suspicion, he didn't have a real picture of what was going to happen—the ferocity of the repression. He had in fact left the country a few days before the coup for a visit to Argentina—yes, Argentina!—and returned a few days after it had taken place. It was simply circumstances that had pulled him away at that particular time. When he returned, the brutality, the murders, the repression were happening in full force. The Minister of Education under Allende was being imprisoned with thousands of others in the Santiago soccer stadium. When Mac (not his real name), my new friend, found out about it he became enraged. To his mind the minister had not been particularly "political." He was simply a very dedicated and decent educator. Mac went to a high official in the Junta and protested vehemently in the man's defense. He helped get the man released. Mac's outrage, his decency, all focused to help this one person who was "innocent." He could, of course, only help this one person. The others he could do nothing about. His culpability somewhat assuaged. His own humanity reaffirmed.

Mac did not approve of the level of brutality unleashed. Though again, he felt something had to be done to defend against the rising influence of the ultra left groups who he felt were being increasingly effective in mobilizing, I suspect, the poorest of the population into some sort of action.

He felt a particular bitterness towards Henry Kissinger who he felt had given Pinochet a green light for the repression. He related to me, God I wish I had written it down, significant details about a highly confidential conversation between Kissinger and one of the leaders of the coup. Kissinger in effect told him that the U.S. will look away. Kissinger said that world opinion was highly selective in what it decided to condemn, very hypocritical. And so while the U.S. couldn't explicitly condone their actions, it would look the other way because a very important job needed to be done.

Another thing he was upset about was that a close friend of his, the U.S. Ambassador to Chile at the time, was, he felt, being slandered in the movie *Missing*, where he was portrayed as someone who was complicitous in the cover-up of a murdered American. He thought the man was honorable and that he had acted in good faith. The Ambassador had sued the film-makers for libel. The trial was just about to begin. Independent of the accuracy of the charges against his friend, he had no real sense of the Ambassador's larger complicity in the horror.

The conversation went on for hours. It was clear he was getting a lot off his chest.

3

The woman gave me a long hard look. Caught a strong vibe. Not sure how she looked. Decided to hang out in the lobby just in case. She looked hungry and sexy. Is it what I want? Do I want to talk to her? Would I be open to being approached by her? It sure would be nice. I have to piss something bad. Is she someone I want to meet? She definitely wants to rumble. With someone. Well will it be me? She's getting up to leave. She wants to speak with me. I have to go over to her. She won't come over to me. She did come over to me. We spoke and then she came to my room. I became increasingly more nervous. Something was off. She was a hooker. I said I'm sorry—a terrible misunderstanding. I inscribed a magazine—for a nice conversation. She asked for $10 which I didn't want to give her. I told her I had no money. I am a little nervous. Maybe I should have given her the money. And here I thought I was so attractive. God what a jerk I am. Even before she said she was a hooker I had lost interest. It didn't seem right—I'm a wildly perceptive person it seems. I didn't know how to put an end to the evening and ask her to leave. I think it might be harder for a man to ask a woman to leave than a woman to ask a man to leave if the man and the woman who are doing the asking are both conscious people—that is if the man is not a prick. Though women are taught to be accommodating. For me to say no to a woman who puts herself forward sexually feels like a betrayal. If I have accepted her advances to the point of saying no. I think it is harder for a woman to do. Obviously it is a betrayal of myself and of her, certainly of myself, to do something, except in rare circumstances, that I don't want to do. Except for the first moment with Betty I felt no heat coming towards me. This unfortunately is the case when things are usual. There is often a strong initial attraction and it either fades completely or turns into something else. I think it could be me that is losing interest. Anyway it can never be rekindled, and going through the motions—like I was ready to do here—never really amounts to anything. I hadn't wanted to sleep with her before I knew she was a hooker on the job. Thank God I had a way out. This was not a great experience. Not an interesting experience. It was simply a bad experience. No bad exchange between us. A simple misunderstanding. It was clear that something was off and I couldn't ask her to leave. I thought I was getting in over my head—not exactly knowing why. I sort of decided to let sex pull me wherever it may. Not the greatest idea. I thought it would be an antidote to a sexual attitude of being too careful. This was really stupid. I don't think I took away any business from her. I was the only man left in the lobby. We spoke for maybe ten minutes. Then she came up for about five. Already I was worried about my passport, my wallet, etc. I wanted to ask her to leave. We kissed—it didn't feel right. She asked me when I was going to leave Argentina. It didn't feel right. I know I didn't want to see her again, let alone not want to be with her tonight, which I thought I could somehow manage. When she came back from the toilet she said we had to discuss a present. I told her there was a misunderstanding, apologized profusely—not overmuch but quite a bit. Said let me give you a magazine. Inscribed it: To Betty—For a lovely if misunderstood meeting—Robert. She asked me if I had any money. She wanted $10. I said I didn't have it. I hope there are no repercussions. It would probably be a dumb thing for her to do. She said this was her hotel. She worked it alone. I thought she was hot, maybe lonely. I thought maybe—why not. I didn't want to be with her after the first three minutes. I let the momentum of the encounter pull me to it even as it was getting more and more uncomfortable. What an unpleasant experience. This cannot be the first time this has happened to her. Unless there is a code everyone but me knows about. It was too easy. Though at times sex is as easy as that. I was pulled by her sexual assertiveness. Again I thought she was in the mood and what could be safer than a man passing through town. My own fear of entanglement—parodied by my fear of having to see her a second time—was enough for me to want it to end before it began. This was not a good experience. The tenth time I've said it. She was so sexually aggressive—Mr. Perceptive here did wonder maybe it was not what he thought though he did think it could be what he thought. She had seen me looking at her. As she left the bar she waved to me with a big smile across the room. I thought maybe she was the recreational director of the hotel. More probably somebody who had stopped for a drink. Maybe another guest at the hotel. Maybe someone who worked in the area. She came over and gave me a big kiss on the cheek and placed her knees against mine. I was attracted to her boldness, though I was quite nervous. Though I wasn't attracted to how she looked. The situation attracted me. Though I wasn't sure. She spoke in Spanish—a little English. I spoke in English, a little Spanish and once or twice in Hungarian. I told her I was a writer—somehow hoping at this point that for some reason that would be a turn-off. Someone making that strong a sexual gesture towards me made it hard for me to somehow put an end to it. And I was somewhat caught up in the adventure. When she asked to see my room I could not say no. Again I didn't want to hurt her feelings—somehow thinking that I had given her a wrong idea—didn't want to punish her for her sexual boldness—I'm not talking about a very sane thought process here—I was getting less interested in the situation and found it more and more difficult to get out. When it became clear what was up, I was relieved. I could say no. Maybe I should have given her the money to avoid any unexpected hassles—like a pimp out to make an example of me. I don't feel I should pay her for taking up her time. I really didn't know what was up. No harm for her trying for a few extra bucks. I did not feel as if there was a threat involved. Though one can always be nervous. This was a big mistake. I don't like to misread a situation as badly as I did this one and allow myself to get caught up in something that is clearly not going to work out too well. This was very dumb. She took it in stride. What a dumb thing to let happen. I think I'm most upset that I had placed myself in a vulnerable situation in a strange country. I could have been robbed—I know I didn't trust what was going on. This was just dumb, simply dumb.

An upheaval of violent dreams. At one point in the night I felt the walls of my psyche shatter. ■

Dave Zirin, *What's My Name, Fool?: Sports and Resistance in the United States* (Haymarket Books, 2005)

Of course there is exploitation but there is fun and beauty too. I mean, what's more beautiful than a 6-4-3 double play perfectly executed where the shortstop fields a groundball and flips it toward second base in one motion, the second baseman takes the throw in stride, pivots, avoids the base runner, and fires it to first on time. That's not a put-on. That's not fake. That's beyond all social analysis of the game. The idea of people coming together and amazing the rest of us.

—Lester Rodney [from What's My Name, Fool?*]*

AS A FRESHMAN SPORTSWRITER for the Queens College *Phoenix* I was sent in 1962 to cover a baseball game. One of the players made a couple of errors and failed to get a hit, striking out three times. I used him as an object of humor throughout my piece. This is what sportswriters did and I was pretty pleased with what I had written. I thought I was very funny. The next time I saw him, he approached me with a kind of seriousness and respect I had never experienced before, and said, "What you wrote was hurtful. I was trying my best and there was really no need to mock me." I apologized and thanked him.

What's My Name, Fool? is written with compassion, insight and love. It is fueled by a profound social rage. Dave Zirin is the type of sportswriter I never encountered growing up.

I have only maybe two or three people I can talk sports with. The conversations are fun and they are in their way intimate. But I have them very rarely. Because there is so much about sports that goes unexamined, I am very protective of the parameters I feel safe inside of.

Reading Dave Zirin's book is like speaking with an extremely knowledgeable friend about a subject I am nervous about. He has very important information and analysis to share but he does not shut down the space where exploration can take place. Often while reading the book, stimulated by something Zirin had written, my imagination just went off in its own direction.

For example, when he writes about women in sports, "On the one hand, sexism of stomach-turning proportions prevails both within and surrounding sports, from cheerleaders to beer commercials. But sports have also provided a critical place for women to challenge sexist ideas about their abilities and potential," I remember a friend, a long jumper who as a freshman in college, in a non-sanctioned meet leapt past the too short sandpit and landed on the ground, breaking her ankle. The meet officials didn't think a woman could jump that far. She recovered but never competed again.

He writes about homophobia and my mind flashes to the time my teammate, trying to get me to play better defense in a basketball game, yelled, "Get up next to him. Fuck him if you have to."

Throughout the book we see acts of compliance and acts of defiance continually playing themselves out. The event that inspired the very title of the book itself highlights the truth of this.

The title comes from a heavyweight championship fight between Muhammad Ali and Floyd Patterson. A faster, stronger, younger and certainly socially more courageous Muhammad Ali beat up on a physically courageous though vastly outmatched Floyd Patterson who insisted on calling him Cassius Clay. "This fight is a crusade to reclaim the title from the black Muslims," said Patterson. "As a Catholic I am fighting Clay as a patriotic duty. I am going to return the crown to America."

Zirin writes, "On the night of the fight, Ali brutalized Patterson for nine rounds, dragging it out yelling, 'Come on, America! Come on, white America....What's my name? Is my name Clay? What's my name, fool?'" It was an assertion of pride, dignity and social/political/personal defiance. It was those qualities of his that electrified the world. But it was also one black man mercilessly pummeling another. In that way the fight

was not all that different from the time when "Southern planta-
tion owners amused themselves by putting together the strongest
slaves and having them fight it out wearing iron collars." What
do you do with all that? I'm not sure. And this is the type of
question I kept asking myself as I read the book.

Floyd Patterson's iron collar that night was very clear.
Muhammad Ali's was not. But the collar he wore, as Zirin
discusses in the chapter on Ali, would take a terrible toll in the
long run. Floyd Patterson survived and when Ali was stripped
of his title and sentenced to jail, Patterson, a soulful and poetic
person in his own right, said, "What bothers me is Clay is
being made to pay too stiff a penalty for doing what is right.
The prize fighter in America is not supposed to shoot off his
mouth about politics, particularly if his views oppose the gov-
ernment's and might influence many among the working class
that follows boxing."

Zirin in this book gives us an answer to a question that seemed
to have eluded millions of baseball fans for decades. Why was it
that for so many years the Boston Red Sox never won a World
Series? The answer of course is that they were the last team to
be integrated. "In 1959...the Sox removed their color bar by
begrudgingly bringing marginal infielder Pumpsie Green up
from the minors."

A digression: To be considered the "marginal" player
who integrated baseball's most racist franchise twelve years
after Jackie Robinson must have taken its own kind of courage
and equilibrium. I looked him up on the Baseball Almanac
website. In lieu of the corporate endorsements he could never
get, I thought where else but *Socialism and Democracy* could the
entrepreneurial fantasies of Pumpsie Green that I saw there
be fully appreciated. "Some day I'll write a book and call it
'How I Got the Nickname Pumpsie' and sell it for one dol-
lar, and if everybody who ever asked me that question buys
the book, I'll be a millionaire." –Pumpsie Green in *Baseball's
Greatest Quotes* (1982).

What's My Name, Fool? touches on, and to a degree discusses, what to me is a crucial question. In a world of winning and losing is it possible to have anything but anxiety, humiliation and failure run rampant?

What happens for example when I watch a Michael Jordan soar through the heavens. Does it make it easier or harder for me to move freely? Can I fully appreciate Jordan's athletic greatness without wanting to extract some measure of revenge? Conversely how could Jordan soar like that and yet be so emotionally closed off to people suffering in Nike sweatshops. And is my asking that question the revenge I am speaking about? A need to steal some part of his vitality.

Even in the little neck of the woods many of us inhabit, in the section of the universe devoted to radical change, people are constantly compared and contrasted. Our work and talents compulsively evaluated as people are assigned their proper place. Winning and losing a constant drumbeat of concern.

I remember a woman saying in a public forum that she didn't feel ugly. She felt mildly attractive. That she didn't feel she was stupid. She felt that she was intelligent but not brilliant. And no one understood her humiliation. She brought me up short. For I always saw her as she described herself. My own silent role in her oppression.

Dave Meggyesy, the former St. Louis Cardinal linebacker who wrote a moving and sensitive introduction to the book, was also interviewed in it. In the interview he speaks of the pain he felt when he was benched for his anti-Vietnam War activity. "...All kinds of self-doubts began to creep into my mind. Because one of the core values in sports from the athlete's point of view is that it is a meritocracy: The best players play.... When someone messes with that, it messes with everything that is great about sports." The big question here is when the most glaring forms of injustice are alleviated and something like a meritocracy is achieved, what impact will that have on that howling sense of inadequacy that so often drives and destroys people in a world as pathologically competitive as this one. Many of the competitive attitudes that we often condemn in sports characterize so much of society in general and in fact even move right into our left academic and artistic universe. It is again something reading this book raises and forces me to think about.

In the chapter on Jackie Robinson, a very deep and complex one, there is a pointed back and forth in public pronouncements between Robinson and Malcolm X where each brings their genius to bear as they struggle out various strategies for social change. The exchange often is quite nasty. Yet, "When Malcolm X was killed, Robinson wrote an obituary that, unlike most, didn't bury Malcolm but praised him. He quoted Malcolm saying to him 'Jackie, in the days to come your son and my son will not be willing to settle for things we are willing to settle for.'"

At one point a comment like Malcolm's would have felt prophetic and inspiring. But knowing the form of the massive tragedies that befell their families—Jackie Robinson's son returning from Southeast Asia "carrying a gun, scared of shadows, and addicted to drugs"; Betty Shabazz, Malcolm's widow, dying as the result of a fire set by their grandson—these words now have less resonance for me than they might have once had. The large-scale retreat from social and political concern by the generations coming after them compounds my despair. Yet the fires of freedom continue to burn and at least a significant number of people still do refuse to settle.

Near the end of the book there is a wonderful interview with Toni Smith, the Division III basketball player who turned her back on the U.S. flag during the playing of the national anthem in protest of the war in Iraq. "But it wasn't just the war," she said. "It was everything before that. It was everything that the flag is built on, everything that is continuing to happen and things that haven't happened yet."

There is a photo accompanying the interview. In Toni Smith's bearing and posture you can feel the presence of so many others. There is Tommie Smith and John Carlos. Billie Jean King, Babe Didrikson, Muhammad Ali, Pumpsie Green and Mia Hamm. Maybe even Floyd Patterson. In the actual photo itself, two of her teammates are giving her support. "Two of my teammates always stood next to me during the national anthem," she said, "one in front of me, one behind me, holding my hands—Melissa Solano and Dionne Walker. They were absolutely and completely supportive 100 percent, and would have taken a bullet for me." The tenderness and strength of their love brought tears streaming down my cheeks.

•

Each night when I lie down to go to sleep I start making up baseball teams. Basketball teams. Tony Oliva, right field. I've done this since I was around twelve. Bill Sharman at guard. It calms me down. Left-handed black basketball players.

After reading this book I have whole new teams to make up. Teams of Resistance. People who inspire me during the day and help put me to sleep at night: Carlos Delgado *1b*, Jackie Robinson *2b*, Roberto Clemente *rf*, Pee Wee Reese *ss*, Toni...

I think this book will bring great pleasure and understanding to any number of people. ■

I'VE WANTED TO WRITE a short story for many years about a young woman who dreams of being a famous poet, of being part of a culture of artists and poets, part of a world-transforming community. She comes to New York from her home in Halifax. Through the sheer force of her belief that that community exists she approaches various well-known poets, artists and musicians without fear or ego. She penetrates their cynicism, their despair, their competitiveness, the wall they have set around themselves, and touches that part of them that is still similar to her. They become transformed.

She rises quickly in their circles. Things fall almost effortlessly into place for her. She is totally without guile. Her confidence soars, her contagious humanity reaching out to audiences throughout the city. She writes a book. She gives a reading at Cooper Union. And here I'm lifting a story Meyer Liben told me about Delmore Schwartz. The place is jammed. The first two rows are filled with homeless people. After the reading someone asks her to repeat one of her poems. Then someone asks her to repeat another. And so it goes until the security guards clear the hall. The curiosity and the excitement of the homeless gives her a sense that she has reached the masses. They of course just wanted shelter from the cold and the longer the reading, the later they would have to go out into the night. At some point it all starts crashing around her. I'm not sure how the story will end. ■

Lavender Dicks

LAVENDER DICKS IS the name of a lesbian detective agency. It could be the name they've given themselves. Or they could have been dubbed that by the tabloids and the handle stuck.

I heard a woman having sex from somewhere in my building. I couldn't be sure from where. I wondered who she was and where the sounds were coming from. I thought I would have to have sex with each woman in the building to find out. Though it was also possible she was just visiting someone. I only heard her moans in the morning. And on three different occasions. Each time while sitting at the kitchen table. The facts are a bit murky. The clues a bit vague. In the story she could be a witness to a crime. A detective who lives on the third floor and had heard the passionate screams and moans is hired to find her. She has to seduce all the women in the building in order to accurately identify who the woman is. Now people make different sounds with different people. This compounds the problem. But she is well trained and quite confident. The arch-criminal has to track her down first. He/she also has to seduce all the women. It is a race against time. Finally the criminal and the detective come face to face. Should they seduce each other, shoot each other or just turn away till another day? ■

Mis-Fortune Cookie

YOUR TALENT WILL BE recognized and duly thwarted. ■

I RECEIVED A PHONE call from Shari last night telling me that Charlotte had died two months ago of pancreatic cancer. Reduced to a dim light in her rear view mirror, no one else thought of calling me or probably even knew I was there to be called. We had fallen out of touch since she moved to Vermont over a decade ago. I am absolutely devastated.

Shari had seen her a few months before, looking very healthy and buoyant. She had just run into a friend of Charlotte's, which was how she found out.

I read various accounts of her death. On his website Stephen McArthur wrote: "She passed last night at home with family and friends. Only a little while before she died, Hannah, her ten year old daughter, who has been struggling as only a child can with this kind of unreal thing, came to her and sang."

When I told my mother what happened she said that she had somehow been thinking of Charlotte all that morning. "You know she had loved you very much," she said. A friend remembered running into her at the now long defunct Elgin, a movie theater in Chelsea, right after Charlotte and I had broken up. She had been sitting behind him. He had just broken up with his wife. They could only make nervous small talk. Halfway into the movie she left the theater.

"I have a sense of the dramatic" was a favorite expression of hers. And if anything ever was true that certainly was.

Charlotte and I were walking through Washington Square Park one day in the late '60s when suddenly a man was stabbed. Blood started spurting from his neck. Within a split second Charlotte ran over to him, put two fingers over the wound and kept them there until help came. Afterwards she wiped the blood off her fingers and pretty much said nothing.

Our relationship had been a potent mix of sexual chaos, love and pain. Not grasping the depth of her love, I betrayed it.

•

Puffy from drink, in the grips of a depression, she was a prisoner in a tiny apartment, in a dangerous neighborhood, living with an insensitive fool.

I could never fully say "our apartment." Even after three years of her living there. Another small humiliation for her.

Charlotte and I would alternate working, with her on balance working considerably more than I did. During this period however she not only wasn't working, she more or less was home all the time. She would be there when I left, when I returned. Always there. Surrounded by her thick depression, I was never alone in the apartment.

Building up in me was an overwhelming need to masturbate. A strange and guilt producing need. There was no time or place to do it. No privacy whatsoever.

One night almost beside myself I raced over to Peter and Patty's apartment, ducked into their toilet and masturbated. Total pleasure, total relief. When I came home an hour later the door was locked and Charlotte wasn't home. So sure was I that she would be there I didn't take my key. I sat on the top step right outside our sixth-floor walkup apartment and waited. A friend dropped by and started talking to me about sex he was having with his sister. "The most exciting sex in both our lives," he said. The wettest she's ever been she had told him. They ate each other but she didn't want to fuck. We talked about that and we talked about other things. My own earlier sexual escapade looming larger to me than my friend's revelations about a little hot incest. And Charlotte still hadn't come home. My friend eventually left and I waited and waited on the top of the stairs. Finally, "You're out fucking other women, you asshole..." A stream of curses and flying objects hurled from her handbag. It turns out her friend Cathy had passionately kissed her, and Charlotte had kissed her back with equal passion. So it was the objects of her desire not mine that came hurtling towards me.

Black and blue mark on her arm where I had hit her. The same black and blue mark on the same part of the arm that I saw on the girlfriend of another friend. The measured, controlled violence of sensitive Jewish men.

One time, a couple of years after we broke up, I visited her studio, a studio full of new paintings whose canvases had been slashed. "You think they're too violent?" she asked. "I think they're great," I answered kind of numb to their power. Later we argued. At one point, looking straight at me, her voice steady and laced with steel, "There's no place you haven't screamed at me. Scream at me one more time—you see that knife—I'm going to take it and kill you." My behavior with her and for that matter everyone else changed on the spot. ■

In Memoriam

SHE DIED AT THIRTY-FIVE much of her insides removed from ten years of cancer operations. Light-skin black woman with huge freckles and bright red lipstick she moved in and out of mental hospitals during those ten years. "Fucking is what I do best," she once said. Her white friends always criticized her for fucking white men. "They treat me better than black men," she would reply. Her heart would often be broken. At times she would wander through streets in a daze, walking in and out of restaurants and shops. A walking nervous breakdown it was called. Terror of dying made her crazy. She died young, angry and bitter. ■

HOW OFTEN HAVE WE seen a man walking down the street, a child on his shoulder playfully kicking against his chest, and a woman walking somewhat to his side, maybe even a little behind, looking worn out and depressed. We have seen this also at parties, the man playing with the child—everyone impressed with what a good parent he is—and the woman freed to have the run of the party will as often as not sit slumped on a couch. Clearly it is an improvement for men to take responsibility for being with children. But often there is some rip-off involved. The man most likely will have more social power in the world than the woman and it is something that he will not and probably could not give up. And now he has usurped her role as nurturer, celebrated for things she is taken for granted for doing. And she is left with nothing. And it is likely that some woman will crack because of the injustice of it all and she might do something horrible to herself or to the child or to the man. At that point everyone will trot out her particular psychological history and try to explain everything away. ■

Uglier by the Second

I HAD A SHORT intense spectacular love affair with a woman from the Philippines when I was in Israel. Her name was Lolita. As I was about to return home I mentioned it to a sociology professor at Tel Aviv University whom I had met a few months earlier in New York. He was kind of a socialist peace now type. So I felt some affinity with him. He said too bad you didn't have an affair with one of our beautiful Israeli women. Bad enough. Then a couple of minutes later as I was about to leave he asked me if I could give him Lolita's phone number. It was absolutely repulsive. I never spoke to him again. ■

Stare

NAOMI LOOKED BLOATED, HER breasts swollen, her face red yet simultaneously emptied of color. Normally she is very contained, stylish, well manicured and I think quite attractive. This day she was wearing a sweatshirt and sweatpants. I had twice proctored her on exams. Both times we were in a room alone together and things went quite smoothly. With some measure of warmth, she thanked me politely each time, but was strangely distant whenever we would run into each other. On this day, while I was sitting at the computer, she flew by me into the tutoring center and spoke in a loud manic voice to a young woman who like me was also a tutor. Her chest was heaving in and out. It looked like multiple internal eruptions were taking place. It was like watching a fire or an earthquake or a raging flood. It was happening right there to the side of me and I got caught up in the intensity of it. I stared at her and in some strange way it was a turn-on. I suspect I was invisible to her until I stared. I certainly didn't want to make her uncomfortable. But it is not hard to see why I did. Which I am sure I did. Afterward she would turn to stone if I ever said hello.

Naomi often reminded me of how my recently murdered cousin looked when she was a young woman. At times I would look at her trying to understand something about my cousin, how certain gestures and styles had skipped on through generations. So again if she was uncomfortable it wasn't like she was imagining me looking at her. Though I think it was more that one time than anything else. In any case I don't think I did anything wrong. That being said I absolutely don't feel good that I had unsettled her in any way. And it is something to be more careful about in the future.

The competing narratives: emotionally unbalanced woman imagining things (Naomi twice expressed discomfort about working with two older women tutors) or predatory male tutor leering at women. I do focus in. I pay very close attention. Sometimes God forbid, the feeling is decidedly sexual. That doesn't mean the close attention is always the same or that everyone responds to it in the same way.

At the orientation session those in charge of the program dealing with students with learning disabilities and students with emotional problems said these students can often radically misperceive situations. They talked about how one woman in particular was bent out of shape by a male tutor staring at her. They said things like that often happen, that everyone, particularly the men, should be mindful of how we interact with the students. The woman they were speaking about was made to sound disturbed and unbalanced. Naomi is far from that. They sounded relieved that the woman, whoever she is, had graduated. No one looked at me when they spoke. And in fact throughout the day they were all unusually friendly and warm.

Whether indeed they were talking about me or about someone else or about a recurrent problem, it felt creepy to possibly be protected by people's good feeling for me at this woman's expense and it also felt potentially menacing that the lens could switch in an instant and everything I do appear like the cold calculations of a predatory male. If for example I am friendly, polite, considerate to someone it can feel like I'm establishing a cover. He's a real nice guy he would never do such a thing. And in fact without trying to establish a cover, you do act differently and have different feelings towards different people. You might in fact violate someone and not someone else and not at all be manipulative about it. Or you might be. Or you might have done absolutely nothing. But once you are seen through that lens anything you do gets interpreted a certain way. In fact while they were talking I was starting to see myself through that lens. Everything I did felt well thought out and calculated. It was a bit spooky. I know people are so filled with guilt that they can believe what is said about them even when it is not true. But the fact is in this case I did make her uncomfortable.

In more extreme situations these narratives can be catastrophic. You saw this happen after the Atlanta Olympic bombings when someone was targeted as a suspect and everything that he did was interpreted as indicating the likelihood of his guilt. They near ruined his life. And even more tragically after the attacks in London when the police killed a Brazilian man whose every action was interpreted as him about to be a suicide bomber when in fact he was doing nothing even remotely close to that. These air-tight narratives, each with their own internal logic, can in fact at times give some insight into behavior and social patterns. But clearly they also can be extremely dangerous. In the confines of my workplace nothing quite so serious is likely to happen. Though being the target of sexual harassment on the one hand or the victim of a false charge on the other can be quite traumatic to say the least.

The tutoring center is overflowing with people. The contact between people is often intense and intimate. It is hard not to watch people, catch someone's eye, be looked at yourself. A bulge in the crotch. A nicely placed tattoo. Breasts flowing out of blouses. It's not like you're not there and don't have a response. Barring someone really being disgusting, a certain amount of confusion, missteps and violation can't help but happen. The best you can be is sensitive to the nuances of these situations. It is easy to misread a look or a word. I once saw Naomi being unexpectedly touched by a student/tutor, a warm, strapping young man, someone I think she liked. She looked a bit startled but then seemed okay with it.

How do you read all these things correctly? A fellow worker called me at home. I hadn't given her my number. She sounded drunk and clearly had screwed up her courage to call me. I'd much rather she didn't call. It made me very uncomfortable. Yet if she were someone I was interested in I would have been thrilled. How was she supposed to know? I certainly don't begrudge her calling me. When it was clear my regard and liking for her was not going to go in that direction, she backed off. It took a while for me to be comfortable with her again. In addition, I thought she might have some pull in the office and I was nervous about some sort of retribution. Time worked it out. It is one of the things that can happen when people reach out for contact, particularly where different types and layers of power are clearly and not so clearly at play. ∎

Jerry Sandusky

This was written before the trial and conviction of Jerry Sandusky, former Penn State assistant football coach, for multiple acts of child molestation.

FOOTBALL IS A BRUTAL sport. Jerry Sandusky spent years teaching people how to scramble brains and break bones. Football is a big business and sports in general is deeply corrupt. There often is a closing of ranks; the old boys network rallying to each other's defense. A hearty pat on the back, a series of excuses, justifications, mystifications and the diminishing of the reality of victims. As well as very selective but probably real identification and concern with the pain of one of their own.

Football grooms athletes to obey authority on the one hand and to feel above normal constraints on the other. Athletes are placed above and beyond everyone. But when they are damaged or outlive their usefulness they often are cynically discarded. And often societal fury driven by envy, insecurity and payback comes pouring down on them.

In the case of Sandusky we don't know yet what happened. We do know that Mary Kay Letourneau was placed in prison for 7½ years for what clearly was a consensual and passionate affair with a 12 year old student, Vili Fuallaau. Any serious damage done came from the response of people around them. How she and her lover were treated was disgraceful. Later when she was 43 and he was 22 they were married.

In the case of Michael Jackson we don't know what happened. Were kids sexually abused, were they not. Was there sexual contact. Was it consensual, or as consensual as any contact between adults and children can be. Was it manipulated, was it coerced. Is any situation involving that much power, money, star power too overwhelming for a kid to be consensual. Could it have been a wonderful experience.

Kids are sexual beings. Calling them "innocent," as so often is said, is an attempt to obliterate that truth. Sexual abuse violates vitality, sexuality and someone's essential being—not "steals their innocence." *The X Factor* has a week of entertainers singing Michael Jackson songs. So if he did abuse children, in his case, well he's Michael Jackson. And if not, then there was a witch hunt against him which might have hastened his death.

One question to a neighbor about whether you are a sexual abuser, or worse a child molester, could stigmatize you for life. So these investigations by themselves are dangerous to unleash. People are very glib about the consequence of such things. Narratives are easy to create. And police often frame people they are sure are guilty.

Oprah Winfrey displays photos of seedy looking men who she says are child molesters. The unshaven school janitor, the cross-eyed handyman, the junk collector. They certainly look the part. So they must have done what they're accused of or even convicted of. I remember a man who certainly fit that description. He would give blow jobs to teenagers on the roof of my building when I was growing up. He told me that his social worker said that he needed his release. The boys would allude to it. But not speak much about it. I didn't like the man too much. My friends seemed more than okay with the experience. Later, and I am not sure that I remember this correctly, someone said they had beaten him up.

Oprah insists that even if a girl says she enjoyed sex with an adult it still has to be rape. She ostensibly was addressing the confusion about experiencing bodily pleasure during a sexual assault. A very crucial issue. But since she extends the definition of what an assault is to include any sexual contact between an adult and kid, no matter what a kid may feel about it, you don't even know what necessarily happened to the girls. If a girl or a boy feels positively about the experience what can they know? The child molester is even lower than the terrorist in popular consciousness, and may actually provide the entryway to the continual loss of liberty.

When Arnold Schwarzenegger was running for governor of California a number of women, real live grown up adult women said they had been sexually harassed and physically assaulted by him. They described the experiences as traumatic. The governor, a champion body builder, a world famous actor, a person with enormous wealth and power, is a pretty scary person to come up against. I wasn't there so again I don't know what happened. The accusations could be true or not. Still Oprah had him and his wife, her close friend Maria Shriver, on the week before the election for a nice friendly chat. This was done to reassure the California electorate that Schwarzenegger was a genuinely decent guy. None of the charges were alluded to. In the world of Oprah Winfrey girls (and boys) who say they feel positive about the sex they've had with an older person can't be trusted. Also not to be trusted are grown women who dare to claim they were abused by one of Oprah's powerful celebrity friends.

In almost every cop or FBI TV show I have seen, the threat of rape in prison has been used as a way to coerce a suspect into cooperating. Sometimes when a rapist or suspected rapist is caught there is vindictive glee in what will happen to them in prison. In addition there is often tacit approval of a beating, as a suspect is being transported from one place to another. Brutality and rape are sanctioned on these shows. There is nothing to indicate that this doesn't happen quite often in real life. In all the fevered talk about Penn State, this part of the story is never spoken about.

How would I handle it, if I stumbled upon a situation similar to the one described in the showers in the Penn State locker room. The scene was described as a young boy face first pressed up against a wall in the shower with Sandusky pressed up against him. How would I intervene. How could I be sure it was what it looked like to me. Would I be able to defy authority. Would I be too intimidated by the power of someone like Sandusky. Would the possibility that it could be consensual (something most people would not be restrained by) interfere with my judgment. Would I want to report something to people who very possibly would cover it up. Which very much could also include the police. Would I be ready to wreck the life of someone, maybe someone I feel close to. Turn them over to the criminal justice system, where people are routinely dehumanized. Dooming the person to public and private ruin when I could be misreading what's going on. Or unleash a series of unexpected repercussions on the victim. And if it were consensual you could be unleashing a torrent of horror on both of them. And in a fevered universe even if it was what it looked like, the consequences to each could be nightmarish. Everyone is so sure about what to do. Most times I become paralyzed in a situation like that.

I once was in a van passing a park where there were a lot of homeless people. We stopped at a red light. There was a man pursuing a woman. It was a slow motion pursuit. Two homeless people among other homeless people. Were they playing? I don't know. She was half naked, wearing only a shirt. And she seemed to be resisting him. Then they had sex or was it rape. My boss/friend was sure it was "just sex." I wasn't at all sure. Imagine bringing the cops into that situation. What should I have done. What could we have done. If it were consensual even strung out, down and out consensual and you bring the cops into something like that, God knows the chain reaction that could have caused. If she was being raped and I jumped out of the van I could have been knifed. How in the world could it be investigated. If she was being raped she would have almost no credibility. If they were out to get the man, if he were innocent he would have no credibility either. She was naked, running away, playfully resisting or was she actually frightened. Or some combination of both. He caught up with her and they started, what? Having sex? They both looked in a semi-daze. She was in a rhythm with him. Still there was no way for me to read it. The light changed and we continued on our way. The image is frozen in my mind. ■

Astor Place

My friend and I
Both hung up on the same woman
Walking and talking, analyzing every gesture
Wondering who had the inside track
Who she might choose

We were lost in our musings
Our energies hotly flowing
Our powers of analysis finely tuned
Our obsessive natures in full bloom

And there she was
On Astor Place

Hi!

We made small talk
Nervous stumbling
A quick disengagement

My friend and I continued on our way
Lost again in discussion
Who will she choose?

Well, she chose me. Not at the time. But now. Thirty-five years
later. Calling me last night at 3:45 am in a sultry voice saying I love
you. Second time in two weeks jarring me awake in the middle of
the night. She calls me over and over again. Recently she speaks in
tongues. Sometimes she just rages. Usually it is the same message:

  If you are hungry may you always have food you choose
to eat and can afford. If you are thirsty have a beverage of your
choice. May you always have a home you enjoy. If you make love
make love with all your heart. Thank you for publishing me.
Love, Karen Cohen.

No matter what else is happening I get a call from her. In person or on my voice mail. It punctuates my life. A repetitive motif in a horrible comedy. "Fuck you," I yelled slamming the receiver last night. This has been going on for over fifteen years.

Sitting in an office forty years ago, a group of us were processing information for the Kerner Commission on the roots of urban riots. Karen returning from lunch break, flushed and filled with energy, grass stains, a couple of small leaves still stuck on her clothing. Lying in the park caught up in the romance of a beautiful day. Who would expect the catastrophe that her life has become. Horrible breakdowns. Wild rages.

Once at the beach—don't even know how I got there—I saw her swim far out in the ocean. Powerful graceful strokes until she was a tiny speck in the distance.

Sex, fucking, making love. For weeks bleeding from the rectum before she checked it out. Picking men up from the bar. She told one that she was tired, would like to do it right, and put off fucking for another night.

One morning I saw Karen in a Ukrainian restaurant on the Lower East Side with two other people just as she was about to go mad for the first time. The three of them looked spent, exhausted, a very nice kind of exhausted. I was sure they had been in an orgy. I was filled with envy.

Over the years I have had to make a peculiar adjustment. I know that what I read as bliss is often the first stages of madness. What looks like freedom often in fact is a person in terrible pain. It is not that I now see that the person is suffering. I see the lifting of repression and a powerful life force breaking free instead.

I was once asked to write a little statement about an opera written by Margaret Yard and Michael Sahl, two very close friends.

"There is a moment in *John Grace Ranter* the opera that has stayed with me all this time. John Grace Ranter part preacher, part squatter, part anarchist, part religious fanatic goes to his fellow patient/inmates and reaches through walls of pain, repression, drug induced fog to touch a place in each that is still alive, vibrant and free. The hospital is transformed into a space of liberation. My God is that rendered with overwhelming beauty and power. But such Freedom is always feared and despised. There is a struggle over the control of the patients. Bureaucratic, technocratic doctors on the one hand and a whacked out charismatic lunatic on the other. Horrible forces released through people who in some ways actually care about the patients and are concerned about their well-being.

"Freedom unleashed is menacing and beautiful. The ending of the opera is tragic. Yet it is the immense possibilities of that freedom, so powerfully depicted in the opera, that remains with me today."

And there it is. My own yearning, wanting some connection, some experience, some release. Fearing the madness, the chaos just lying there ready to be unleashed.

Karen as a young woman had long curly black hair. A beautiful dark-haired Jewess would be how she would have been described in an earlier time. She had a sense of style and of adventure. A small firm body. A very cute ass. She came to Goshen where a group of us were living out in the country, and had sex with Carl. Two tired world-weary veterans of the dating wars. Both in their late 20s, they fucked and sucked and walked in the country holding hands. But it was clear it would be only for this short time. It was a script each knew well. Karen initiated a three-day juice fast. I joined for a day. But it seemed too manic for me.

Years later her hair wild and gray. She gained a lot of weight from anti-psychotic meds, has a set of false teeth that at times falls out when she gets too excited. Until recently she chain-smoked, her apartment reeking from stale butts and smoke. It also stank of cat shit. Even now though there is a bounce to her walk. And she writes music and creates beautiful collages.

Years before and I don't know why but she was the first person who had been a friend that I didn't cross the street to say hello to. I hadn't seen her for a while and had absolutely no desire to do so. Clearly something had soured or deadened in my feelings towards her. Another time later I ran into her and a friend and she whispered something about me to her friend and they laughed. It surprised me. Not going out of my way to greet someone has happened since then any number of times. A faint feeling of hurt, lethargy, a general demoralization. Usually though I will cross the street to say hello.

Karen wound up in 1968 occupying a building during the student strike at Columbia. How did she get there? Did she know these people from before? She wound up or already had been connected to a radical group centered in Newark. It was a group similar to the Weather Underground where emotion ran wild beneath ideological constructs. No matter what, she kept the mannerisms of a well-educated upper middle class young woman. What happened to her? What was the particular source of her bitterness? She clearly had been scared out of her mind by something. Was it drugs? Did she get involved with gun running? Was she in a group where instead of monogamy being smashed she was the one being smashed?

She again startled me awake twice last night. Just as I was about to fall asleep and again early in the morning. Called her now to complain but her telephone has been disconnected. ∎

Out Front in the Lead

MICHAEL DURANT BROKE DANNY Stein's nose at my ninth birthday party. Mike never picked a fight, but he never backed away from one either. Danny had been somewhat of a jerk, but his father didn't see it that way and threatened to sue my father. Michael was the best athlete on the block. He was a terrific baseball player who later had a tryout with the Yankees. I have a vivid memory of seeing him once when he was a teenager, in his baseball uniform and spikes, walking, with an air of athletic worldliness, out of our building to a waiting car. There were times he would go to a new ball field to join a pick-up game. At 5'9" he looked slight. He might be one of the last players chosen, then electrify the other kids as he tracked down fly balls in the outfield, threw runners out with his strong left arm, and hit doubles and triples and an occasional home run from both sides of the plate. He smiled a faint, interior, almost invisible smile after each catch or hit, a smile I think that reflected both pride in his accomplishment and pleasure in the surprised gasps from the other players.

As a high school cross country runner he won many medals, though he never came in first. In shorter middle distance races he didn't do quite as well. I remember listening to a track meet being broadcast from Madison Sq. Garden. Knowing he couldn't win, Mike raced out to the early lead. "I like hearing my name," he told me a couple of days before the race. After the first three laps, and after the PA announcer called out his name at least ten times as the leader, he faded out of contention.

Michael did very badly in school, got into a shitload of trouble and as soon as he could, joined the army. He was put into the infantry. He fought in Africa as well as Vietnam. He fought in secret imperial wars and was wounded at least twice. "Being shot at is no fun," he told me. And it was only then that it occurred to me that he could be afraid of anything.

In Vietnam he sometimes had to eat rats and it was there that he was sent into peasant villages. "If anyone, an old man, a child, anyone looked at me cross-eyed, I would shoot them," he said. One mistake in judgment and it could be "me that was dead."

My mother sometimes sees him in the post office hanging out with two homeless men and one homeless woman. He turns his head away when he sees my mother; he is almost toothless now.

Michael's father was a fireman who carved nightsticks with very ornate patterns on the handle. Sometimes if you held one in your hand the handle would cut into your flesh. I remember seeing Mike Sr. once crouched behind a car spying on his wife. He put a finger to his lips so I wouldn't speak. I had never seen a grown-up with a face as young as his. Another time I remember him pulling a burning sofa out of the lobby of our building into the street and knocking the flames out with his jacket. He died at fifty from a heart attack.

As a kid Mike would vomit large white chunks whenever my father would take us on a car ride. He was a couple of years older than me. We would have goosing fights. His body seemed to change almost overnight. I remember the first time I grabbed his newly developed cock and balls. We rolled laughing, sprawling all over my parents' bed onto the floor. At sixteen he had his girlfriend's name tattooed on his arm. I would see her name tattooed on the arms of other boys. I remember Harry Bower breaking off with a girl he had sex with. He hung up quickly after telling her he didn't want to see her again. As I am writing this I remember the rage I felt towards Steve Schwartz when I saw that he had grown pubic hair. I saw his black pubic hair as he was putting on his swim suit at the St. George Hotel. I still hadn't grown any pubic hair. For years I tried to obliterate him for this. To my shame I hurt him very badly. He too went to Vietnam. He served there as a cook. Howard Ross went to Vietnam and had both his legs blown off by a mine. Another friend, John Franco, told me of having to pile up dead bodies there. And the horrible feeling he had shooting blindly into the jungle and not knowing if he had hit someone or not.

A couple of years ago, after losing a job I went to the unemployment office. I saw a handwritten sign which looked strangely familiar. As I was waiting I saw Steve Schwartz behind the partition talking to another worker. He mumbled hello and said with obvious discomfort, "I'm here and you're there." It was for some reason more than he could handle.

Michael once hinted to me that he and his friends had possibly murdered someone during a fight in a parking lot on Long Island. Another jerk it seems who picked a fight with the wrong person.

I wrote this piece sixteen years ago. My mother called me the other day to tell me she had run into Michael's mother who told her that Michael had died a year ago from lung cancer. ■

Sabbath Gift

I SAW HERMAN LEVY looking stunned, shattered standing frozen in a corner of his father's living room. His marriage was over. The emotion was so raw that its intensity was almost comical. He never recovered. I met his brother Harry at my brother's wedding in 1992. He said Herman lived for 30 years as a hermit in Florida before he died. Their father was a total jerk. Telling my mother after she went back to college what a hippie waste of a human being I was. Blamed her going back to college as the source of my turning out to be such a failure. This I didn't know until recently.

Found band-aid inside Mrs. Jacobson's hallah baked for my mother as a Sabbath gift. Her husband Ben Jacobson was a sanctimonious DA in Queens, a fanatic death penalty advocate, nasty and mean. Another of my father's friends in the synagogue. On the High Holy Days there is a prayer where congregants beat their chest to purge the sins committed during the year. Ben Jacobson pounded his chest with a fervor unmatched by anyone. When I was accepted into the army I was in a state of shock, falling rolling thrashing on the living room floor of my parents' apartment, shrieking uncontrollably. Smashing down a lamp shattering the glass shade. The only thing my mind could grab onto was the image of women in shock running from burning buildings, and my knowing they had recovered. At some point my mother sent me over to Mr. Jacobson's apartment, very naively thinking he would be of help. He had total contempt for me. For my fear, for my weakness, for my lack of patriotism. Later he told my mother I was a cancer on society. I never should have gone over there in the state I was in. My mother's judgment in that instance was terrible. My father was in Japan. I remember him coming home almost immediately. Greeting him at the airport, he waved with an air of someone who would take care of everything as he descended the steps from the plane. And so he did. And so did I. And so we did. And later after some real effort I was finally rejected by the army.

So many of my father's friends from the synagogue were incredibly messed up. Not everyone to be sure. What was happening there? My father wasn't that way. He was expansive, humorous, friendly. He paid attention to people. He paid attention to people other people didn't even know were there. He was a little dissociated. Very high strung. Nervous. In some important ways confused. But extremely funny, generous and loving. And at times pointed. Once in the car while he was driving I was going on and on about the army. My fear of dying, of being hurt. Until my father turned to me and said, "Old age is like the army." He brought me up short. And I shut up.

My mother at that time was more private, more internal. More overtly depressed. Not being a "phony" she succeeded in simply being unfriendly. Much more uptight, puritanical than the rest of the family. I picked up my father's friendliness and my mother's brooding. Both my parents' fear and anxiety. My father's playfulness and humor. My father's interest in politics. My mother's radical rage. My father's absorption in the news. And my mother's anger about my father listening to the news on the radio during meals. The oppression of the dinner table was suffocating. I would leave the table as soon as I finished eating. My father at times had severe outbreaks of hives. And as with everything else involving either of my parents, only the remotest corner of my brain would register it.

I think the need of some parents to protect children from bad news can leave foggy vaguely unsettling gaps in understanding. Similar and different from the amnesia drug they put in the anesthesia where terror trauma is wiped from memory, while the impact on the psyche might not be. ■

My Fourth of July Weekend

THE JULY 4TH WEEKEND was pure pandemonium. I had to go for an endoscopy on July 3rd. I had seen the stomach doctor, Dr. Rosen, about a week before. He was the one who was going to perform it. A day before, I got a call saying he was no longer working at the clinic and another doctor, Dr. Chaffey was going to do the procedure. There was a backlog of people when I got to the hospital. I was the last one in the room and I spoke to someone who told me that Dr. Rosen had jumped out the window a few days before and killed himself. I had some premonition when he examined me. Something about him upset me. I couldn't locate it. He seemed to me as if he had a big secret. Some thoughts flickered in my head. I really don't know what it was that I picked up. I do know that I was in a very oblique way worried about him.

Something in his face. *I was looking at his lower chin, his lips, the space above the lip. A little bit of dark hair, a five o'clock shadow was beginning to appear. Don't know what caught my attention first. Maybe the light powder covering both his stubble and a dark birthmark near his mouth. I fixated on the powder and the birthmark and stubble. Dr. Rosen was extremely pleasant. But something was off. I don't know what. I asked if I should have an endoscopy. "Well if you want one I will do it," he said. He didn't feel entirely there. He said he could do it that Friday. But I was busy. So we set up the appointment for the following Thursday. As we spoke there was a split second, almost infinitesimal delay in our exchange, almost like a phone connection slightly off. I was a bit apprehensive. I sensed there was something wrong. Some big secret he was keeping. A sexual harassment charge. An illicit affair. A gambling debt. Drugs. Possibly an illness. Maybe a friend in some kind of trouble. Something very large. I was a little concerned about being injured when he did the procedure. I felt he was in deep pain and I made a decision to be particularly nice to him afterwards. Not necessarily say anything different than thank you. But a thank you with more emotion.*

Carletta's cousin Laura also went to him. We discovered this at our joint birthday lunch that Carletta had made for us. Laura said Dr.

Rosen's face at times could be very red. Maybe that was what the make-up was about. He projected an image of the perfect doctor—a combination of competency, politeness and care. And in fact he may have been all those things. Laura liked him quite a bit. The paper said he was highly emotional, that he would often cry if a patient died. He loved going out dancing with hospital staff.

I would not have recognized him from the photo I saw in the paper. Laura said it looked like him. She had been to him a number of times. "Thank God he wasn't my psychiatrist," she said. As for me I only remember his mouth, the chin, the powder, that split second delay.

After the procedure, which a third doctor performed because of the backlog, I checked the Internet to see what happened. According to the one article I read Dr. Rosen felt overworked on the job and had another job lined up. He had a meeting with his boss who called him a traitor for wanting to leave and the boss possibly had tried to block him from changing jobs. Someone in the article said the boss was pretty ruthless in getting whatever he wanted. Dr. Rosen then left the meeting and jumped out the window in the corridor, which was on the 17th floor. There were no other details. My guess, based on nothing really, is that the boss held something over him and threatened to reveal it.

Turbulence, turmoil, leaping from the 17th floor. Laura said she heard that Dr. Rosen's boss' mother had died shortly before this had happened.

When I was told what happened I wasn't fully shocked. But obviously it was very upsetting. The third doctor, Dr. Siegel, was pretty jerky after the procedure. But I saw Dr. Chaffey yesterday who told me that the test turned out ok.

Anyway that was on the 3rd. On the morning of the 4th I went to sit with my friend Elaine who was having chemo. I had to be at the hospital at 8:30. But Elaine had given me the wrong address and I was running all around from block to block trying to find it. Finally I came home, saw I had remembered the address right, but before I went out again decided to look it up. And then found the right one which was located nowhere near where I had been. I was so worried about having stranded her. Finally got to the right place.

It was a difficult morning. Very painful seeing her ill. Very lovely hanging with her. Elaine and I sat within inches of each other. She is there for chemo and I am visiting. The chasm so enormous.

Then I took her home. I stayed a couple of hours at her apartment and went home. About 3 pm I got a call from my mother's caretaker Livia who said my mother had gone berserk, that she couldn't work there another minute and that she was going to leave. I talked to my mother who was hyperventilating. She told me between gasps for air that Livia was going to kill her and then hung up on me. I called back and told Livia to try and keep her distance because whatever she did would only agitate my mother further. My mother was calling her a murderess and a drug dealer. And Livia was calling her a crazy woman. For three hours on the phone between hang-ups and phone calls I finally calmed Livia down; my mother also calmed down. I told Livia that she couldn't leave my mother alone in the apartment and that we would find someone else as soon as possible. It was the 4th of July weekend so she would have to give us a little time. I told her that I wasn't going to try and trick her into staying. That this would soon be part of her past. I called Kathy, the person in charge of the agency, who fortunately was at home. She said she would try and find someone but that it was the worst time possible. Told Livia that Kathy was now on the case and it would be sooner rather than later, but we needed a few days. Then I went to a party to watch the fireworks.

The next day, Saturday, I was at my niece's birthday party when we got a call from Kathy saying she got someone. On Sunday the new caretaker, Ildi, was to come and introduce herself to my mother. When I got there my mother was at the door in her wheelchair very frightened. Livia was hovering anxiously over her. I told Livia to take a break, go out for a cigarette and not worry. I had called Nellie, a friend of my mother, someone who sometimes works for her, to come by and help with the transition. When Nellie arrived things calmed down even more. While waiting for Nellie to arrive Livia was very anxious. She looked both worried about my mother as well as worried about what my mother might say about her. I constantly had to tell her what a good person she was and that she had done a wonderful job. In fact in many ways she had. But she was high strung like my mother and did get locked in with her. A few hours later my brother and sister-in-law and their two kids arrived along with their dog. Finally Ildi came with her son and his very pregnant wife. That made eleven people and a dog.

Ildi immediately went into the bedroom where Nellie and my mother had gone to be alone. The three of them got on very well. Ildi couldn't start that night to Livia's extreme disappointment because her son and daughter-in-law had planned a surprise dinner for her. She did start early the next morning, Monday July 6th, and so far she and my mother have gotten along very well. So let's hope for the best.

That was my 4th of July weekend. ∎

Shit

"I'M ON MY THRONE," my mother jokes when I call her while she is sitting on the commode. A lifetime fearing shit and now in old age life is organized around it. She said if she had the energy she would write an essay on the different ways caretakers talk about her body and her bodily functions. Some are clinical, some "crude like a sailor," others using childish euphemisms. Since it is all in Hungarian it is not altogether easy to translate.

I am grateful to Livia for daring to remove my mother's diapers. Livia was very fucked up in a lot of ways but that act of daring or insight has made a big difference. I hesitate to say it gave my mother back her dignity. Because a person who needs to wear a diaper has dignity. But it was a very significant development for my mother's emotional well-being.

The smell of one's own shit is often pleasurable. "That person is so filled up with themselves that they are in love with their own shit." I think that is true of most people, even the ones making that statement.

The fear of shitting in one's pants in the street or when one is in a public place or has no access to a public toilet has imprisoned many people in their apartments. Pete showed me an amazing piece written by his friend Sidney Morris, a playwright who had AIDS and was incontinent. It was about the things he would do when going out in public which for example included wearing dark clothing. I read the essay many years ago and don't remember the details. But it was funny and very serious and extraordinarily important. I had asked my mother before the crisis if she would write a similar piece. She said she would call it "The Strategy." But it was a bit too embarrassing for her to do. ■

The Dumping of Old People into the ER

MY MOTHER RECENTLY HAD two brutally traumatic experiences in the ER—one at Elmhurst General Hospital (Queens), the other at Mt. Sinai (Manhattan). Both experiences probably caused her some real damage. In each case I was somewhat foolishly comforted by the notion that this was a common response of older people thrust into a dramatically disorientating new institutional setting and that the reaction wouldn't be permanent. But in truth the ER was not something that my mother, at 89, very easily got over and I'm not too sure in what ways it might have made an already precarious situation infinitely worse than it had to be. Also her experience at Elmhurst made me more reluctant to bring her in a second time. It could have been a fatal mistake if I hadn't. But a part of me feels that if I hadn't brought her to Elmhurst, had waited a couple of days until she would have seen her regular doctor, my mother's condition would not have deteriorated as swiftly as it had. Of course there is no way of knowing what would have happened. And because of the extreme fragility of my mother's condition, it feels almost anything I would have done would have been the wrong thing.

Still my mother spent 36 terrifying hours at Elmhurst and at least 20 at Mt. Sinai. At Elmhurst they moved her from place to place to place. They did not feed her any food. When a friend and I went back to look for her the hospital staff couldn't find her. Finally we discovered her alone in a room kept open by a bin filled with dirty laundry placed against the door. One crazed patient opened the bin, scavengered through it and started throwing the dirty laundry up into the air. A 300-pound security guard was sitting just outside her door. He was placed there because my mother had grown extremely frightened and agitated. She was sure she had been kidnapped and tortured.

My mother's experiences in Mt. Sinai were not this extreme, but quite humiliating and traumatizing nonetheless. Both at Elmhurst and Mt. Sinai my mother was calm enough in the beginning. It was only after a number of hours that she began to emotionally come apart. If my brother and I hadn't been with her at Mt. Sinai she very likely would have gotten off her bed and fallen. In both cases she trusted my judgment and went into a place she felt would almost certainly destroy her.

The day after her ordeal in the Mt. Sinai ER, I visited her in her room. She had calmed down considerably, but thought she was a character in a play. A great play as it turned out. "Why would they choose a skeleton to be the leading lady?" she asked me. She referred to the ER, as she had the night before, as the Drug Store. Which was not a bad description of where she had been and she wondered if scenes from there would be in the play/movie. Maybe they will be.

All this to suggest that for older people there should be an ER that at least tries to mitigate as much as possible the nightmare dislocation as well as some of the horrible spin-off damaging effects of being there. In truth the ER is a horror for almost everyone, including the overburdened medical staff. The dearth of available hospital beds compounds the problem by keeping people there far longer than otherwise might be necessary. Deep structural changes in hospitals around the country would be needed to shift a borderline criminal situation in any meaningful way. But something far short of that might be possible. Already separate ERs are in place for children as well as for people with asthma.

Once again: Since reactions such as my mother's are extremely common, I think, at the very least, a special ER should be set up just for older people and other people at high risk for the type of responses my mother had.

Once my mother was moved from the ER to another room, the attention she received improved. How much and in what ways is open to discussion. But what is clear is that much avoidable damage had already been done. Sadly, there's no way of escaping the fact that what happens on the bottom floor of a hospital has an impact on what later happens on the upper floors. ■

Sent a version of this as a letter to a doctor in a senior position in the geriatric unit of Mt. Sinai. He said he passed it on to a number of people.

Later a shorter version of this got published in the letter section of The NY Times. *They had an editorial that day about conditions in ER rooms. Told people about it when I visited my mother in the Mt. Sinai rehab center. They said there was a lot of talk about my letter in the hospital. A couple of years later I read that they had implemented just such a program at Mt. Sinai. Felt good to have been part of whatever momentum helped move that decision along. Though I don't know how it has worked out in actual practice.*

Won't Write a Great Poem
Even if I Could

The city is flooded
Pain abounds
Common outrage
Common sorrow
Pulling together
We do our best

It takes a poetry website
Devoted to change
To call for ecology poems
Where brilliant poet/editors
All socially aware
Are there to decide
Whose work will appear

Compulsive criteria
A kind of hysteria
That even a natural disaster
Can't relieve

It is foolish
I guess
To expect more
In a world
Where
Solidarity ends
At the critic's door ∎

Leslie Klein's Petition

Arnie Sachar and I wrote this story in 1979.

❋

THE FOLLOWING SPEECH WAS delivered at the Caucus for Radical Concern during a three-day conference in Schimmel Auditorium, N.Y.U., in February 1985.

Several years ago the gay and feminist movements came along and introduced a new form of consciousness. Pain and anger were expressed over concerns that weren't thought about before. Feminists and gay activists spoke out with deep seriousness; they were ignored and belittled, but they insisted on the truth of their complaints and the validity of their demands. It was embarrassing and uncomfortable. It was a long process but much of what they said and did has been incorporated as a regular part of our thinking.

Now in that tradition I bring a new problem and a new concern, difficult and embarrassing once again, something that will cause confusion and hostility. Let me explain the background here much in the style of the earlier consciousness raising.

I live with my father in a middle class neighborhood. I go to the neighborhood park and people say to me: What do you do? How do you earn a living? I say I have significant contacts, people in an active intellectual ambiance, people whose work appears in the *Village Voice*, the *Nation*, the *New York Times Book Review* as well as several small periodicals devoted to social change. They say that sounds exciting. Does it pay? Are you respected? Do you enjoy being with those people? I say it is intense and exciting. I may be on the verge of something very big. But it's complicated; these things are hard to spell out exactly. As I say this to them I am filled with confusion and there is pain in my heart. I am telling only a half truth. I do have some connections. I know some people respect me, but I have no real sense of security and dignity.

I sit alone at home often frustrated and sad. I feel left out of everything: parties, study groups, conversations, meetings. Everything. Most of you never even phone me. I feel neglected. It is with this in mind that I come before you today. I feel extremely angry and frightened. I am also very embarrassed. What I am asking might seem presumptuous, but all such things will appear presumptuous at first. I repeat again that a legitimate response to what I ask might demand a new consciousness and outlook.

I can't seem to do coherent and sustained work. I try. Occasionally I do call up the talk shows on the radio and make an intelligent statement, and every so often I will write a reflective essay. I feel the neighbors mock me behind my back, and I use my contact with you to justify myself with them. But I really don't know how I am seen in your eyes. This is a problem, I think, for many among us, which makes it a problem for all of us. This is why I have chosen to present a formal petition. In doing so I feel hesitation and ambivalence. I don't know if I will be listened to. If I will be paid attention to or will be rejected and ignored. Also even if I am listened to I don't know how much trust I can feel.

If I am rejected and ignored I will be filled with pain, confusion and finally bitter rage. I will then likely reach out to all those similarly betrayed who will join me in my rage. I hope we will never have to come to this point.

Now I will offer an explicit set of demands that are particular to my situation, but hold out the possibility for a solution to the problems of isolation, neglect and abandonment that I have raised. It's not a rigid formula or blueprint. On the other hand, I would not want to whittle down the force and essence of the demands I am here proposing. I want the substance and essence of them preserved without dilution or compromise.

1. I would like a phone call once a month from a prominent person.
2. I would like to appear three times a year on significant panels.

3. I would like at least a couple of my reflective essays to be published in respected journals.
4. I would like a small weekend symposium devoted to a critical review of my work and its overall coherent pattern.
5. However little or much writing I do must absolutely not be a criterion for attention or acceptance by members of the Caucus for Radical Concern. ∎

Torn

AKEMI VISITED A FRIEND in the hospital who was dying of AIDS. The man made some comment about Japanese women and their abilities to nurture. He spoke of their self-sacrifice as if it were an entitlement. It was these very expectations that had driven her out of Japan. Her frustration was acute. She wanted to help her friend but felt humiliated and angry. When she came back to my apartment she fell on my bed and wailed uncontrollably. ■

Schwartz Bros. Funeral Parlor

SHAVINGS OF WOOD WERE still resting inside the coffin, making it feel even flimsier than it was. Five years earlier I had seen the very same shavings and remembered thinking the coffin had been made to look as if it would fall apart as soon as any dirt was thrown into it. My father, an orthodox Jew, wanted to be buried in a very simple plain pine box. The second most simple plain pine box, looking much sturdier than the first, was double the price. It was the one my family decided to buy. ■

Hospice Care

In response to an article about hospice care in The NY Times. *Bernie's comment appeared under mine in the comment section.*

MY MOTHER WAS REMOVED from home hospice. Her health remains precarious. She is bed bound and almost totally emaciated. Sometimes even when the most skilled hands move her, a swath of skin tears off. While on hospice care visiting nurses were able to quickly identify serious changes in my mother's condition and help shift the direction of treatment. One or more major catastrophes had been avoided because of this. The purpose of hospice care is to treat terminally ill patients with dignity and bring as much comfort as possible to them. In the process, a person's life might be extended to a degree. This should not be treated as a punishable offense. It is beyond ridiculous to think my mother's condition has shifted in any serious positive way since her initial diagnosis. She has a powerful life force. But that can only carry her so far. There is a hideous paradox here. Her good care, care obviously in a decent society every seriously ill person would get, not just terminally ill ones, has probably extended her life. Taking it away creates an imbalance that seriously jeopardizes her life.

From Bernie Tuchman:

Your comment is excellent, and covers territory not touched by anyone else. The article and most commentators focus on the fight against invasive unwanted and unnecessary treatment. But the positive side of hospice care is care itself—a person's right to be noticed and responded to. Negligence is the by-product of metric-focused protocols—in medicine, the environment, education—in fact, everywhere. Tying hospice care to a fixed protocol kills its very purpose. It is an ironclad determination not to notice living human reality.

Footnote: To underscore the total insanity of this system my mother died almost three months to the day after she was thrown off hospice care. Three months hospice care is designed to be there for the last three months of a person's life. ■

Photograph by Bill Cofone

My Mother's Death: Three Months Later

IN THE CAFE I look in the mirror. A gray fading face, its contours unchanged. On the cusp of looking old even to myself. As I walk down Bleecker St. a huge sadness comes over me. I remember walking down 8th St. three decades ago. The street almost deserted, except for a young teenage girl across the way. The light from the street lamp cast a soft glow over her. She had iron hooks for hands and she was just standing there crying, wiping her eyes with her arm. She looked so forlorn. I am so forlorn. The pain is overwhelming. ∎

Xenophobic Productions

I WANT TO WRITE a piece about a friend of mine who was dropped from a play because she had an accent that friends/advisors to the director thought was too heavy. None of my friends who saw her performance had any trouble understanding her.

The play is an adaptation of a novel originally written in English then translated into French. Relatively unknown in the United States, the book became a best seller in France. And then in turn received a modicum of success back in the U.S. The director's dramatization of the book is based on the original English. The French embassy put money into the first production of the play.

The play is about a young boy put into a facility for troubled children. The first version of the play encased you inside an opaque horror that explodes at the end revealing the monstrous crime that the boy had committed. It was as close to a radical play as you're going to see outside of your own imagination and still see produced. The play in significant ways was about sexual repression and the adult hatred of children. The director was told by her advisors that the play moved too slowly, was often unclear and that my friend's French accent was at times too difficult to understand.

The play of course was not intended to be confined to a run of three weekend performances. The director wanted it to be produced Off-Broadway. At least $100,000 would be needed for such a production. So the objections of these people had to be seriously considered. A showcase for potential backers would have to be set up. I overheard the director say this in the lobby of a theater after she and I had just been spectators at another play in which my friend had appeared.

The showcase production, which was produced a number of months later, moved at a much quicker pace. Instead of encasing you inside a sense of horror it moved you quickly, forcefully toward the denouement. It was clearer; things were stated more explicitly than in the first play. And my friend's character, a young girl, was referred to by another kid who said, "She's foreign, she has an accent." Certainly something a kid might say. But in the context of the play it felt to me like an apology, something tacked on to mollify an objection. The story takes place in Detroit in the late '50s. French music is laced throughout. A tap dancer emerges at crucial moments. Adults play children. Men play women. The set is made of string resembling the children's game of cat's-cradle. Its configuration changes from scene to scene to provide varied playing spaces for the actors. From one angle nothing about the play made any sense. But of course everything about it made perfect sense. Yet the only thing that needed to be explained was the foreign accent of a child in a classroom. The line at the time made me a little nervous for my friend.

Both versions of the play were special. Though I preferred the earlier one. Possibly because it was the first one I saw. Possibly it was because I knew the changes came more out of a need to accommodate the market than out of the creative impulse of the director. And if it grew out of her creative impulse, it still came from a kind of market pressure as the impetus. Or possibly I felt my friend's role was subtly eroded, key moments reduced or eliminated. This might be totally ridiculous because her role was a very big one. A bunch of friends who saw only the second version liked it enormously. My friend was the co-star. She was breathtaking. Electric. Beautiful.

The director is hip, super conscious, young, maybe a little older than young. Sophisticated, determined, ambitious. Clearly someone with a deep and profound insight into the world.

The night I saw the director in the lobby of the theater I told her how much I liked the play. I told her that I'd encouraged all my friends to come. She said cuttingly, "Well how many of them did come?" I said all of them. But in truth two did come. And I asked another friend to mention it on her radio show. I was a little stung by her comment. But I know how much people bullshit each other. And clearly she was frustrated. But still I didn't like it. And so some of what I'm writing could be springing in part as tiny payback for being slightly, unfairly nicked.

Months after the first showcase performance a second one was planned. This time my friend was dropped from the play. "Jessica was given to an American girl," was the way my friend described what had happened.

I don't know if the director made the decision herself, was pressured into it or had no choice. Possibly in her mind she felt that my friend had enough time to improve her English. I do know she didn't want the play to be confined to a few spectacular performances when it had the potential for a lot larger audience. It was clear that the play spoke deeply to her. And she wanted it out there.

The whole thing upsets me. The cutting comment of the director, while mildly stinging at the time, feels more unpleasant now. Again a look at my own biases. Personally I would feel more than satisfied, exhilarated really, if I had been part of anything as significant as the first production of this play. A two or three week run of sheer beauty and power. But then again that is not why the director and others connected with the play are doing this. The next step is hopefully Off-Broadway. And the compromises intensify. The choice might have been drop my friend or not have a play. There is no way the replacement won't be exceptionally good. All the actors in this play are marvelous. And the director is very demanding in how she wants this to be. But my friend's particular genius will be missing. And that is a terrible loss for a terrible reason, independent of what the substitute might bring to the role.

The play has become a rapid-moving, crystal clear, xenophobic production. The last of course is not in the play itself. It is in the capitulation to what was perceived as what might be necessary to get the play produced. What capitulations, conscious or unconscious, occurred in response to the French embassy's original sponsorship I don't know. But in this case it is clear that the director yielded to the low grade xenophobia in her environment. Sexual hatred and repression of children can be resisted; not low grade xenophobia. It is this of course, more than the quickening of the pace of the play and the need for a certain kind of clarity, that is the deeper problem. Though a friend of mine from Bulgaria feels that they are all of a piece. Part of a cultural dominance. And in her life here she feels oppressed by the whole package. It is very disturbing whenever cruel, hard-headed decisions are made. When they are a capitulation to a form of prejudice it is even more disturbing.

I wouldn't presume to speak about the choices that the director felt she had to make. So much effort. So much creativity. Such emotional investment. It is the environment I am addressing more than any particular person's response to it. That being said there is now a corruption at the very core of this play, along with what clearly is so very profound. I'm sure the director can live with her decisions. If not she might as well pack it all in. But something serious and real and beautiful is gone. And it really is gone. And that is why great art has a much smaller impact on me than it might have once had. ∎

A HIP, TRENDY RESTAURANT industry needs all that young energy to shore itself up. The waiters are "on." It is a place to emote as well as work. The customers appreciate the performance. The grace and charm and sizzling energy of the waiters. Even washing a window is done with a dancer's grace. It is the dream of making it in a hope filled exploitative universe that feeds the restaurant industry with an endless supply of young creative people. The entertainment industry provides the hope. It too is continuously reinvigorated by the influx of young people hoping for a break. So what is exploited in the restaurants, in addition to their labor power, is the charm and talent and hope of the people working there. The atmosphere at least initially can appear positive. Other actors and theater people exciting each other with their presences. The expectations of the life ahead of them. A connection is formed.

Ears to the ground the culture of actors/waiters find work for each other. Acting jobs, better restaurant jobs etc. And at times the pay is good. Hours are often flexible. Accommodations are made when a person has a gig. People cover for each other. But very likely there is nothing like job protection or health benefits.

The natural energy of the workers can lead to a fluidity, a kind of community. Often it extends into a night life. And one day a person wakes up into the reality of the dream.

Those that stay, if they have not made it, may find a satisfaction in doing things like commercials. Since many of the same ingredients of skill and talent, the completion of a task, are at play it can feel in its way like a creative undertaking. And of course since most of what is at this point considered and might actually be great art often has the same moral core in its actualization as a cigarette commercial, you might as well be doing one as the other. And the people moving inside the shadow schlock universe often through a kind of pride and shame elevate their work into a caricature of a true calling which itself is often a caricature of what it once might have been. ∎

Column Inches

—How many column inches do you think I will get?

—Well, if you had died twenty years ago quite a lot. Now probably a two-line mention on the front page and about half a page in the obituary section.

—Yeah, twenty years ago it would have been a screaming headline. Mohamed Atta could picture his own obituary. He had real imagination. He came from nowhere. And look how much space he got.

—While on the subject. What if Osama bin Laden is dead. And no one knows it. There won't be any obituary for him.

—All that for nothing. What a waste.

—What if you are part of a category? Ten thousand people die in an earthquake. Or better yet, in an oil spill where there is an ongoing investigation. Does that count for much? You don't have a name. Maybe you are mentioned. Maybe a little portrait of you.

—Well that might be okay for some people. Not for me.

—What if you are part of a movement? The death of the counterculture.

—Well, you're still alive so it doesn't count.

—Are you that ego driven that you think you are larger than social trends? Or cataclysmic historical realities?

—Don't get nasty. Let me ask you a question. How do you feel that you were not even mentioned in Joseph's obituary? But in your obituary you will be described as a friend of Joseph's. You will be defined in some way in relationship to him.

—I'll take those inches any way I can. Besides my life isn't over yet. But it is true that at the height of my powers I would have gotten a whole page in the *Times*.

—Don't delude yourself.

—Look at Jack Abbott. He was found hanging in his cell. There was a fair sized obituary for him.

—Now he is a funny case. He is written about because he knew Norman Mailer and he murdered someone. So Norman Mailer is written about in his obituary.

—But also remember there is no way he won't be mentioned in Mailer's obituary. Now think about it. Not bad for one murderous act.

—If you were one of the people slaughtered in Sabra and Shatila a lot would have been written about you. Okay. Probably not by name. Still. "A child with one shoe lay on the side of a dirt path." So it could be as specific as that. And as a group you sure will be mentioned and not just as an afterthought. Probably as much as a paragraph in Sharon's obituary.

—How about the fact that I have ten books in the library and Joanne only has two? That should count for something.

—That doesn't mean you will get more column inches. It just doesn't. I'm not saying it might not be a factor. But what do I know. I'm not the one making the decisions.

—Look at Max. He spent the last ten years working in a soup kitchen. Nobody even remembers who he is. So now probably there will be only a bare mention of him.

—There was a big article about the death of altruism.

—That was written five years ago. Still, working in a soup kitchen might be an interesting angle. You don't know about these things.

—So what do you think my life has amounted to?

—Maybe one column inch.

—Don't you think I exist somewhere in the collective imagination of civilization?

—Yeah, as a nameless shadow.

—I'll be really discovered after I die. My poems, my writings, my good works. Reams and reams will be written about me.

—Think that if it makes you feel good. But for now we are talking about your obituary. Not some fantasy how history will treat you. We are talking about the number of column inches in your obituary. Not the peculiar distortions and mystifications that time will create. We're talking about authentic original response.

—Yeah. But a lot of it might have been written years before.

—Don't get technical with me. Because it will be your obituary that your Maker will read. For that is what God looks at. The obituaries are the guide. God does not have the time or the patience for "future evaluations." There are no appeals. Future evaluations are only that. They are not obituaries. They do not rise to the level of an obituary. Obviously they matter. And I don't want to diminish any valid measure of human worth. I hate comparing these things. But obituaries are what we live for. ■

Castrated Bulls

IN THE SOUTH OF Holland thirty years ago I saw castrated bulls on the top of a hill. Each with the saddest of eyes. One then another would start a charge. Three, four steps down the hill and then they would stop.

Sometimes I gather myself, gather myself. A faint memory of an emotion, a faint sense of who I once was. Three quick steps. And I stop. I feel the most horrible sadness in my eyes. ∎

Gutsy little bird
Walks into the café
Eating crumbs
Off the floor ∎

On the Eighth Day

ON THE SEVENTH DAY the Lord rested. And then there was chaos. Left on their own the creatures of the world all became unhinged. Bees attacked the flowers. Flowers poisoned the ants. Clouds burst upon the deserts. The deserts bloomed the flowers. The flowers graced the wilderness. Creatures groped and touched. Anxiety introduced itself to the lions. Love erupted from the caves.

On the eighth day the Lord decided never again to rest. But it was too late. ∎

Dirty Old Man

"DIRTY OLD MAN" is a sexual slur. It doesn't have the same force as calling a woman a slut. But it is a punishing description of sexual desire. It is a form of policing sexual feeling. As I get older it is a term more seared in my consciousness than I had ever realized. And I'm furious about it. ■

Stupid Cupid

Stupid Cupid
Where have you been
Lost in time
Lost in space
An arrow flies over my head
And hits a tree instead

Silly Cupid
What do you know
A swollen head
An empty bed
A terrible ache
That can't be fed

Erotic Cupid
Drunk on beer
Loosen up
Lose your fear

Ancient Cupid
You've lost your glow
More slings than arrows
Your gnarled hands throw

Low flying Cupid
Wings tangled in a tree
Twisting and turning
Unable to get free

Mean green Cupid
What have you done
Brought love to their hearts
Then pulled out a gun.

Sad eyed Cupid
Caught in the rain
Taken for granted
Lost in pain

Lonesome Cupid
No hearts left to touch
Lying forlorn
On psychiatrist couch:

The steady aim
The world wide fame
It was never a game
For me

Moonlighting Cupid
Tired as hell
Down on your luck
Driving a truck

Working class Cupid
You're taxed to the hilt
Corporate greed
Trumps any other need

Fearsome Cupid
All in a rage

Take a moment
And turn the page

Dapper Cupid
Donning new threads
Dreadlocked Cupid
Smoking weed
Wild eyed Cupid
Roaming the streets
Junked up Cupid
Eating sweets

Smooth muscled Cupid
So glowing and sweet
Desire on hold
Starts growing bold

Or

Smooth muscled Cupid
So glowing and sweet
Desire on hold
Starts growing old

Your Cherub's face
Always a mask
Hiding desires
I dare not ask
Still tell me quick
If you will
What flowing rivers
Make your loins quiver

Quivering Cupid
Taking the lead
Wings catching fire
From all that desire ■

Smart and Tart Juicing

Libretto: Robert Roth & Carletta Joy Walker

Music: Michael Szpakowski

2

Dirty Water

I was a janitor in a building. My father was in a coma. While I was mopping the floor, a tenant came up the stairs and said, "It's always dirtier when you finish." She clearly was very pleased with her own cleverness. Probably the line flashed into her head one night in bed and she was just waiting for her opportunity to say it. It wasn't at all playful; it was straight out nasty. I glared at her. I was in too much pain to answer. In other circumstances I might have said something. I wasn't at all prepared for it. So there it was. A nasty gratuitous comment delivered to someone whose father was in critical condition. Anytime I would see her afterwards I turned to ice.

I never before had any unpleasant feelings towards her. Seeing a familiar face I smiled. Maybe even hoping for a little sympathy. "How you doing?" "Not well. My father's in the hospital. He's in a coma." "I'm very sorry to hear that." Nothing more. Maybe not even that much. A nasty gratuitous comment was the last thing I needed. The violation was clearly greater than the intent. How would she know? It certainly would be a lousy thing to say under any circumstances. But under these circumstances the impact was not one she would have wanted.

A couple of weeks before while mopping the building I accidentally kicked over the bucket and all the dirty water cascaded down the stairs, floor after floor making a colossal mess. I cleaned everything up. But the floor was in fact dirtier than when I started.

I would never speak to her again. I would make way for her on the stairs, looking only at her feet as I continued to mop. But otherwise in no way acknowledge her. I think she may have made little conciliatory gestures towards me. Knowing myself, if she had said what she did at any other time I eventually would have let it go. ■

Titles

Added Expenses

Wax in the Ear Dialogues

From Here to Uncertainty

Misdirection

How Certain it Once Seemed

Leaking Roof in Arkansas

It Should Be Warmer Tomorrow

Squirrels in the Attic

A Corpse in the River

Untied Shoelaces

Big Pharma, Bad Karma

Sandstorm Over the Atlantic

Under the Kitchen Table

Belligerence

How High the Morning Sky?

But Why? Dear

Wrong Turn Down a Winding Road ∎

Endings

Everyone applauded.

He stared vacantly. The time had come. He closed his eyes.

How else could it end?

The waves hit the beach. The moon rested heavy on the clouds above.

The riverbank was still wet.

She looked at Maureen. There was not that much left to choose from. The disappointment was bitter, but also sweet.

What could he say? The hour had come. No one was left. The emptiness of the streets spoke volumes.

The sadness was overwhelming. The hearse moved through the streets slowly. From nowhere someone threw a rock. The silence of the mourners soon became the shriek of a blood-curdling mob.

One man lay dead, another severely injured. The silence would never again be broken.

How could it be? Well, it was.

Bargain basement deals don't come cheap. ■

An Interview with *And Then* Magazine by Kika Stayerman for *Who Seeks Finds*

ON A PLEASANTLY SUNNY day in May this year, I sent out an email to my dear friend Robert Roth, asking if he would be willing to be featured in an interview for my blog.

"Definitely would like that!" he replied almost immediately.

I first met Robert when I attended his reading at the KGB Bar with our mutual friend, Ian Vollmer. It was a love at first sight.

I remember listening to his outstanding reading while he stood behind the wooden podium with a lamp that kept the darkness more than it dispelled it, and I wondered at how fortunate I was to have met him.

We prolonged the night with a few friends over at a Ukrainian restaurant and indulged in stuffed Varenikis, during which I sat closely to him, inhaling his every word and thought.

I was then invited to contribute to *And Then* magazine and my first piece will be published in the coming Volume #18.

In the midst of forming and shaping this interview I asked to meet Carletta, the co-editor of the magazine. I felt a physical need to see her in person and nod to all the beautiful things I've heard about her.

We scheduled to meet in mid-July at La Libertad Café, and when she opened the door and entered, the place lit up.

I have never seen such a calm, gentle and smiling face, such pure beauty and evidence of one's name, Joy. The rich conversation that followed left me wanting more. It became clear to me again, how fortunate I am that as life would have it, our paths have crossed.

Since its founding 27 years ago, *And Then* has sought to showcase the kind of intimate and arresting writing that can shift a worldview and instigate a safe platform for all opinions, thoughts and cultures.

Robert and Carletta, I am endlessly in your debt for this honor.   –Kika Stayerman

An Introduction by Robert Roth:

Kika, thank you so much for doing this interview.

Arnold Sachar (Arnie), Shelley Haven, Marguerite Bunyan and I started *And Then* in 1987. Shelley designed the first 13 issues, while Marguerite the last five, including the one we are working on now. Marguerite has done the desktop publishing from the beginning and Shelley still designs the covers. Both have written and done artwork as well as inviting other people to contribute their work to the magazine.

From 1987 until his death in 2009 I co-edited the magazine with Arnie. Now my co-editor is Carletta Joy Walker who has been a very vital, basic and enormous presence in my life almost from the very first words we spoke to each other. She is a person of sizzling creative energy and deep sensitivity to people. She also was a very dear friend of Arnie and good friends with Marguerite and Shelley. Carletta will join us in the interview.

In addition Myrna Nieves and Ralph Nazareth have been enormously involved over the years and even more so now. Myrna and Ralph are among the most extraordinary writers I have ever read, and along with Carletta, have wide networks of friends and connections to various communities. All this has deepened even further the richness of the magazine.

I would also like to mention Jim Stoller and Carol Jochnowitz who have worked on the magazine pretty much from the beginning.

For my part I want to make it clear that when I say anything I am speaking only for myself. Not for Carletta, Marguerite, Shelley, Ralph or Myrna. Also, I know at times I will be speaking about Arnie as if he were still here doing it with us. And I am not speaking for him either.

KIKA: What do you think of the written word of today?

CARLETTA: Hmm? I like written words configured in interesting, thoughtful, informational ways; also like handwriting or fonts that are beautiful, artistic and/or intriguing as well as readable. I think there are a lot of words written today.

KIKA: Can you tell me about the origin of *And Then* magazine?

ROBERT: For many years Arnie and I talked about starting a magazine. Arnie had a profound prophetic imagination. And an extremely active and insightful political mind. But he also felt very insecure and disrespected and could talk about his insecurities until you were about to collapse. So one motivation on my part was for us to set up a vehicle where a lot of credit and appreciation would come towards him. Obviously I wanted that for myself also but a good part of my motivation was to shut him up or maybe to put it in another way to make him feel better about himself since he was someone I loved very dearly.

Each year it would seem we were inching closer to doing it. My friend Gary Sheinfeld, who was very good friends with James Baldwin, showed him a piece I had written. Baldwin liked it quite a lot, which made me feel incredibly good. It was a piece that had recently gotten rejected from a publication. I said, fuck it, if James Baldwin likes what I wrote why don't we just do the magazine. I then spoke to Marguerite and Shelley, both extraordinary artists and very close friends of mine whose work I admire beyond words, and they also knew how to get things done. When they agreed to be co-creators of the magazine, everything seemed possible.

Before we began I told Arnie that no matter what we do people will say that the magazine is uneven. That this piece is derivative and that that piece is original. That people are compulsively critical and generous at the same time. That there is no way to guard against the negative. Let's enjoy the positive and let the chips fall where they may. So over the years people have said the magazine is uneven, but always uneven for different reasons and there hasn't been anything like a consensus on any piece.

Each issue of the magazine takes on a life of its own and it's only as we begin to put it into an order that we get a sense of what we have. Multiple currents run through each issue. Volume 1 was in part a kind of manifesto. Many of the pieces formed an internal critique of radical social movements. One woman wrote an article about how other women inside the women's movement responded to, or more to the point, neglected the book she wrote.

The magazine exploded onto the scene. That it wasn't blurry and could be read at all seemed to surprise everyone. Someone had access to a typesetting machine in the bowels of a major corporation. We are an underground magazine after all. So over a period of time a whole bunch of people on weekends and weeknights would sneak their way into the building to input their own and other people's pieces.

At some point paranoia slowed us almost to a crawl and we thought we would never finish. I sometimes wondered what would happen if a wrong button was pushed and all this radical material wound up as part of that corporation's annual report.

In addition to our having access to a typesetting machine, another friend, Joel Cohen, who is a printer, offered to print up the cover for free. So as it turned out it was cheaper to have the magazine typeset and have a nicely printed cover, than to do it any other way.

The first issue was in a way the most painful. Though each issue has had serious problems. Communication between me and everyone else was totally lousy. Too many people misheard, misunderstood and forgot things that I thought had been agreed upon. And vice versa. It was clear that I was doing something wrong.

Everyone was working for free, donating time, energy, and enthusiasm and yet with all that we had to do the work as if it were a paying job. Any mistake on someone's work could ruin the whole experience for that person.

CARLETTA: The origins of *And Then* are from the congregation of social-political ideals in Robert's mind and Arnie's deep listening wanting to dance seamlessly with freedom, create a home to express, introduce us to each other.

KIKA: Can you tell me about your role and how did you become the co-editor of the magazine?

CARLETTA: I co-edited issue #17, and contributed significantly to #16 before "officially" accepting the role. Robert co-edited and co-published *And Then* with Arnie Sachar, who died a few years ago. They were great friends and political allies.

Robert and Arnie invited me to contribute my first piece as a result of becoming familiar with me through my weekly radio program (Tuesday Night Live Eclectic Radio) on Pacifica Radio, Wbai.

Participating in a talk at the Brecht Forum during Women's month programing is where I first met Robert and Arnie. It was the late '80s, my mother (and father also) were still alive. Robert recounted an interesting story that highlighted, to me, where race, class, immigration status, power and gender can and do drift together and dance in our everyday lives. After we became friends, Robert shared that the comment question was intended to engage me. It did, and when Robert and Arnie approached me after the panel, I was very open.

Robert later mailed me the first two issues and invited me to contribute. I thanked him. I read the issues cover to cover; I was very impressed and quickly responded. The pieces were a compelling mix of information and emotion—which gave them a refreshing air of honesty. I don't remember specific art but felt the flow of it throughout. The attention to presentation and detail was evident.

I became a regular contributor, and part of the *And Then* community. The respect my work, and me, was accorded was (and remains) remarkable. It was clear to me by the time I met Robert and Arnie that writing/contributing to a commercial magazine was of little interest to me. Having an article published and widely available when coupled with a pre-established, and fairly restrictive template was not comfortable or satisfying. It opened writing/publishing possibilities at a price: diminished regard, consideration, inclusion in process.

And Then adheres to standards of excellence, and its existence and evolution speaks to the possibility and reality of distinction that is not arrogant or imposing. It is cooperative, organic and contemplative.

KIKA: What is the main focus or purpose of the magazine?

ROBERT: *And Then* is a mixture of prose and poetry, artwork, fragments, music. I feel there is something like a shimmering field of freedom inside the pages of the magazine. You never know what someone will come up with. What form their expression will take. You expect an essay, you get a poem. You expect a poem, you get a musical composition. People almost always give us something of particular importance to them. Very rarely does someone give us a piece with the attitude, "Well, I'll just give them something that I have around." The readership of the magazine is serious, engaged, playful and responsive and people know that what they do will have an impact.

The magazine has people from many places, many cultures, and many states of mind. The age range is from 5-94. In one sense it could be called multi-cultural but I think, at times, it would be more accurate to call it multi-anti-cultural. Many of the pieces are by people trying to break free from the repression and oppression of cultures they grew up in or are still a part of. And this includes almost everywhere on the planet.

Sometimes I think of the magazine as a big communal gathering. There are so many people in each issue. And it is nice to see them all hanging out together. Sometimes I like putting two pieces together only because the thought of those two people sharing a page just delights me.

CARLETTA: *And Then* focuses on maintaining a valuable and valued space to voice unfettered written and produced words and arts.

KIKA: What's your day/week like as an editor?

ROBERT: It is nothing like a formal job. With Arnie, we spoke about it day and night. Carletta and I have a more structured arrangement when it comes to talking about the magazine. Like with Arnie, she and I can talk endlessly about almost everything. Still we set up times to talk specifically about the magazine. It is a different way of doing it for me and a different rhythm. We are figuring it out as we do it. We have worked on so many important things together over the years that we have a very good feel for each other. Still it is an adjustment for me.

CARLETTA: As an editor, the magazine starts to live in my mind as an in-progress entity. When I am not working on it in the foreground, as the focus of what I'm doing, the pieces are "running" in their workspace in the background. Additionally, because I am co-editing, there is also a consideration/inclusion of aspects of the editing process that have primacy for Robert. Hence, we two are in a dialogue, and also Marguerite, as the designer and typesetter who, along with Shelley, shares art editor functions.

Then there are the scheduled meetings; with the amount of work I do, being scheduled is very important. For the current issue, Robert and I meet once a week, between meetings I return the magazine to the background where it processes and tinkers with what we've done in our work meeting.

I am also, most probably much less so than Robert, working on the next issue. I think about people I'd like to contribute, specific pieces I would like someone to write—the asking conversation.

KIKA: Are you formally educated or was it something you developed by doing?

CARLETTA: Not certain of what is meant by "formally" educated? I studied English in college, not with any thought or connection to editing. I do think editing is a skill that one develops—one develops an understanding and sensitivity for the written word, its relationship to the writer, the writer's intent. Important and vital is to have an understanding and clarity of one's own intent when holding and handling someone's work. Editing in my thinking is collaboration, a partnership—which includes conversation, discussion, question—time and space.

Writing and editing (and art and publishing) have been integral to my adult life. Communication is essential ingredient in all communication—words define, can limit and/or expand the parameters of existence. Defining, evolving one's self-definition can be empowering and liberating. Editing with intent of facilitating cohesive flowing voice among other voices to have a chorus of sound is an essential skill in producing *And Then*.

KIKA: What makes *And Then* different from other literary magazines?

ROBERT: Probably one big difference is we don't reject pieces and don't in any way insist on people changing their work. If people want us to comment on something or work with them that is another thing.

Here I am speaking only about myself. Unless someone wants to discuss their piece with me I am very reluctant to say anything. I certainly don't want to have someone dangling out there with something that might embarrass them without pointing it out to them. But I am very hesitant and it takes quite a lot for me to do it.

Sometimes when I talk to a person about their piece they are appreciative. Other times their bodies tense up. And even if later they might change something it doesn't feel great even when in some sense it might be a relief.

In the early days of the magazine, once in Volume 1 and then again in Volume 2, I spoke to two authors, very close friends of mine, about their pieces. Both wanted to know what I thought. The wording in one person's piece implied that childbirth was a self-evident good and the other wrote "crack kills" 5 or 6 times in a period of heightened anti-drug hysteria. The person who wrote about childbirth thanked me for pointing it out to her, saying that's not what she had meant to say. She changed her sentence but made a little pointed comment about me and freedom of expression. From the beginning it was clear she didn't have to change a word. And it was a change she wanted to make. But in a small way it felt to me as if she capitulated to my position of authority as editor of the magazine. The other person asked me and Arnie to be as honest as we could about his piece. We asked him why all those crack kills; in our mind, it fed into a nationwide anti-drug, law and order hysteria. He argued. We argued back. Again it was clear it would go in any form he wanted. He took out a couple of crack kills. It was clear to me that our role as editors had more weight in the discussion than it should.

Except with people I am working very intimately with on their pieces and where it is very much wanted, I have never argued as forcefully again. That is except with Arnie and my mother who when they were alive I offered passionate unsolicited advice whenever the mood hit me.

Basically I love the anarchic feel and unpredictability of what people do.

CARLETTA: It has tremendous variety, range—race, gender, age, ethnicity, religion, ability, experience … there is an inchoate quality coexisting with aged wisdom; harmony with singularity; integrity with multiple voices … it's lasting, thoughtful, it has a timelessness, and yearning urgency … *And Then* does not privilege anyone over anyone else, or try to define, direct the readers' response.

KIKA: What other literary magazines/platforms do you appreciate?

ROBERT: There are many, including your platform, *Who Seeks Finds*. I think among the other magazines I am closest to are

Home Planet News, Socialism and Democracy, The Sun, White Rabbit and *Hawansuyo,* my friend Fredy Roncalla's blog which is infused with a profound free-wheeling poetic humanism.

CARLETTA: I read lots of stuff; these I read regularly, or in clusters: *The New Yorker* (I accepted a gift subscription), *The Sun* (I request Robert save for me), *The Chronicle Review* (part of *The Chronicle of Higher Education.* Started reading school copies), *Home Planet News, National Geographic,* and *Scientific American.*

KIKA: How has the magazine been doing? Do you see its readership growing?

ROBERT: Each issue has a lot of new contributors mingling in with people who have appeared before. Most everyone has someone or some people they are close to. And to that extent the readership and involvement of people keep expanding. In terms of actual numbers, we are printing less and selling less.

CARLETTA: The magazine—meaning the core producers and the community of participants—has lived and sustained for nearly 30 years. I'd say it's doing okay.

Certainly, continually expanding; in my view, and actions, there is an intentionality in the growth process, one that honors the cohesiveness of community. When one is "invited," it is an invitation to be part of something—for that moment/issue or for more; whatever, one's presence has entered the magazine.

KIKA: How has it evolved and changed from the first issues till now?

ROBERT: One of the changes is that many of the contributors, those who can do it at all, take much longer than they did 27 years ago to climb up the steps of my building when they come to pick up their magazines. This time it was almost comical. I live on the third floor. I would hear heavy breathing. Faint movement below. I waited on top of the stairs—sometimes for quite a while—to greet whoever was arriving. There always was a smile of exhausted achievement when they finally made it. When we started, people would bound up the steps and might be at the door even before I had a chance to open it. Now more of the contributors are in their 60s, 70s and 80s.

In looking at who writes for the magazine Arnie and I would do our own demographic study. Some of the categories were pretty obvious ones. But some not so obvious. We would go over and over it again. It is very easy to fall into patterns. Into patterns you are totally unaware of. We wanted as great a variety of people as possible. Age, of course, is one of them. The age range has been between 5 and 94, but as the magazine got older, so on balance did the contributors. So we had to make a conscious effort to get younger people involved. Race and gender are of course crucial concerns in terms of who is in the magazine. But there are other things as well. Published, unpublished for example. There are so many, and each in its way is very important. With Myrna and Ralph as well as Carletta all inviting contributors things have opened up very dramatically over the years.

I once wrote a piece that I only showed to about five people about the demographic makeup of the magazine and the people who have worked for it. "And Then: The City/ A Demographic Study." This is one area where I feel it is very important to be obsessively focused. Because if you aren't, very pernicious aspects of the society get replicated almost immediately without you even being aware that it is happening.

One important change that I should mention is that there is more artwork than when we started. This has had a profound impact on the magazine and its power and since Volume 2 almost every issue has at least one music piece.

Another quite lovely development is that people have developed followers over the years and others have been curious about what they have to say. And also about the life changes they have gone through.

For example, one contributor, Legacy Russell, first appeared in the magazine when she was nine years old. I met her when she and a couple of other girls came to an *And Then* party. They were each carrying balloons and all working on novels. At some point they lost control of their balloons and watched with such sad panicky faces as the balloons floated to the ceiling. Every few years Legacy writes something else for *And Then*. She is in her mid-twenties now and has grown from this glorious kid into this soulful wildly creative young woman.

In the coming issue three granddaughters of longtime contributors are appearing for the first time and the younger brother of one, who will soon be three years old, is waiting in the wings.

Recently my friend Lee Cronbach (am listening to his magnificent *Angel Blues* recording as I am writing this) got inspired to start reading the magazine from the very beginning to the present. He wants to write a piece about the changes the magazine has gone through over the years. It will be very interesting to see what he comes up with.

CARLETTA: Yes and No: it is more of what it was, and has lived into its intent to be an orchestra of sounds.

It requires work to be inclusive, to truly represent through inclusion, not by speaking for the multifaceted cultures that exist. Robert and Arnie, in my view worked consciously and consistently to have *And Then* look and read like it does—ages in low single digits to the nineties, a rainbow of colors, identities, Jews, gentiles, orthodoxy and wild edges of takeoff all inside honor of the open invitation.

KIKA: Do you have an idea of a certain theme for each issue?

ROBERT: Themes usually present themselves as we create the order of the pieces. Sometimes it is startling what we discover as we are doing it. And sometimes the themes are invisible until they're not. Occasionally months after the magazine has come out I might notice some theme or pattern or connection between pieces that I had not noticed before.

KIKA: How do you determine what goes into an issue?

ROBERT: It's pretty much a first come first served kind of thing. But we might ask someone to write something about a particular subject. Or give us a particular artwork. We don't reject pieces. Pieces though need to stay within a certain space limit.

KIKA: Can you take me through the process of an issue from idea to print?

CARLETTA: Earlier on pieces are being read, taken in for their intellectual content and emotional content; relationships are being made to other pieces. Some essence in made relationships connects to the essence of another contributor's piece. When the majority of the pieces are in, they are sent to Marguerite for typesetting. A second group of pieces get typeset; first proofing occurs and the work of creating an issue intensifies.

Although there is no intentional theme, often a theme of sorts emerges. The work then is to create a flow that isn't dominated by the emerged theme but integrates pieces such that all fit and shine. Duos grow into trios and quartets; another theme emerges. Short pieces are placed in as sharps, flats, and codas. Art accentuates, ignores, begins or ends a configuration, yet always receives its due. More pieces come in, the sound shifts, the configurations respond. I have to not attach to something we did earlier; I have to be mindful that inclinations toward my idea of efficiency do not constrain or short circuit my ability to realize, remember that enjoyment. Slowly, with constant review, reading, familiarizing, trying arrangements out, intuition, the issue feels like it is emerging. Robert and I pay attention in different ways—intellectual, emotional, spiritual content—part of working is harmonizing intention. Bringing held, unarticulated ideas, expectations, and assumptions to the surface awareness, clarity and voice is important and ongoing.

Robert is in conversation with Shelley about the front cover; he is in contact with Marvin about the inside back cover;

he is in regular contact with Marguerite; he is scheduling out with proofreaders; he is in contact with key people who have gathered contributors (this particularly so after Arnie passed), so he is a "manager" in addition to editor. He doesn't do this alone, but he keeps all aspects in his head.

With the exception of an occasional modest fee for specific expertise, *And Then* is a totally volunteer produced and self-sustaining publication. It neither receives nor seeks grants, a source of revenue for many small literary magazines. This means production is both scheduled and on a timeline, while having to consider the fullness, and need for most to work for income, of the lives producing it.

Three of us (Robert, Carletta, Marguerite) meet, at least twice, for the final look at the flow of pieces, how they look, and fit, flow design wise receiving important input from Marguerite.

KIKA: Is there anything you haven't done at *And Then* that you wish to do?

CARLETTA: I would like to figure out a reading that included all that wanted to participate, yet didn't get overwhelming. Also, the idea of a set being published…

KIKA: What was the most surprising thing you learned while running the magazine?

CARLETTA: The magical mystery of it all coming together…

KIKA: Is there any certain piece you particularly love and cherish?

ROBERT: I think each issue is a creation unto itself. The pieces interact with each other and create some remarkable whole. Once an issue is out I can't imagine any piece in any issue not being there. And I love them all. So I don't like to single anything out, certainly not in a public way. I do find it interesting that Arnie and I would fixate on different pieces as we put an issue together.

That being said I do love the piece that you just gave us for the magazine. It will go into issue #19. I won't say anything more about it. I will leave the world just hanging there in suspense. I am totally excited that you wrote it. Carletta is the only other person who has a copy of it.

Speaking of love and cherish, my mother wrote for every issue but one. Early on a group of black women (and some men) loved her work. She was very excited and touched by this. In response she ordered a subscription to *Ebony*. "To understand oppression it takes more than to say people are oppressed. You have to understand the details of daily life. They are interested in what I am writing. I want to understand what is going on in their lives also."

Ebony didn't quite fit the bill. But she devoured and responded very profoundly and viscerally to the work of those women (and one man in particular). She would sometimes quote sections of pieces in her heavy Hungarian accent. It was probably the single greatest pleasure I have gotten out of doing this.

KIKA: What are some of your favorite writers or poets?

CARLETTA: There are writers I return to, want more of; and, there's being engaged with the writer/poet (artist) I'm with in the moment. Toni Morrison, James Baldwin, Chinua Achebe, Judy Grahn, Bapsi Sidhwa, Virgil—*Aeneid*, Thich Nhat Hanh; the many writers in *And Then* whose works are favorites, live in my ears and thinking—Kato Roth.

KIKA: What does the future hold for *And Then*?

CARLETTA: The present.

ROBERT: That is hard to know. The magazine keeps growing in size while the number of people buying it keeps shrinking. The cost keeps going up. From the get-go I promised myself if the community wanted it to exist, the community, consisting of whoever wants it to exist, would have to support it to the point where we break even. Having said that there seems to be a lot of energy coming towards us. So that in itself provides a strong impetus to continue.

KIKA: What are you looking for from authors who submit?

CARLETTA: I want a unique voice and representation on what may or may not be a unique subject.

ROBERT: One thing we are nervous about is people fixing on a notion of what type of thing we want. There is nothing really that we feel is an *"And Then* type piece." What I mean is, if someone wants to do a straight out scientific analysis of the makeup of a leaf, that would be as much welcomed as anything else, as would a piece written in heavy academic language. There is a danger that people will pigeonhole the magazine and say this is where I can express my deep feelings. Not that we don't want people to do that but we don't want the magazine boxed into that.

Now for the subjects written about, Arnie and I have had a very definite political point of view, maybe too definite and this is often, though not always, explicitly reflected in the things that we write. It certainly informs almost everything we write. The contributors come from a wide cross-section of people with an even wider cross-section of perspectives and to say the least, some people have political and social attitudes much different from our own. Arnie and I had to fight against our own ideological rigidities in how we responded to some of the work people give us. Fortunately while our politics were almost identical, our rigidities were not. So we could calm each other down.

One thing that I really do appreciate is that no one has consciously given us pieces that they know we would not like, just to get them published. This is particularly true of certain friends whose politics differ very sharply from our own. These friends simply have not given us pieces that they know would deeply upset us to publish. They save those pieces for other publications and other venues. And so we can get offended in peace and fight it out elsewhere. In truth it almost did happen once, but our friend, clearly as an act of love and I think kindness, eventually withdrew the piece.

We won't reject anything. Period. Not exactly a full period. But a basic guideline. If something is absolutely messed up we would. But nothing close to that has ever happened. We ask people to contribute. We don't, for the most part, want unsolicited material, though some wonderful pieces have come in that way. So once we ask someone to write for us we are obliged to print what they do. This is the risk we have taken and to renege on that would make it very difficult to ask anyone else to write for us again.

In asking people to write for the magazine I promise them that their piece will get in. This allows for a certain amount of freedom and some risk. And since I ask all kinds of people to write for it the risks are significantly greater. For example if I ask a firefighter what it is like to save the life of a person by running into a burning building, and I don't know his or her attitudes about any number of things, who knows what could slip into the piece.

In fact, just before 9/11 I met two firefighters at an art opening in Hunts Point. We had a long talk as we drove back into Manhattan. One owned a gallery in Chelsea and was pretty liberal. The other was quite reactionary. He was also lively, colorful, friendly, with a very strict moral code in terms of honor, integrity and service. They spoke about the dangers they faced at times when working as an EMS. The hostility of crowds even as they were trying to save someone's life. They also spoke about meeting in the basement of a high rise, coming from two different firehouses. The almost slow motion dance, as fires were raging in various locations in the basement. They both said they were extremely calm during it all. How in control they felt. How in sync all the firefighters were. Both situations were extraordinarily interesting. Now what if

I asked the second guy to write a piece. There is no way that it wouldn't have been interesting. And there would be a real possibility that all types of attitudes about politics and culture that could have been very disturbing could have entered into that piece. So the question is do you take a chance, not exercise control after the fact and just live with the consequences (the consequences of course could be spectacular) or wait until you come across a firefighter whose politics and social attitudes are roughly in line with your own. I lost touch with them after that night. I pray they are both okay.

I think it is precisely because we tell each person that they can write as freely as they want and guarantee we won't clamp down on them that so many extraordinary pieces have been written. Again I am speaking only for myself, not Arnie, Carletta, Myrna, Ralph, Shelley or Marguerite who also ask people to contribute.

If I wanted to have a magazine that reflected my politics more explicitly or just have writers that I am in agreement with write for it, maybe three pieces would appear. If I were a little looser then obviously many more. But the range would still be quite limited. But we are doing something different. Sohnya Sayres described it as giving people a space on the wall where they are free to create whatever they want. Obviously there is a significant element of control in doing it that way since we generally do the asking but I feel the less control the better.

Sometimes we ask people way outside a certain "consensus" to write for it. And that in fact is a risk because they don't know what not to say and what not to think. There might be no one else in the world who can speak about what they are speaking about in the way they are speaking about it. It is what makes the magazine special and includes people who most likely couldn't appear anywhere else. And what am I supposed to do if I don't like something the person says. It is not like after putting so much of themselves into something they can easily get it published somewhere else. In opening things up as much as possible my own sense of freedom is expressed. Even if some other aspect of my politics could be undercut or potentially even violated by some of the pieces. There is a deep contradiction here. Certainly a potential one.

Obviously this is a subject I keep going around in circles with. Analytically and emotionally my mind is pulled in various directions. Because as I said there is a deep contradiction that can't be fully reconciled. Certainly I haven't been able to. And probably really don't want to.

For example, I can very much see myself working on a magazine that explicitly represented my own political/cultural perspective. Some of the most important shifts in consciousness as well as deep and profound changes in society have grown out of and been inspired by just such publications. Much of my own work appears in publications such as those. And I feel very identified with them.

But that would, of course, involve a whole other way of doing things. Much more scrutiny of how language was being used, what positions were being taken. Nuanced differences can start taking on very huge importance. Sometimes very justifiably. Sometimes neurotically. Sometimes destructively.

Within the contradictions I have been discussing I almost always come down on the side of openness. I have seen how easily people's expression gets clamped down on in very coercive and intimidating ways. How the imagination can become constricted. And how people's spirit can be broken. Not only by the dominant culture but sadly at times also by movements responding to and challenging that culture.

Sometime probably in the early '70s I attended a puppet show in a friend's apartment. The puppeteer was a single mother raising a young child. She was on welfare and thought doing these informal puppet shows could bring in some extra needed money. In the audience were other parents with their kids. The apartment was pretty small so we were all packed in. Robin Morgan, feminist writer and organizer, was there with her husband, Kenneth Pitchford and their young son. One of the puppets in the story was an evil witch. After the performance

Kenneth and Robin, first Kenneth his body shaking with rage, then Robin started attacking the woman. Didn't she know that women were burnt at the stake as witches and that this was a horrible reinforcing of a vicious stereotype. The woman had no idea what was happening or what they were talking about. Kenneth and Robin saw this as a teaching moment as well as, I suspect, an act of great integrity and bravery on their part. They intimidated the children, unsettled the parents and probably cost the woman needed income, since many of the people made a quick escape. Separate from the validity of their point it was a horrible act of bullying. Kenneth with Robin's permission could unleash whatever misogynist rage and hostility he had towards women, here a very poor woman, and could get off on it. And still feel very virtuous.

Unfortunately in situations like that, secondary and tertiary agendas are often at play: it could be envy or a need to prove one's intelligence or maybe a need to settle a score. Mixed in with genuine awareness and commitment it also can be an opportunity to assert a poisonous sense of one's own integrity. Whatever the motivation, it can be tremendously destructive— independent of the validity or lack of validity of the comment.

Here in *And Then*, my political/cultural perspective is reflected in the opening to expression and keeping the space as open and vital as possible.

I am not suggesting that other people should do this. The negatives could outweigh the positives for them. My feeling extends not only to political positions and attitudes but to the whole idea of standards etc. This makes many people equally nervous. That again isn't an issue for me. In truth I don't even know what that means. This is a whole long story. What it comes down to is I wouldn't want to do this if it involved policing and rejecting people's work. For me much more would be lost than gained. I can certainly understand why someone would feel differently about it.

KIKA: What do you NOT need more of in terms of submissions?

ROBERT: Anything and everything is fine. Even if two people say the exact same thing with the exact same words it is never the same thing.

KIKA: Why is it important to keep publishing lit magazines today?

ROBERT: I think literary magazines as well as all other forms that are available for people to express themselves are quite crucial. I certainly don't think any one form is better than any other. The more ways the better. At their best they provide powerful vehicles for people to be heard as well as feel connected to other people.

CARLETTA: Corporate media/mass media homogenizes—difference become sameness and even attempts to shift stereotypes end up reifying them.

KIKA: What is on your nightstand now?

ROBERT: Piles of paper, some books, a dusty candlestick holder, a box of tissues, my phone.

CARLETTA: I'm surrounded by books, magazines, manuscripts and notebooks, art-notebooks—the people mentioned in response to your question on my favorite writers, a book on history of architecture, plus several issues of *And Then*—currently rereading issue 2.

KIKA: What is your favorite drink?

ROBERT: I make some sort of tea concoction every morning. Throw in something that is around. Could be blueberries or garlic, seaweed or whatever. Makes me feel like a great chef.

CARLETTA: Current favorite is freshly made pineapple juice.

KIKA: What is the most fascinating thing that happened to you this week?

CARLETTA: Waking up laughing.

KIKA: How can people subscribe to the magazine? What are the costs?

ROBERT: There is no way to subscribe. We come out too infrequently. We have a big party. Hopefully we can sell a lot there. And hopefully the friends, family and lovers of the contributors will buy them. As well as people who are familiar with it. Or whatever new people we might meet. ■

I ALWAYS RACE FROM here to there even when the there is here. ■

I'D MUCH RATHER BE caught in someone's promiscuous net than be rejected by someone more selective. ■

IF SOMEONE ACCUSES YOU of something you know you haven't done but they are sure that you have, you know something about them that they don't know about themselves. ■

TIMID EXPRESSIONS OFTEN FEEL like ferocious assertions to the person who makes them. The effort is often extreme and brave. ■

"I LOVE YOU SO much I would even fall in love with you if you wanted me to." ■

Conversation with Death

GET LOST I DON'T need you in my life. ■

What's Age Got to Do with It?

You're old, they think you're senile then they feel they can wipe your mouth while you're talking.   —*Kato Laszlo Roth*

The following is a review of Margaret Morganroth Gullette's Agewise: Fighting the New Ageism in America *(Chicago: University of Chicago Press, 2011).*

I

WHEN I WORKED IN a day care center many years ago it struck me how almost everything involving children created anxiety and panic. This often resulted in sure-footed theories and frozen attitudes. Clashes were inevitable, some over very small things. The large thing of course was the culture of hatred towards children, the need to control them, impose on them guilt-laden values and insecurities. Tame their energy, their sexuality, their curiosity. In that way all the theories were the same. Though of course some were much worse than others. But even those with the most enlightened theories didn't examine their own underlying emotions too closely. There was also among everyone genuine concern and more than a little tenderness.

The same happens with aging and old age. It is a subject so fraught with confusion, mystification, love, anger, hatred, ancient hurts, vulnerability, pleasure, need, revulsion, desire, fear, and wild projection. All taking place inside an ageist and freedom-hating culture.

When my mother was gravely ill in the hospital, the two questions I disliked most were "Did you visit your mother today?" or "Are you going to visit her later?" I almost always felt there was a hidden judgment in the question. That it was asked to see if I were a dutiful son doing the right thing. I bristled. In retrospect I don't know why people asked me that question. What it stirred up in me of course was more to the point. Still I asked people not to ask me that question. In fact I asked people generally to let me be the one to bring up my mother's illness altogether.

Reading *Agewise* I would at times bristle in the same way. Feel guilt-tripped, dragged into a consciousness of rectitude and obligation.

I would have to calm down. Was it something I was projecting (often), was I responding to an attitude that was actually in the book (sometimes maybe), or possibly some combination of both (sometimes maybe also)?

If only for that reason alone, this is a very important book. It touches raw nerves. It reaches deep into the culture; it explores a difficult and dangerous terrain. It stirs up emotion. Margaret Morganroth Gullette has thrown herself headlong into the subject. A formidable achievement. A combination of sharp analysis, the marshaling of significant information, and social outrage. Written with literary flair and eloquence.

Gullette's mother Betty Morganroth appears intermittently in *Agewise*. She is 94 when the book begins. And suddenly near the end she is 96. It was exciting to realize that two years had passed and she was essentially still feeling good about her life. Much of the polemic force of the book seems fueled by their love.

In *Agewise*, Gullette argues that ageism and middle-ageism have grown more pernicious, more lethal, more life-deadening in recent years. The assault on older people has expanded to an assault on those of middle age. She paints a very grim picture of the economic/social/political realities that many older people are faced with. In one chapter she analyzes and discusses a hidden truth about the devastation inflicted by Katrina and the criminally negligent response to it. Of the dead, 78% were people over 50. The book also focuses on the manufacture of medical need such as the successful marketing of unnecessary and dangerous "hormone replacement" medication for women experiencing menopause. There is a chapter on the wide and wonderful range of sex older people are having. She also analyzes those jokes about aging that are part of what she calls "decline narratives." The anti-aging propaganda that helps set external and internal conditions for harsh social policies and personal/communal collaboration with them. She speaks of various ways this can be resisted.

II

Carolyn Heilbrun, a mystery writer, a feminist scholar, a well situated academic, a greatly admired figure, committed suicide at 77. The chapter opens at a memorial service with a young woman delivering a eulogy to a huge audience. She is deeply distressed that Carolyn would kill herself "to avoid old age." She begins to sob.

Carolyn Heilbrun's death created anger and confusion and a sense of betrayal among many women who admired her, and who saw her as an inspiration and a guide.

"It's the kind of decision," Gullette writes, "that might leave people who hear the story—including quite young people —with the idea that despair is a rational response to normal aging and that feminism can do nothing to alleviate it."

Well, feminism in Carolyn Heilbrun's case did not alleviate her despair. And other feminists could not convince her not to commit suicide. In Heilbrun's mind feminism in fact helped reinforce her sense of agency. It allowed her the freedom to choose under what conditions she wanted to be alive. She argued that the right to commit suicide was similar to a woman's right to have an abortion. Gullette argues back, "This appeared to be a feminist argument about control," but "feminists presumably would want to distinguish more sharply between ending fetal existence and ending an adult life of achievement and connection." This of course raises basic questions about what constitutes "achievement and connection." And why Gullette thinks they are so crucial to a person's sense of self.

Elsewhere in the book her definition of what constitutes

achievement can feel very expansive. It can apply to any number of people, in any number of circumstances. Here however the meaning is extremely clear. Achievement means institutional and corporate (publishing house and university) validation of what you've done. And "connection" means connection to important, powerful and unusually brilliant people. Are those things hollow or real? I think usually more hollow than real. But that is for another time.

Gullette feels that ageism very possibly played a role in Carolyn Heilbrun's despair. Her writing career met new and unexpected stumbling blocks. "Older writers, however well established, are driven into silence by increasingly age-ist attitudes in the increasingly feeble publishing business…in today's youth-oriented climate." Another among many blows occurred after her retirement from Columbia University. "She had resigned from Columbia University's English depart-ment, famously, because male colleagues were not advancing her protégées. They were denying her the influence that her seniority merited and thwarting her ability to help the feminist movement." After retirement, "she should have been able to join that small coterie of top men who resist ageism through traditional patriarchal means, retaining connections, prestige, and honors."

As if guilt-tripping a ghost, Gullette wishes that Carolyn had "found a different image to live up to: not as an older woman who justified her increasing determination to die as stoic, but as an antiageist who would feel guilty about the legacy she might leave by saying age was the cause."

In talking about suicide in general, Gullette makes a very sharp distinction. She is arguing against the "duty to die," the pressure on older people or people with serious disabilities to choose death, rather than to be a burden either on their loved ones or on society as a whole. This as opposed to "physician assisted suicide" or "the right to die." Though she thinks the right to die can be less of a free choice than its proponents might think. So there is great truth when Gullette writes, "The prospective fantasy of suicide operates without any hint that sexism, classism, racism, ableism or ageism might deform it."

She continues, "Many people thought that Dr. Kevorkian, who assisted people in suicide, was a hero. As Kevorkian went on, a few feminists pointed out how young some of those dying were, how relatively well many of the patients were—one was said to have played tennis the day before—and how many were women and/or recently disabled." That all might very well be the case. But we are left with the other truth. It could really have been what those people wanted to do. She argues that even in an ideal situation, "counseling—more than two visits to a doctor—therefore becomes mandatory before one can get medical assistance with suicide, even with an illness diagnosed as terminal." This might be a reasonable suggestion, but it hardly is without a potentially terrible downside. For any real delay might be subjecting someone to an unbearable hell. No matter how understanding the person you are talking to might be, the urgency and the pain are yours. All the theorizing in the world won't mitigate that fact. To interfere with their decision could be a very profound violation of someone's dignity and autonomy (as is forcing teenage girls to get permission from their parents to have an abortion or for women to be required to see the ultrasound of a fetus). For a person in physical or psychic pain an hour can be an eternity. Let alone having to endure multiple forced visits to an empathetic soulful well-trained professional. Even in the best of circumstances, the policy Gullette advocates is extremely coercive. Her reasonableness is not as reasonable as it sounds. Nor for that matter is my unease with her reasonableness all that reasonable either—because people are in fact coerced, manipulated, treated with contempt, and are easily discarded. Ugly bottom line calculations are often at play. Secret and not so secret family and institutional agendas often create momentum in one direction or another that is hard to resist, particularly when you are in an extremely vulnerable and fragile state. Wherever you come down on this, for me at least, when actually faced with real situations, it is all one horrible, bewildering, nightmarish mess.

Gullette's chapter on the terrors of forgetfulness starts with her escorting her mother to a table in a residential community where there was an empty seat. Over 30 years separate the youngest from the oldest resident. People are in various states of health and "cognitive functioning." As they approached, one of the women at the table said, "Jack won't like that!" She meant that Harvard-educated Jack, a man in his 70s, "wouldn't like having to pass a dinner hour next to my mother." Gullette still placed her at the table, while nervously mentioning how good her mother was at Scrabble. Gullette's response was a protective, visceral rage, but she couldn't be sure how her mother took it in. The paragraph winds up with Gullette, as she is leaving, glaring at the woman who made the comment.

In a succeeding passage she writes eloquently about the "growing dominance of cognitive hierarchies" which can start in infancy, later reinforced with grading and testing in school, and which just continues and continues right to a table in a residential community. This whole system of evaluation of intelligence and functioning is brutal, dehumanizing and pervasive.

Eventually Betty Morganroth "often chose to sit with people who had more serious cognitive losses—people who spoke less but welcomed her with smiles. This was hard to watch." Why was it hard to watch? We know absolutely nothing about the inner reality and complexity of the people she is writing about. Ironically, her assessment of them feels steeped in all kinds of ageist assumptions, assumptions similar to those often made about her mother.

Over the next few pages she writes movingly about the multiple dimensions of her mother. The powerful impact she has on people. Her wisdom and insight. Her sense of humor. Her courage. All while from a certain angle her "cognitive functioning" could be described as in decline.

In an extremely important observation Gullette writes, "How is it possible, that a mind can be...so uneven?...Having so huge a gap between one mental state and another may not be common, but some disparity between states is one of the things people discover who have a loved one with memory losses." How true, how true.

A remarkably similar thing happened to my mother. One part of her brain felt like it was decomposing only to feed another part that flowered in spectacular and remarkable ways. I spoke to her about it as it was first happening. She said she felt it herself. Was both frightened and awestruck by the change. The last few years, she is 93 now, have been for both of us painful, difficult but at times beautiful beyond description.

IV

A young fashion designer from Africa with incredible flair and charisma through the graces of the gods (and the harsh realities of xenophobia and capitalism) stayed with me for a number of months.

The Nation and *Elle*. *The Nation* and *Nylon*. *Socialism and Democracy* and *Bazaar*. *The Sun* and *Cosmo*. Something from IKEA for variety. And *Vanity Fair*. I never knew what would arrive in my mailbox.

Glamour magazines all piled in a corner. High heels. Red. White. Lavender. Gold. Torn jeans and army coat. Stop-traffic-dead dresses. In some way my small apartment became fashion central. Each time Aziza looked in the mirror, with just the tiniest of adjustments she would totally change her appearance. It was fun to see her do it. Yet the harshness of the fashion world, as well as its playful energy, was constantly being played out in front of me.

There was a photo shoot on the roof of my building. All the key participants were Asian and African women. The model was a broad-shouldered muscular rock musician in her mid-30s. So in some ways a part of the age, racial and body-type biases of the fashion industry was challenged. But only in a very limited way. I also heard accounts of the increased oppressiveness of actual working conditions in the big-time fashion houses themselves.

Aziza wrote a wonderful poem about both her need and her ability to create beauty inside an industry essentially designed to keep women in constant states of insecurity and self-loathing.

And it just keeps getting worse. In her chapter on plastic surgery Gullette writes, "To the control of the male gaze and the white gaze has been added the age gaze. . . . Advertising that promises people they can pass as younger is overt, normalized, unashamed." The use of the term "anti-aging" is everywhere.

In describing a very touching personal moment Gullette writes, "In the shower one morning I was twisting to get soap and looked back and down my side. In the shower you can never see your whole self, only parts. Suddenly the curves of my hip, buttock, thigh, calf, and ankle came into view—startlingly elegant, powerful and voluptuous. It was an angle of myself I had never before observed." It was also an angle that she had never seen depicted anywhere before. Not in photos, not in paintings, certainly not in any anti-aging advertisement.

"The assumption of our culture is not just ageist but middle-ageist, that bodily decline starts not in old age but ever younger." She concludes the paragraph by saying "I haven't yet gotten my face to seem astonishingly lovelier, but every time I look down at that arrangement of hip and leg I am rewarded by a jolt of pleasure."

Her chapter on plastic surgery is fraught and complex. It is called "Plastic Wrap," which in my mind at least, is a particularly ugly and punishing title. Plastic wrap is a description someone gave of how faces look after plastic surgery. The chapter describes in detail the physical dangers attached to the surgery. The things that have gone wrong. The injuries and deaths that have resulted. Also the psychic injury often involved. The financial interests in pushing it. The cultural interests designed to reinforce what she calls the uglification industry, the need to make people feel ugly and inadequate. A feeling that can drive people into the arms of a plastic surgeon, to have surgeries that can cause long-lasting bodily harm and at times can be even fatal.

The chapter examines pressures on people, mostly women,

but an increasing number of men, to look younger and in general to feel inadequate about their physical selves. In recent years, the number of people getting plastic surgery has significantly decreased, which she is happy about. The reasons for this decrease are multiple. Some positive, some not so positive. Websites with names like Plastic Surgery Disasters show photos of people, women mostly, with botched surgeries. The websites are vindictive, mocking and hateful. What is driving people to do that would be interesting to know. There is no attending to the pain inflicted by those images. And no attending to the forces that drove the people to seek the surgeries in the first place.

More benign, but still stinging, are the responses of "the resisters [who] think 'normal' is the way their friends used to look before they succumbed. A woman described a friend who she says lost 'the most gorgeous, beautiful eyes, they were her redeeming feature....The bags are gone but the shape is different.'" If your dear friend thinks you have one redeeming quality, and it's a quality that she cherishes, you just might tell her to go fuck herself. I can see why her friend who had the surgery ignored her and did not pay much attention to whatever she said or maybe even started to hate the one characteristic that she approved of. And then there is the argument that, with so many eyes now trained to see such things, "even if you don't dislike the way you look 'after,' you may dislike being scrutinized for telltale signs."

To live in a culture where no matter what you do or don't do, people continually look at you through some life-distorting microscope, is as much a problem as anything else. Because the obsessive judging and looking and scrutinizing are laced with a poison that is not good for anyone. It might be an advance that fewer people are turning to plastic surgery, but in truth it is essentially cosmetic in terms of addressing underlying dread and humiliation.

Another reason for the decline in plastic surgery is that other "anti-aging" alternatives, such as Botox and various assortments of creams, are being aggressively marketed with growing success. This of course does nothing to challenge the basic oppression of "lookism."

The most vivid positive response to age shame in the chapter comes from Joan Nestle, a lesbian S&M activist who has written astoundingly powerful pieces over the years. She writes, "Gray hair and textured hands are now erotic emblems I seek out. As I curiously explore the lines on my own chest running down to the valley between my breasts, I caress the same lines on the chest of my lover."

I saw a show, a couple years ago, where two women with facial hair were being interviewed. One was a white, maybe Jewish, woman with a full beard. She was a dancer and a performance artist. I had seen her over the years walking through the streets looking to me like a dashing prince or one of the Three Musketeers. So narrow is the range of images available to me and so limited are my powers of description. But that's how she looked to me. And it was exciting to see someone who felt almost like a friend on TV.

I felt that I knew her. I had once seen her do a performance piece about her life and what it was to be a girl and then a woman with such an abundance of facial hair. Her girlfriend, a lithe, athletic blonde woman, was in the audience. The dashing prince and the gorgeous young damsel. Again that's the image that flashed in my head.

The performance was powerful, at times very funny. Two friends upon seeing it started talking almost immediately about everything that they felt was missing in the performance. "It has no class analysis" being the most ridiculous. This was the very first time any of us had seen such a presentation, and rather than be deeply appreciative, the loony critique/distancing/getting-on-top-of-everything mode kicked in.

The other woman on the show was young, much younger than the first. But she looked considerably older to me. She was a black woman, heavy set with thick patches of hair on her face. Her expression was one of pure torment. At some point she started to cry uncontrollably. She spoke about how painful it was for her to be seen in public. She felt that no man would ever want her. It was probably an act of tremendous courage for her to be on the show. She was in no mood to get to a place of "self-acceptance," let alone pride. Clearly no "progress narrative" was going to soothe her pain. She was simply tormented and wanted to get rid of the hair. She wanted to be normal. She wanted and could not afford electrolysis treatment to remove the hair. The host told her the show would set it up for her. The etched pain immediately turned into a smile.

What do we as a community have to offer the second woman? Certainly not reassurance about how much we "appreciate her redeeming qualities." There is the age gaze, the white gaze and then there is the progressive/radical/paternalistic/patronizing gaze. Subtle and not so subtle presumptions of power are the salient features of that gaze as they are of the others.

Reading *Agewise*, the whole world can seem, at times, like one big academic conference. Engaged and thoughtful academics are quoted throughout the book, along with an occasional line or two by a brilliant novelist or poet, or a profound insight by an informant or someone being helped by people of heightened consciousness. It is a stratified universe that I feel very alien from. And this is true regardless of how much I may admire, love, learn from or even be inspired by any number of the people who make up that world. Everything is a "discourse." Any serious human concern seems to wind up as a department or a sub-department at a university. Suicide studies, menopause studies, one "studies" after another. If you're not privy to the constantly shifting constantly refined distinctions, there is no entry place in the discussion. The universe that is Gullette's reference point can feel like a variation of the table that shunned her mother.

I needed to get that out of my system. For Margaret feels to me like a second cousin, someone I don't see too often but admire from a distance, whose values and politics are similar to mine, but different enough to more than occasionally get under my skin.

That said, Margaret Morganroth Gullette has written a significant, deeply engaged book on a massively important and nerve-wracking subject. She is a powerful advocate. And "family" tensions aside, I am grateful that she wrote it. ∎

Acting Debut

(In George Spencer's Tom, Sally and the Marquis de Sade*)*

The Critics

RECENTLY I WAS LASSOED into acting in a movie. I was so uptight and wooden in the early stages of the movie that any critic would seem ridiculous saying anything negative about me because you have to be a certain level of "good" to be called "bad." As the filming progressed I got somewhat better. Now if a critic said I was bad I would take that as a powerful affirmation of my progress.

Sex Scene

I guess the tip-off was him stripping to the waist and asking me to stand behind him placing one hand on his shoulder the other around his chest. Obviously something sexual was going to happen. But my co-star was wearing pants so I just thought it was an intimate somewhat physical scene. Didn't realize that the impression in the movie was that he was naked and that we The Marquis de Sade and Thomas Jefferson were fucking. I can be pretty dense at times. If I knew what was going on I would have been a bit more believable than a kind of cardboard character making a few purring whispers in the background. Of course this is not nearly as bad as actually having sex with someone and not knowing it was happening. ■

Celebrations

1.

blow job in progress
in old run down red car
early Sunday
gay pride morning

sticky lip smile
two contented faces
windows and wheels roll by
one block later

2.

I went to Queens College which some people said had until recently been mostly a girls' college. Rumor had it they lowered the requirements for boys in order to get more balance, an early form of affirmative action. I had been one of the bottom fifty students in my high school class of about 800. Stuyvesant was an elite all-boys science high school that taught me how traumatic space multiplied by time could be. Still it may have played a part in getting me in.

The college had many stringent requirements. And a whole series of comprehensive exams that needed to be passed in order to graduate. Each year another requirement was dropped. And even if I failed one of those schoolwide tests it didn't matter. Because once it was dropped it ceased to be a requirement. I got a D- in the last class I needed to take in order to graduate. On my final paper, something about Shakespeare, I copied chunks of material from the very book we had been assigned. Later, I think I saw my teacher blissfully banging drums during a giant Be-in in Central Park. I was stoned out on acid so it's possible it wasn't him. But I hope it was. ■

The Museum

Story One

I WENT WITH MY friend Miriam to the Guggenheim Museum. It was one of those huge exhibits that draws thousands of people. Allen Ginsberg was there responding, taking it all in. There was a lightness and intensity in his response to the work. Miriam rented a headset with a tape that walked her through the exhibit. She was unfamiliar with the work. I didn't know the work and I didn't order the headset.

Subtext: Allen Ginsberg, world famous poet. An artist. Philosopher. Photographer. Buddhist. Political activist. Middle aged Jew. Homosexual. Responding to, connected to, breathing with, continuous with the works on display. He wouldn't be bogged down by headphones, which either were going to tell him things he already knew or if he didn't would interfere with his reactions by superimposing a grid through which he would see the work.

Miriam is a linguist. In the beginning of a career that has moved her into something like the third tier of fame in international academic circles. A feminist. A Jew. She has a deep alertness. She has powerful responses to music, art, literature etc. She didn't want to take in the work in ignorance. The tape allowed her the freedom to have a response.

Me. I was caught in the idea that a great artist doesn't need an uptight, academic guide on tape. But I had no idea what I was seeing. Nothing to help me have an orientation. I wanted to be like Ginsberg. But he was free. Miriam took care of herself. I succumbed to ignorance.

Story Two

I went with my mother and father to the Guggenheim Museum. It was one of those huge exhibits that draws thousands of people. My mother walked me through the exhibit explaining things to me about the painters and the paintings. I knew one or two of the people who had also come to the museum. One was a quite famous, sensitive left-wing writer and psychoanalyst. My father sat on a bench, looked at the paper and then dozed off as parts of the Sunday *Times* hung from his lap.

Subtext: My mother was my guide. In fact that is what she did two times a week. She worked at the Guggenheim as a volunteer. One of her jobs was walking people around and giving talks on the various exhibits. To see my mother possess such presence and focus and knowledge was a bit unsettling. I really only knew her inside a space of wild, often bitter, always tumultuous emotions. She felt great dignity working at the museum. Working for free, I think diminished this feeling to a degree.

My mother guided me through the exhibit. Her explanations helped me respond to the work.

My father was exhausted and he was bored. No amount of stimulation, certainly not in this context, was going to pull him out of this state. His exhaustion seemed to me a kind of rebellion. It was a rebellion that kept him ignorant. And yet knowledge would integrate him into a system of subjugation.

Beneath the subtext of two interrelated stories:

Allen: On the world stage. Has stature comparable to artists whose works are displayed. Out there. Bad boy. World-transformer. Has sense of entitlement. Father a poet. Even in his defiance very attached and nurtured by powerful social institutions. Also over the years put himself at risk both physically and psychically.

Miriam: A woman with big ambitions. Yet confined to very narrow terrain. She was just beginning her academic climb that at 50 has brought her to a place of being almost famous. She comes from an upper middle-class family. She is very aggressive, combative, always jockeying for position. But when she is not feeling threatened is incredibly generous and responsive to other people's work. Odds more against her than they had been against Allen. Though Allen operated on a much larger scale. Her striving more harsh than Allen's. Probably because his sense of entitlement was more secure. Both Miriam and Allen move in and out of places of resistance. Allen more fluidly. More securely. He had the run of the museum.

The Museum: Deeply stratified Cultural zone. Artists selected, separated as more special than almost all other artists. Work is brought in this case to thousands upon thousands of people. There to give pleasure, expand understanding and secure a structure that keeps people in places of deep insecurity and obedience. Allen is probably one of the few people on the planet who could walk with such ease inside the museum. He was there as an equal. Miriam was, in her way, very obedient to her place. Well educated, curious, intelligent—a deeply responsive viewer.

Recently a friend of mine went with a group of artists with whom she regularly meets to a museum. The work of two well-known artists was being displayed. One died maybe twenty years ago. The other was still alive. Each had a floor to himself. There was much heated discussion about which artist was better. The artists from the group all work very hard and respect each other's work. There was in the discussion the unstated assumption that none among them would have work that belonged in the museum. And none could question whether or not this type of place should even exist. Or what does it mean that the separation between them and the artists on display was so marked and complete?

My mother as a housewife was cut off from the world. She had gotten a master's degree in art history at 45. But in her mid-fifties, she was dying of boredom in her apartment. She began to volunteer in the museum. Her vast knowledge of art history was put to good use. She learned to speak in front of a group. Her confidence increased. Groups wrote letters to the museum praising her for her fine work. But as a volunteer she was a source of free labor allowing the museum not to hire someone to do the job. So on the one hand she was brought out of an arid isolation. On the other hand she functioned as an anti-labor tool.

In the museum my father felt utterly estranged. A man in his seventies, still in business, tired in most places, coming alive when a deal needed to be made or a politically charged subject came up for discussion. An orthodox Jew. He had worked since he was thirteen. He was there in the museum with his wife and his son. He never deeply resented his wife going back to school. Never resented too deeply what she was learning. He did not in any way try to sabotage her working as a volunteer. But neither was he curious as to what she could now teach him. I doubt there was a moment he asked her any question about what she knew or let himself expand with what she had to offer. He knew very well he was in alien hostile territory. Still he could not stretch himself toward her.

Their son thinks of himself as a writer, an artist. Political activist. Feels wildly estranged from the energy in the museum. Feels half asleep. Bored as if in a classroom. Physically uncomfortable. Resentful.

As for his heart: Heart beat excitedly as he watched Allen move through the museum. Though it ached slightly for a time before he understood how much Allen belongs to the museum.

Toward Miriam there was a feeling of affection and a kind of shut down sadness for the time that they had been lovers.

For his mother, he felt joy for the pleasure she had in sharing her knowledge and her ability to appreciate as she showed him around with such confidence and flair. She opened his heart to the pleasures of appreciation of the work itself.

For his father his heart felt pure unadulterated love—not even a trace of embarrassment—as his father sat schloomped on the bench, an old Jewish businessman, wrinkled newspaper hanging from his lap as all that engaged energy moved in and around him. Inside the citadel of culture a figure of pure resistance. ■

Killing Time

Checking e-mails,
Watching Egypt erupt
Watching FBI show on TV
An occasional old movie
Too nervous to write
Anything to kill time
Talk on the phone
Anxiety level through the roof
This is only thing I can write:
A BEGINNING, A MIDDLE
IS IT THE END ∎

Anniversary

THE WORLD TRADE CENTER is one more tragic burial ground resulting from the grotesque dance of death the US is very much a partner to. To call that ground "hallowed" and "sacred" is obscene. That would only be true if something miraculous and transformative had happened to the consciousness of the nation as a result of that horror. Nothing like that has remotely happened. To pretend otherwise demeans and dishonors the dead. ∎

Round and Round It Goes, Where It Stops...

HAMAS IS BRUTAL, CYNICAL, misogynistic, homophobic, Jew-hating ethnic cleansing wannabes. It is not for lack of trying that they cannot inflict the same level of carnage that Israel is inflicting on Gaza. Though with such determination they one day might.

Israel is brutal, cynical, racist. A rampaging colonial regional power. When its leaders talk about "mowing the lawn" their deep contempt for Palestinians is revealed. Ostensibly they are talking about decreasing Hamas weaponry. But they know and don't care about the death and devastation they will cause. They sound glib, smug and repulsive. Very much like thugs who are very comfortable strutting their power over people they have contempt for and are used to oppressing. ■

2014

Into Another Time

FOR THE FIRST TIME in my life have been disliking what I have been writing. Usually I either like what I write very much or feel frustrated that I can't express something that is important to me or am embarrassed by something I once wrote. But this is different. I actively dislike it.

A couple of years ago my friend Ralph, the publisher of my book *Health Proxy*, showed me a new collection of poems he was working on. What struck me about them was they were not as "good" as the poems he wrote in his 40s. Those poems had a wisdom and a depth and a power to them that the new work didn't have. I spoke to Ralph about it because it was clear to me that the deep truths that he was in touch with no longer had the same force or resonances for him. The new work reflected that. Obviously the new work was tremendous beyond measure but what I meant by it was that it didn't have the same sureness of insight of the previous work. And I don't mean in any way there was anything glib or facile about the previous work. It was genuinely beautiful and powerful. As for myself, I think I have lived beyond the time where my explanations and insights work as well as they once did.

When the demonstrations in Egypt were happening for example there was much exhilaration and hope. I told my friends I feared that at the end of the day the military would replace the military. Which tragically is what happened. Now is that something that someone should risk getting hurt or dying for? At one point in my life I would say (and still do) it is horrible that things turned out the way they did but some spark has been ignited. If not now somewhere else at some point in the future or somewhere else someone will be inspired by it, gain courage from it. But the enormity of the actual loss in Egypt and elsewhere is larger and more destructive than I had ever before fully grasped.

Just the other day a friend on her Facebook page asked people to tag the names of banned books they have read. It was Banned Books Week. It resulted in a very lively and friendly and fun discussion. I wrote back, "I think there should be a week called 'Couldn't Get it Published Week.' I know many people who have written important things that very probably will never see the light of day. I feel very fortunate I have been able to read their work." This expressed maybe a quarter of what I was actually feeling. Obviously it is more than important, it is very crucial to fight back against repression and be in solidarity with the people whose work is banned, people often enough who are arrested, and sometimes even killed. But there is almost always inside that, the assumption that certain writers are more worthy to be published than others. In a sense you are aligning yourself with organizations who are in serious ways oppressing you. On Friday I went to a friend's reading. Someone whose work I feel deeply connected to. She was introduced by someone from some big official grant-giving agency who said the competition for the grant was fierce, that thousands of people applied for it, so her getting it was such a huge honor. Such pernicious bullshit. And what do you do with that? I was happy for my friend. But still in some serious way I wound up clapping against myself.

I often wince when I hear people's achievements listed before a reading. I don't like it and I genuinely wonder why people are so in the grip of the need for that type of validation. Particularly when it is in the form of governmental or corporate validation. Publishing houses, universities etc. I usually give only the bare minimum for myself and don't particularly like it if it is embellished in any way that plays into that. I do like it if the person actually talks about how they feel about me and/or about what I have written. Sometimes when I have to introduce people at an event I need to take a deep breath when I list what feels to me like culturally sanctioned achievements. If I can get around it without hurting their feelings I will do that. But only if I am sure they won't feel slighted. Otherwise I do feel it is an ideological imposition on my part towards no particular end.

I am a bit of a fanatic on the subject. Which sometimes has bad consequences. Many years ago I didn't mention that a piece I was reading had been published. After the reading, the editor of the publication was upset and told me so pretty firmly. He was right. I was being very disrespectful of all the work he had done to put the magazine out. And blithely ungrateful for him publishing me. Having been co-creator of *And Then* for many years, I know how he felt. It does feel good when someone mentions the magazine. And it does feel particularly bad if they mention other magazines and leave us off the list.

Over the years I have felt almost any conversation about books or movies or music was feeding the machinery of official (or alternative) culture. That painting is great. That book is lousy. It is critically acclaimed. It is about time they give an award to...What do the critics know about anything? How could that piece of shit win an award? He is an award winning author. It is just stodgy academic nonsense. Prestigious journal. Prestigious gallery. Prestigious label. Prestigious company. Got a fellowship to a writing colony. What a powerful cutting edge series of poems. I liked her early work better. It is the same old nonsense. It is part of a new surging world transforming subculture. A truly remarkable discovery. That was a great book it deserves to win a Booker Prize. The class bias is just outrageous. It was such a powerful affirmation of life. Don't understand why it didn't win an Oscar. That writer opened up my world. What reactionary culture-bound nonsense. She is without a doubt the most brilliant composer of her generation.

Even deep actual discussions would have the same impact on me. It feels like a closed circle. No matter what you do there is no way to be free from the machinery, no way you are not legitimizing and feeding it. My separation from all that in some significant ways allowed me to create. This also meant of course that I would miss out on some important work. But even more to the point, that type of discussion facilitates a certain type of connectedness with friends and other people. Talking about movies and books and music and art and dance gives people some common activity, something to share, some way to excite and connect with each other. As well as to create and learn and be inspired. It is not that I want that type of connection, it is more my separation from it is not providing me with the same alive space that existed in me before.

I feel in recent years I have been semi-closeted in many situations (not all) that give me a lot but where I can't fully say what I feel or think. This took on comical proportions a few months ago. Involving two different events. One in the morning, one in the evening.

In the morning I went to the synagogue. I go there essentially to be near my dead parents but also because I like the people and have developed a real closeness with some of them. Usually it is okay being there. When things heat up in the Middle East it can be treacherous. There is a part of the service, though, where every week people pray for the American government. And then pray for American soldiers who are "defending freedom everywhere." And then a special prayer for Israeli soldiers. That part of the service is particularly hard. Not because I wish anyone harm, but because there is an explicit assumption that the Israeli and U.S. governments are essentially in the service of the good; the brutality and crimes of those governments are not only downplayed but are virtually whitewashed out of existence.

While there, I say my own kind of prayer. Pray for Chelsea Manning, pray for the soldiers not to get hurt, pray for soldiers who are resisting their orders not to be harmed, pray for the victims of American aggression. The same with the Israeli soldiers. Pray for those resisting orders, pray that all the soldiers don't get hurt, pray for the people of Gaza they are trying to hurt and do hurt. I pray for the safety of the soldiers of Hamas and I pray for the safety of the people they are determined to hurt. I pray that the global dance of violence, power, greed and death stops. But the silent prayer I say in my mind only works up to a point in comforting me. Since everyone else is saying their prayers out loud, it is somewhat self-deceiving (and not very convincingly so) to think I am not betraying myself to some degree.

Back to the morning in question. There was a visiting scholar who came to the synagogue to give a talk. I was familiar with his work so I was hesitant to go. Many years ago when he was very young he was essentially pretty liberal. A few years later he made a sharp turn to the right. And in recent years has moved kind of to the center. He was born in New York but has lived for decades in Israel. He said that these days regarding Israel he is both hawkish and dovish depending on circumstances or what mood he wakes up in each morning. In the course of it all, he said he thought Netanyahu was getting a raw deal.

Someone who I like came over to me later and told me how much he liked his talk. The tone of the talk, if not the content, was non-combative, humorous, sweet and reflective. "What a gullible jerk you are," I thought when he said what he did. Felt bad about what I felt.

That night I went to a jazz concert where two people I love dearly were performing. One of them runs the jazz series there. Wrote about the place in a piece I wrote a few years ago. The concert takes place in a highly politicized radical environment. Between sets the head of the organization, a charismatic, colorful, humorous, passionate black woman, gave an impassioned talk about heroic African leaders, particularly Robert Mugabe who she felt may be the greatest hero of all. All this within a very astute description of how the U.S. and Great Britain are trying to regain a neo-colonial foothold in Africa.

The audience applauded with real enthusiasm afterward. What got me was that people not part of the organization, but people who were there who just loved the music, were clapping with such enthusiasm. Don't even know if they knew what they were clapping about. Felt the same way towards them that I felt towards the man in the synagogue. Don't like feeling that way at all. A quiet contempt to hide my own sense of powerlessness and complicity. So on the same day in two very different situations, both situations I get an awful lot from, two brutes were being celebrated. This is where my life has taken me. Don't quite know what to do about it (obviously this is not the whole truth).

Recently I jolted someone, someone I care very deeply about, with a comment. It just spilled out from me. Felt bad about it. Not that I said what I said, but that I didn't prepare her for something that she wasn't expecting and that she would seriously disagree with. Apologized for springing it on her in that way. She is a genuinely gracious person and said let's put time aside and have the conversation. Am afraid of actually having it. But will take her up on it. ■

Shooting Baskets

For Scott York

THE FLUIDITY IS GONE. Before it was a matter of subtle degrees. I could shoot a jump shot but not jump as high. I could make quick stops, starts and turns but maybe a little slower. But at the level I was playing at none of that really mattered. I might get out of breath more easily but not that bad. Now it felt more than just a matter of degree.

I turned 70 in December. I started shooting baskets again when I had trouble tying my shoes. Bending over, kneeling down I would get out of breath and find it difficult to do. Needed a stoop or a ledge or something elevated in order to do it comfortably.

The last time I played was well over a decade ago. I was shooting by myself when someone came over to join me. We kept taking turns. He would shoot a few, then I would. Suddenly I couldn't miss. He kept feeding me the ball. I hit maybe 8 jumpers in a row from every place on the court. Then one pass hit the tip of my fingers. Two of my fingers felt like they shattered. Not like the swollen multicolored sprained fingers I would get when I was younger. These fingers felt broken. Don't know if in fact they were. But they do look somewhat crooked to me. The feeling of them shattering made me worry that maybe all my bones were fragile and if I fell, something I am prone to do, I could hurt myself pretty badly. For years I was discouraged from playing. But periodically I would want to. But my ball lost a lot of air and I didn't know how to get a pump. Tried a couple of ways of finding one but got easily discouraged. And it seemed too daunting to buy a new ball. Spoke to a friend before the summer who had an extra pump. Started to play with my old ball. It lasted about six weeks. Then the outer cover started to seriously peel away. Bought a new ball almost immediately. Something I could have done all along.

As the summer progressed I could tie my shoes very easily. I could bend over and not get out of breath. My fingers themselves felt like they had more dexterity. At first if I tried to turn or run I felt like a "doddering old man." It was very unsettling. As the summer progressed I got more fluidity in my movement. Nothing like I used to have. Still it came back somewhat. I started trying to hit 50 shots before I called it a day. That went up to 65, then 75, then 90 and finally a hundred plus a couple extra for good measure. My shot got longer and more accurate. About half my shots would have to be from behind the foul line, more would be okay but at least that many. Then a few from behind the key. And I was able to reach from that distance fairly comfortably by the end. For the most part I couldn't jump more than a milli-inch off the ground at best. If I were ten pounds lighter it might have made enough of a difference for me to feel at least I was getting off the ground. Any jump shot I would take would be pretty close to the basket. No more than halfway to the foul line. Every so often I could actually elevate to a degree which felt incredibly good. And I think it was happening a bit more often before the cold weather came.

Since the weather has changed, even on a nice day I haven't played at all. The other day I had trouble tying my shoes again.

Over the summer I had many aches and small pains. None too bad but they did give me a sense of foreboding. My knee hurt a bit, then my lower back, then my foot. I might take a few days off and feel better. But I still needed to be careful. Maybe too careful, maybe not. Occasionally I played when I thought it might be a little risky but generally felt better afterward.

There is a small full court in the playground that is surrounded by a fence. There are a bunch of baskets all around the playground outside that area. During the time I was playing they put nets on the baskets inside the fenced area. It felt great when a shot swished through the net.

I would almost always go out early to avoid the summer heat. When I first started playing, there were a man and woman dressed in black playing in the enclosed area. So I shot on one of the other baskets. They were shooting baskets as well as doing exercises and running pretty much full court. They were in some kind of nice rhythm with each other. I could not tell their ages. In fact their ages seemed to change pretty dramatically depending on my angle of vision.

They would occasionally imagine there were 10 seconds left in a game and do a countdown for the last shot. I would kind of play along in my head. The man at some point looked to me like Bruce Springsteen. Very much like him. He looked younger and a little thinner. But in truth I know very little about Springsteen except what you can't help but know. They played there for a while, then stopped.

Recently my curiosity got the better of me and I looked up Bruce Springsteen on YouTube. The very first one I clicked on he came on stage with a basketball while "Sweet Georgia Brown," the theme song of the Harlem Globetrotters, was playing in the background. He talked a bit about basketball and then began the concert. So who knows.

In the beginning when I first started there was another man with thick white shoulder length hair who was skating from one side of the park to the other with a hockey stick controlling a ball then shooting it against the fence. He also only played for a couple of weeks, then stopped for a long while until he started again. He was graceful and looked quite strong and clearly had been and clearly still was an impressive athlete.

It was summer, so maybe these people went on vacation. Or in the case of the first two maybe being here was the vacation. Occasionally I see the hockey player walking two very expensive looking dogs in the Village.

I started going earlier and earlier. The playground was now mostly deserted. Occasionally it made me nervous. Because the court was in a confined space. Sometimes some high school kids hung out in the park. Sometimes someone would be shooting baskets in the enclosed courts and I would shoot on one of the other baskets. Or sometimes some people who might be homeless hung out on some distant benches. The thought occurred to me that I was very vulnerable and if someone fixated on me for any reason I could be hurt. It was I think basically paranoia. Two times I got particularly nervous. Each time a different sullen looking kid came to the court to play. Both times I said hello and they didn't respond. Very likely they picked up on my anxiety. But again who knows. Then there was another time when someone in his 40s approached me early one morning. He had been sitting on a bench pretty far from where I was playing. He was well dressed but he looked like a junkie, a word I never use and yet it was the fear that word can connote that entered my head as he walked slowly towards me. He asked if he could shoot baskets with me. I said sure. Got nervous, missed a lot of shots but also felt stronger and more energized. He said he had a fight with his wife and came to the park to cool off. That fight had to do with where they would be living. He wanted to stay in the Village. She wanted to move somewhere else. He had been a basketball player at a New York City high school and then a professional fighter whose uncle trained him. He moved to Florida. His uncle asked him to take a dive with promises of an important fight in the future. Don't remember if he did or not but it really upset him; he felt betrayed by his uncle and quit fighting soon afterward. He said he had been hooked on drugs (and alcohol) for a number of years but was off it now. We kept shooting and talking. Me keeping a kind of slight distance as we were doing it. Eventually he left. Aside from my anxiety he was a nice, very interesting guy and fun to talk to.

One other thing I was worried about was the ball getting stuck in the rim and I would have no way to get it down. This happened three times. Once a park attendant (after opening up they were not

265

always there) jumped and knocked it loose with his hat. A second time the couple in black threw me their basketball and I knocked it loose with their ball. The third time I found a long wooden plank reachable from a construction site just outside the playground fence and I knocked the ball loose. As long as I could reach a piece of wood I was okay even without anybody being there. But when that was no longer the case and when no one else was around I had no idea what I would do. That to some extent controlled what kind of shots I would take. Occasionally I took a chance knowing if the ball got stuck it would be because the shot was taken from that angle. So I took extra care and fortunately it didn't happen.

Another time a man with a dog—at a certain hour people with dogs would come to the park—asked me how long I would be shooting. Even though the basketball court was primarily there to play basketball I still felt somewhat like an interloper. He said don't rush but that his dog usually ran inside the enclosed area I was shooting in. I said maybe five minutes. I had five baskets left to make to reach my quota. Of course the pressure got to me and it took me longer than normal. But still well within the five minutes. He then said don't worry. I saw him a couple of times later and said I would go to one of the side baskets. He said it was fine and he just played with his dog in the outer area.

The next to last time I played was somewhat later in the day, maybe 11 am or 12. Two young long-haired men with head-bands were playing on the full court. This time the park was filled mostly with women with children. A few extremely tiny kids with wild energy on scooters scooted right under me as I was shooting on one of the side baskets. These kids were totally oblivious to me shooting. I kept an eye out for them but still continued, worried the basketball might hit one of them on top of the head or that I would run over one of them or trip over a scooter and hurt myself. But in the end we all managed okay. ∎

Shooting Hoops

Written by Tobin Simon

No ballet dancers we, Steve and I
Stumble after the elusive basketball.
Preschoolers and mothers peer
Through the iron fence at the two Parkies
Congratulating each other on made shots,
Including chippie bank shots,
I, in a body way, remembering fast hands.

Shooting hoops is new for Steve.
Still he bangs in a surprising percentage—
Bombs from afar—
And those that miss mightily I chug after
In retrieving mode—a thought merely
To my zippered chest.

Steve shows no emotion.
Facial muscles much in place,
His voice gritty.
Says he brings his granddaughter to the same park
Now that she doesn't fear the gravelly voice.

We're tired, secretly check our watches
Declare it's time to get to the Jewish Center
For our movement class.

We laugh at the sight of us Parkies
Getting into (and out of) cars.
Steve drives—very mindfully.

I day dream for a moment about the time we were one game
        away from the state championship.
That was 1958. Also remember winning our college
Conference, 1963. No question then for moving feet.

But that was then.

A cup of water and I'm set to labor ninety minutes
with our movement leader.

Next Monday before class, Steve and I
Will shoot hoops again.
We're looking for other Parkies

To go two on two against us. ■

OF COURSE MY MIND and heart are still engaged with the story I read yesterday about Arnie. I met him when I met you. He seemed like your sidekick then because you and I had in common the same experience of Shulie at the same time. That was the remarkable thing we shared at that moment.

But I liked Arnie just as much as I liked you, altho he is different than you. You were both such nice boys, and so clearly good friends. The warmth and friendship between you was palpable.

And so it was like a warmth the two of you together offered to whoever you were with or meeting (me!). I liked you both very much. And then I read both of your poems. And I still remember Arnie's poem and how much I liked it.

Of course the Arnie I met in the East Village when he was your sidekick and friend who I liked and who seemed like a lovely warm friendly guy, is not the same Arnie I met in your story. All those unfathomable depths, and so much going on at every level.

He is more like another Shulie. So intense, so deep, such an intellect, so passionate. So much high drama on an internal level.

Altho it is nice thinking if the 4 of us (me and Shulie, you and Arnie) had all met up together before we took ourselves and life so seriously, we could have had a nice time just schmoozing and hanging out, just being friendly and warm with each other.

You know I am a Queens girl. I grew up one block from Queens College. I walked thru the campus of Queens College on my way to and my way from junior high school every day. Altho I chose to go to CCNY.

I had no idea Arnie was a Queens boy till I read your story. But maybe that is why I instantly felt so comfortable with him and liked him so much. Us who were weird for Queens always had so much in common. ∎

This piece was written after Anne read "The Wolf at the Door," which begins on the following page.

The Wolf at the Door

"THE WHORE YOU CAN fuck but not be seen with. The man you would never fuck but turn to in the middle of the night to be reassured, excited and affirmed."

The lines flashed out of me the night Arnold Sachar died. I was shocked at their intensity and my bitterness.

I first saw Arnie at a Free Speech rally at Queens College in New York City during a student strike. I think it was in 1962. This beautiful and intense figure moved from person to person, group to group, listening, speaking, engaged in the event with a seriousness much different than anyone else seemed to have. It was as if a spotlight followed him everywhere he went. Wherever he stood, it seemed as if something historic was at stake.

The next time I saw Arnie was in Spanish class. He looked spaced out, dazed, lost in some deep internal chaos. The only person more spaced out than me. Each day we would go around the room and have to translate a sentence from English to Spanish. Arnie was always the ninth person called on. I was always the twelfth. Neither of us ever got the answer right. One day I saw that the translations were in the back of the book. So I started memorizing answer 12. But Arnie never knew answer 9. So it really was answer 11 that I would have to give. Finally it dawned on me to memorize answer 11. Of course, that was the one time Arnie got the answer right.

Another time I saw Arnie was during the Cuban Missile Crisis. A solitary figure on a desolate corner on the campus, he spoke with extraordinary eloquence about the insane criminality of everyone involved. "Mr. Kennedy, Mr. Khrushchev, Mr. Castro" all complicit in a profoundly immoral dance.

His great oratory skill was something he shelved. He knew he had the eloquence to move a crowd but felt he did not have the experience or wisdom to do so. Particularly if it involved the risk of significant danger.

Over the years, he would speak and write about alienation, yearning, repression, community, transcendence. Much of his work was an examination of psychic pain and its social/political roots. He could speak beautifully about the nightmarish structural oppression that can flow out of that pain. He articulated the ways in which people resisted and acquiesced to their condition. You often could feel the rawness of his nerve endings whenever he spoke about this.

2

My own nerves are shot. The tragedy of my dearest friend lying in a coma on Long Island. His body flooded with fluids. His head swollen, covered with bandages, tubes and a face mask.

The tragedy of his life. Always spinning his wheels. Never able to appreciate himself. The humiliations and traumas of childhood ridicule. Physically awkward, nervous.

It is now four years after Arnie's death.

I've been writing this piece since before he died. Not all the time but going back to it. Reading parts of it to him when he was still alive. Trying to figure out what to say. How to say it.

My own body is breaking down. Two teeth broke recently. I am missing appointments. I am scared of what can happen next. And what can happen can happen very fast.

3

Arnie could be a bottomless pit of need. No matter how much you poured into him it could be as if nothing had happened.

As much as I loved him, admired him, respected him he would

convince me how marginal, how disrespected, how ignored and isolated he was. I would say that's ridiculous, but start, more than start, to actually believe it. So much so that when someone would ask me how he was doing or having heard him on the radio say he was terrific or God forbid just have a nice feeling towards him, I would grow livid. "So now you feel good. But I don't feel good. I had to go through days listening to this. And you get the compliment. And what good does that do me. You feel good and I am just exhausted." He lived with ghost images, fear, deep insecurities. And a mind that could both take flight and simultaneously be imprisoned. He was always looking out the door to be validated by whoever was not in the room. Whoever was in the room lost the ability to affirm him.

When we were much younger, I would run home to tell Arnie anything and everything. Call him up and talk endlessly. Almost living my life to talk to him about it. Living experience to relate it back to him. He would do the same. My other friends resented this. And lovers resented it even more.

His experiences mostly life inside his apartment. It was lonely. But also very rich. Talking on the phone, listening to the radio, making calls into the radio. Developing a following from those calls. Transforming the role of the caller with his insight and eloquence and urgency. His room in fact could feel like control center. He being at the center of everything without moving an inch from his room.

Very occasionally he would talk about a neighbor or a restaurant. Though there was a period where he would sit in the park outside his apartment engaging the neighbors in political conversation. At times he would venture out from Forest Hills to Manhattan. And inevitably some drama, some excitement would occur. He would also come in for things we did together. And he would often stay in my apartment. Sometimes for a day or two. Sometimes longer. We organized discussion groups and writers' groups over the years. We would write public statements. We would also write petitions on very volatile and to us very crucial issues. And then gather signatures. The process was in many ways gratifying, nerve-racking, exhilarating.

Arnie knew by heart almost everything any number of people had written. He would read things over and over again. Study them, constantly engaging what he was reading. Naturally people would be very flattered by this. I remember him calling up the radio, it was Paul McIsaac's show actually, and asking Carl Oglesby how he reconciled something he was saying with something he had written twenty-five years earlier. Oglesby laughed and said, "I wrote that? It sounds pretty good. But I don't remember a word of it. I have absolutely no idea how to reconcile the two."

On the phone he was always summarizing things he had just read. As well as reading me passages of something that particularly grabbed him, and on occasion he would read me a whole article. There was however a three year period when I had forbidden him to read me anything, except maybe something he had just written.

My stricture was a result of Arnie having read to me for five hours an autobiographical piece in *Working Papers* in which Elinor Langer describes her experiences as a social activist in the '60s. Arnie had a good speaking voice and a love for anybody who put words to paper. And so when he read me Langer's piece I just didn't know how or when to ask him to stop because he was enjoying himself so much. But for the last two hours I could hardly breathe and I didn't want to have that experience ever again.

4

The last year I would call and get off very quickly. I did most of the calling but I ran away from him. His obsessiveness mixed with the direness of his condition was harder for me to take. He grew both more mired, attached and simultaneously liberated from his demons. I felt bored and disconnected. Something I had never experienced before. I would yell at him. I felt at times it crossed over from frustration and a wish to shake him out of repetitive patterns into abuse. I got off on it. Looking for any traces of what was bothering me, then going after him. He mostly said it didn't upset him. He thought I was trying to ground him (not grind him down), bring him back to some sort of reality. I felt I was crossing a line. Being more caught up in a drama than trying to help him. I didn't trust myself. I was locked in.

The horrible panic of that last night. I was too depleted, too exhausted from all the years of reassuring, trying to calm him down. It felt often that he was crying wolf. But the humiliation, fear, panic was there and it was real. Terribly, terribly real. Trying to be talked down from his panic insecurity. But also really fearing the wolf in ways I couldn't fully grasp. Sometimes crying wolf because the fear was familiar and in some strange ways felt safe. The horrible security of a familiar even very negative state. Now the wolf was really here and it was gorging out his insides. And I no longer had the energy needed to help in the way I might with someone else.

His last night before the accident he called me six or seven times. Every twenty minutes he would call me frantically from the hospital, trying to calm himself down. He was having a hard time breathing. He also said he felt as if sitting, lying, standing, walking were entirely different functions, totally divided from each other. No connection at all between them. This terrified him. Terrified me. A couple of weeks before, his doctor put him on a small dosage of an anti-depressant that seemed to throw everything off. People speaking to him the week I was in Montreal said he sounded different. Less connected. And just as arbitrarily they took him off it. No blood test, no nothing.

As we were talking his doctor came by. The two of them started laughing. The laughter made me nervous. For I had a feeling the doctor in some way accepted Arnie's picture of himself. Not exactly laughing at him but not entirely with him.

Which may have made the doctor a little too cavalier. In reassuring Arnie, in a need to settle him down, he might have misjudged the actual severity of his condition.

Arnie got off the phone but not before I told him I needed a break. The whole thing was exhausting me. Wanted to watch some TV to regain my equilibrium. I remember thinking that this could be the last time we ever spoke. Paul called me very early in the morning telling me that Arnie had fallen, cracked his head against the hospital bed and was in a coma. I think his death was one part negligence. One part inevitability. That last night that we spoke he told me that he thought he would be dead in two or three days.

In the early years of our friendship, I ran home to tell Arnie almost anything and everything that happened to me. I would call up and we would talk endlessly. I remember calling Arnie once from a pay phone upset about something Denise Levertov said at a reading of hers. Almost living experience so that we could relate it back and forth to each other. This led to resentment from other friends. And some deep resentment from lovers.

Arnie would do much the same. But his experiences were largely listening to the radio, calling up shows, reading the newspapers and journals, talking to various people on the telephone and interactions with his parents. Occasionally he would venture out. And always something dramatic would occur.

The last year of his life was the first time I felt even a little estranged from him. Very connected but not excited to speak to him. It was like falling out of love with someone you still loved very much. In the last year I felt that I was abusive towards him. We would have wild fights. I felt continually provoked by him. I hit back. And I started to hit back at a shadow presence of a previous consciousness. Because he was in some ways changing. I was addicted to the dynamic. I apologized at times. He felt though that I was trying to help him, ground him, help him shake the frozen state he was in. I often felt he was one small turn of the screw away from doing something that would pull him out of the places he felt stuck. But that one screw turned the wrong way could also unravel everything.

One night about a couple of years before he died, Arnie fell flat on his face while we were walking and talking in the rain. He bruised his lip and his face.

He often was in extreme states of anxiety, and had a fear that at times bordered on terror. His insecurity was real. The SELF-LOATHING was real. The self-almost rape was real. "Robert you don't believe that I feel the way I say I do." Often someone exaggerates a feeling to get the kind of affirmation or attention to pain they think they deserve. And I think it is important to respond as much as possible to the pain felt and not get bent out of shape by what can feel manipulative or dishonest. Or in my case feel mocked and diminished. Because in truth you are not exactly there at those moments. This is all much easier said than done.

What do I do with him. There is just too much pain there. He dies; it all is unresolved. He had both a frozenness and an immense ability to feel. A solipsism and powerful empathy. An insecurity and an extraordinary confidence. A prophet scared of his own shadow. And then he would get up in a room to hushed silence as people waited to hear what he would say. Years of eloquence and profound engagement creating the anticipation. Knowing something extraordinary was going to come. For me that moment at my book party—him ambling up, getting into his composure—was overwhelming. His eloquence and seriousness breathtaking. His affirmation so loving and deeply vital to me.

Late at night after appearing on Carletta's radio show we screamed at each other on the streets down by Wall Street as we walked back to my place. He started talking about how desolate his life was. "Who is ever celebrated the way we were just celebrated," I answered. "Well it was only one show," was his fall-back position. And we screamed even louder. Who has people like that speaking so warmly about what we have done. Carletta putting all her magic into the show. And then there was Ahmed, the great trumpet player and bandleader; Monique, an exquisite poet singer, partner with Ahmed; Eleanor, Arlene's mother, making her media debut from her apartment in Brooklyn—first quiet soft almost inaudible gaining strength as the show went on. "The magazine is real for real people," she said. Creating instant anxiety in Arnie that the magazine was shallow. Arnie wincing, his insecurity, his neurosis tapped into. He should have been able to wince without me jumping on him later for it. Since I knew also how much he really appreciated the comment. "Do you have to notice everything?" he said.

"I can't put myself down without putting you down. You have me boxed in," he then said, half laughing. "Fuck you," I said only a quarter joking.

But now Arnie's gone. It is extremely painful for me to be working on the magazine without him. I feel very incomplete. I feel lost at sea. We would talk five or six times a day. When new pieces are coming in now I can't call him. If there is a problem I can't call him. If we get a compliment I can't call him. I won't be able to work with him to figure out what order the pieces should go in. I won't be able to work out political and social ideas with him. I can't argue about things as openly and completely with any other close friend. There is no one else I can obsess with. No one else I can argue with in the same way. Anyone else I would drive crazy.

Arnie had a profound prophetic imagination. And an extremely active and insightful political mind. The great pacifist/anarchist Igal Roodenko said that we are all instruments in the orchestra. Arnie's presence lingers and has become a part of many of us. But in its fullness, it really can't be there. That section of the orchestra is silent. And the music I play sounds tinny and very lonesome and totally inadequate without it.

5

"Coming into political consciousness I had imagined a radical movement similar to the beggars' march in The Threepenny Opera. *It would be a home, a place to gather for the despised, the grotesque, the disenfran-*

chised, people in pain, outcasts. Together we would menace the society in our very being, in our very acceptance of each other's humanity, in our essential beauty and defiance." (Robert Roth, *&then*, 1987)

He was often filthy. He at times smelled of shit. He would cut himself up shaving. Splotches of raw razor cuts in between thick black untouched facial hair. Finally he went to get a weekly shave. He loved the warm towel and neck massage from the barber. At one point he would buy He-man shirts designed specifically for heavy set men. They were sexy and colorful. And a surge of compliments would come towards him. Until the shirts were tattered and torn. And somewhere in his mind when he put them on he expected the same excitement. He was genuinely confused about why it wasn't happening. Further confirming his belief that nothing he did would change how people perceived him physically.

We walked down 8th Street. He had mismatched shoes. One possibly four sizes too big. His foot was swimming inside the shoe. He was almost shuffling down the street. His pants falling, the cuffs tattered from being stepped on. Ran into Sohnya who panicked when she saw him. Thought that he would be a target. That he looked so spaced out and homeless. She dragged him into a shoe store and bought him a pair of shoes.

One night, it was an isolated incident, he shit all over my bathroom. Somehow it wound up on the walls. In an attempt to clean it up he was smearing it everywhere. He looked almost like a kid fingerpainting. I gagged. Yelled at him. Ran out in the middle of the night to a bodega for cleaning material including a painter's mask. Felt horribly guilty. Squeamish and uptight. He said he didn't blame me for yelling. I didn't even realize he was in touch enough not to take offense.

Years later when he was sick, brought him home from the hospital. His apartment was reeking of shit. All over the floor. In every room. I was shocked and horrified. Again I ran out of the apartment gagging. Again I was ashamed of my squeamishness. Felt someone else could have handled it better. He did not even know that it was there. The floors covered with shit. His bed beyond filthy. He described his apartment as "messy." I convinced him to hire two close friends to clean it.

At times there were moments of recognition. He saw himself in the mirror and saw he had grown significantly bald. It surprised him and upset him. He had looked that way for years.

·

The constant stigma of Arnie's life. He craved a certain normalcy while simultaneously defiantly living outside the world.

Whenever he was relaxed a calm came over him.

> Delicate hands, almost fragile
> Beautiful spirit soaring

6

The searing humiliation of himself as freak. Me never knowing how to fully engage that feeling. How to help him through it. How not to get caught up in the compulsive self-laceration. And through it all we thought together, created together, worked together. Tried to engage the world, to help change the world together.

"Can't you ever accept people's love. You just torment me with all this nonsense," I would yell at him. "Okay then you're right; you are just a repetitive bore. You only speak in headlines, and say the same fucking thing the same way over and over again. Who the hell would want to talk to you. Everyone should be bored with you." Then I would catch myself and laugh. "And if they're not bored with you then something must be wrong with them."

It was a tough time between us. His inability to accept or embrace our various joint achievements as well as those of his own felt like a putdown. But it wasn't. It was just some horrible internal dialogue flowing out of him towards me. In a world where so little affirmation was coming our way it still felt like a putdown.

Because even if you feel somewhat confident and proud about something, one slight negative gesture and you can dissolve into nothingness. One step out of a bubble—is it a bubble, or is it a community of shared consciousness—can unsettle you and make you feel totally inadequate. I needed his support. I needed his affirmation. I felt abandoned by him in those moments.

And yet the stigma he carried was greater than mine, as painful as mine is for me. Don't know what to do with it. It is so hard to think about, so hard to relate. How does someone who feels ugly but knows the world thinks of them as beautiful feel as opposed to someone who feels ugly and the world confirms that feeling almost every minute of every day?

A line I wrote once but never used in a fiction piece I was writing about someone whose body looked "lopsided." "It is where the spirit broke free from the armoring of the body."

How not to live vicariously through his "freakishness." Thinking of it as a manifestation of freedom. Him bearing its brunt while I'm drawn to it as liberation. To have him play out my fantasy of someone totally outside the world. I once wrote that for some left-wing people the only good oppressed person was a dead oppressed person. Here was my version of that.

We betrayed each other in some core place. Betrayed is a strong word. Probably too strong. A word unfair to either of us. And yet there was an aspect of betrayal certainly on my part not knowing/understanding the depth of the stigma, the humiliation he experienced almost constantly.

My friend Harilyn Rousso said that Arnie carried the pain for both of us.

7

Twenty-five years ago when Akemi saw the condition of the sheets in my apartment where Arnie slept, she was outraged. I thought well what does he know? He is so oblivious why bother cleaning the sheets. A strange fatigue on my part. They'll get dirty again in no time. Something deeply punitive in my own passivity here. Can't fully locate what it was. He just accepted the humiliation of his condition. Expected almost nothing from the world. When I changed his sheets he expressed his appreciation without me even saying that I had changed them. So he was much more aware than I realized. And so there it is. What that "it" is is probably something I don't want to look too closely at.

8

Michael Sahl just told me at a concert of his at The Cell one of the people in charge said, "Who *is* that?" referring to Arnie, whose dentures were falling out as he became all excited by various friends being there. Especially excited to be with Michael and Margaret and celebrate the concert and their achievement. Michael pretended not to have a clue who or what the person was talking about. The cool hip trendy edgy sophistication of the place violated.

Edgy. That is what *The New York Times* says about plays or books or music or art. Or they might complain that something wasn't edgy enough. Or subversive enough. Such bizarre terminology emanating from the belly of the beast. Very much also the terminology of the fashion industry: Revolutionary, cutting edge. Nothing means nothing. Don't even know where to go from here.

I do remember one night my dear friend Aziza, her father very much involved in liberation struggles in Africa, she just beginning her career as a fashion designer, sitting in my living room, listening to me go on and on about this very point. Until she lifted her head from a sketch she was doing, flashed a smile and asked "How about 'Self-determination' for the name of my new line?" Brought me off my high horse. And we both started laughing.

Back to my high horse. Raw exploration, deep insight

wind up as a blurb or an ad. Everything is commodified. People themselves are constantly referred to as "brands." It feels almost stupid to say something that obvious. And yet it is so taken for granted, so pervasive, so unchallenged.

But even in the purest form where those terms actually had the power and authenticity of people deeply engaged in struggle there was often something hollow and manipulative about them. For example, "Power to the People" too often morphed into "Sorrow to the People."

Almost anything you do politically runs the real risk of you becoming the "useful idiot" of forces larger than yourself. The alternative often is to fall into a world-weary cynicism. A know-it-all fatigue. A terrible resigned despair.

Arnie and I would together always attempt to negotiate a political/social terrain fraught with this danger. We would talk constantly. Working out ideas, discussing things. Writing public statements. Our conversations at times could be so rarefied that someone overhearing them would not know what we were talking about. Some of the concerns were constant. We'd go back to them over and over again. But as much as we talked, it does not really help me now in figuring out how to address a problem that is new. The same basic principles might apply but that helps only up to a point.

One day I was in a café and obsessing about a problem that I knew only Arnie would fully understand without me having to lay out the givens that we had worked out over decades. And I was really in pain that I could not speak to him. So I called my friend Bernie and said I need to discuss something, something I could only talk to Arnie about. I'm in agony about it. You are my second choice, a very distant second. Do you mind? I knew Bernie was a dear enough friend and someone rightly confident enough in his own thinking that he wouldn't take offense. He laughed and said sure. And it was exactly what I thought it would be. The very best second best conversation imaginable.

9

I loved Arnie's parents. They looked entirely different from each other. But in a room of thousands you could pick them out as Arnie's parents. He looked exactly like each of them. When they weren't fighting they very much enjoyed going out dancing. They were also great story tellers. Roz had a particular gift with words. Being able to take words that were in the air and give them her own particular slant. She also was continually giving away gifts. She would create spontaneous parties anywhere and everywhere at any time of any day. A present could be a tiny trinket wrapped in tin foil. Or something significantly more valuable. When she died Dave beyond grief kept repeating how he could never give people gifts the way she could.

Roz in very real ways was very brazen, she would speak her mind. But she was also incredibly fearful and her feelings got hurt easily. A fearfulness and sensitivity to slights she passed on to Arnie in an extreme way. Arnie had enormous courage in putting his ideas out there. But he could fall apart over almost anything in an instant. As for Dave, a veteran of World War II, I remember him going to an early teach-in about the Vietnam War and getting up and saying "My fucking son is right about this fucking war." This to the great delight of the audience and to the extreme embarrassment of Arnie.

One time I along with my lover, Charlotte, and her mother, Betty, who was in from Minnesota, visited Roz and Arnie in Forest Hills. At one point Betty referred to Arnie and his mother as husband and wife. A look of primal horror crossed both their faces. I literally fell off my chair laughing. Another time Arnie rolled in the middle of the street kicking his feet against the pavement in response to something his mother said— a four-year-old throwing a massive tantrum. Until her death they would spend hours in the kitchen talking.

Dave was kind of a tough guy, wiry and small. He was also

an athlete. He told me a story of being in the bowling alley hitting strike after strike. Until he was a frame away from a perfect game. The whole bowling alley gathered around for the last frame. He got so nervous he threw a gutter ball.

He had been a bat boy for the NY Giants and also once delivered some dry cleaning to Mae West. It would be story after story. And here he had a son who would do nothing but spend hours on the phone in his room calling up the radio. Being extraordinarily eloquent and in his own way having a significant influence on the political and social movements of the day. This both amused and worried Dave. He did not know what would become of Arnie when he died.

Arnie's special gifts were appreciated early on. His father was an accountant. Some of his clients were mobsters. One was called in front of a congressional committee investigating organized crime. He asked if Arnie, who was fifteen, could write his introductory remarks. When the time came he read Arnie's words as if they were his own. It was in large part a paean to the greatness of the country. His gravelly voice became more and more filled with emotion as the senators and the gallery grew increasingly spellbound.

•

The Forest Hills Streaker—I got a call once from the managing agent of the building Arnie lived in. He heard complaints that Arnie was running naked through the building. I told him that couldn't be true. But I asked Arnie about it. He said his belly was so big and wearing pants so cumbersome that when he had to throw out newspapers he would poke his head out the door, look around and when he saw no one, would dash or sort of dash out of the apartment totally naked, make his way up one flight of stairs to a recycling area and then return to his apartment as quickly as possible. He was surprised anyone had noticed.

•

Arnie Sachar at Riverside Church. I remember attending a major political event at Riverside Church. There was a young black woman always rising from her seat cheering every comment that had any passion, integrity and militancy behind it. When Arthur Waskow spoke, he threw out what he clearly thought were a series of show stoppers. But they had virtually no impact on her. She remained glued to her chair. Just polite tepid applause at the end. I asked Arnie would he rather be praised by one of the high-powered left intellectuals he was preoccupied with, but not have her budge from her seat. Or have her rise with wild enthusiasm and have the left intellectual barely acknowledge his words. He said I was being totally unfair and started to giggle.

•

One time we were at a party. Arnie was in a corner talking with one of the sexiest, most beautiful women imaginable. She took a real liking to him and asked him to dance. She held on to him and started grinding against him. His face flushed, his body tensed. Arnie getting more nervous by the second started quizzing her compulsively about her position on various issues, trying to find the one issue that could drive her away. She ignored the bait and continued dancing. After a while though she did get discouraged. Not that there was a cause and effect, but a few years later she wound up in a torrid affair with a higher-up in the Carter administration.

•

His father told me a story of Arnie playing softball as a kid. The last inning, the bases loaded, two outs. Standing in right field completely lost in his thoughts, his glove absentmindedly stuck out in the air, when without him even knowing it a fly ball landed in it. He was the hero of the game. The whole team ran out to him and triumphantly carried him off the field.

•

He wrote a magnificent piece about what it was to feel ugly when much of the world actually saw him as ugly, freakish. The places he shut down, the places he soared. The places he embraced his "freakishness," the places he craved to be respected and accepted in deeply culture-bound terms. It was here—in his need for that acceptance—that the greatest tensions and struggles existed between us.

•

In camp the counselors and fellow campers would seek Arnie out late at night. In the darkness, they would talk intimately about their desires, pain or intellectual interests. Sometimes in the case of the counselors the conversations turned to books or politics. During the day he was often shunned, mocked, had practical jokes played on him or, in the case of his fellow campers, he was also at times physically assaulted. Not to the extent of causing serious physical injury but enough to leave lasting harm to his psyche.

•

Twirling a pen. A pencil, a swizzle stick, for a time a dirty toothbrush. Twirling ever faster, while rocking back and forth, the more excited or delighted or upset he would get. It would unnerve some people. Others simply enjoyed it as a basic feature of any conversation. Another friend, Paul Meyers, a wonderful poet, did that also. But not as noticeably. He had a different rhythm. Used different fingers. It was fun to see them in a room together.

•

Early on we attended parties at David McReynolds's apartment on the Lower East Side. Dave was deeply involved with the War Resisters League. He helped organize massive worldwide protests, was a political theorist and a very out gay man. When we wanted to discuss some pressing political issue with him, we would go to the WRL office. However, whenever Arnie attempted to get into a discussion with him at a party, Dave would always say, "Arnie, no talking at parties."

•

Arnie walking crossing the street as cars were whizzing by looking like Jesus walking on water. He never getting hit not even close. His doing this caused no small degree of anxiety in many of us. Though at least in my case it was clearly offset by the knowledge that nothing had ever happened so it was very unlikely that it ever would. He did get a jaywalking ticket for crossing Queens Blvd. once. There had been a large number of deaths and injuries so the city cracked down. His day at court was filled with one adventure after another which he recited with great gusto and humor.

•

Arnie, beside himself with excitement, was talking with the ex-lover of a woman he was totally hung up on. As they were walking down the street, he nervously pointed to his pants, now wet with semen. He had ejaculated without even touching himself during the conversation.

10

The chief rabbi of Poland was visiting the chief rabbi of Warsaw. They were in the synagogue. The first rabbi, suddenly overcome, ran up to the ark, threw himself on the ground and said, "Oh Lord I am nothing in the face of your glory." The second rabbi overwhelmed by the sight of the first rabbi followed suit. "Oh Lord I am nothing in the face of your glory."

The Shammes, the caretaker of the synagogue, totally transported by the sight of these two wise, holy men prostrating themselves with such fervor, stopped what he was doing and threw himself on the ground. "Oh Lord I am nothing in the face of your glory."

The first rabbi turned to the other and said, "The nerve of him to say that he is nothing."

In their book *Bound by Love*, Lucy Gilbert and Paula Webster talk about how those men who could not dominate on the athletic field would assert their patriarchal power through their intellectuality. Arnie and I would talk about that often.

A Buddha, Arnold Sachar
By Louise Rader

When I first met him
I felt unnerved
by his intellect's power
to pierce illusion,
by his rocking roundness
as if prayer were a physicality,
by his ungoverned giggling
echoed in the swizzle stick
he twirled fizzing air,
by lucence then sudden
constriction in his eyes
stunned at a society
with love, joy, communion
shackled,
by his refusal
to put on constraints.

Decades
of his longing, written,
his voice from the radio,
the presence he bestowed
on a moment,
          a teaching,
                    a touchstone.

Here, each leaf falls
into a ground mosaic.

Arnie was timid. He was fearful. He had a soaring confidence. It was like he was always rehearsing for the State of the Cosmos Address. The one that at the precise right moment when called upon he would deliver to the universe. And it would also deliver him from the humiliations and pain of the world. So a conversation with him could be like watching someone rehearse in front of a mirror with you being the mirror. He could be very repetitive to say the least. I would roll my eyes at times when he read me something he had written. In conversation there were way too many times when he wasn't speaking with you, but at you.

That was the down side. My friend Andy calls it the talking sickness. It is hard at times to distinguish hysteria, compulsiveness, real insecurity from a bullying insensitive arrogance. A very not uncommon trait of forceful people in the grips of massive insecurity.

Arnie was always pitching to be brilliant, more than brilliant. At times it felt like his life depended on it.

"I am not James Baldwin," he would declare. As if not being James Baldwin was the next best thing to being him. That the failure of the intent was much greater than any other achievement imaginable.

What do you do with that? What could James Baldwin do with that?

Other times Arnie was expansive beyond measure. His face relaxed. His anxiety lifted. He could separate himself from his fears, his insecurities. In fact he had separated himself from that aspect of a radical/intellectual culture that could feel almost pathological in its need to compare and evaluate and situate people in a hierarchy of consciousness, intelligence, understanding, location and power. A movement acting in many ways as a parody of the dominant culture. The depth of Arnie's warmth and appreciation for people at those moments was a thing to behold.

Even people with virtually no power in the world can function as conduits for forces that oppress you. And the actual powerlessness of the person doing it can be forgotten. Or even if you fully understand the absurdity of it, that understanding might only deflect a little the injury you're experiencing. This can work in all directions.

Every slight in the street, in the supermarket, at school would somehow be overcome by the sheer force of Arnie's brilliance. That the affirmation of a small select group of "special" people would undo or provide salve for that injury: He funneled so much of himself into that hope. Really only a partial hope. Because he understood how toxic it all was. Trying to get out from under it. He was in fact bitter at the end that he had bought into it as much as he had.

Simultaneously, unaware of his own power Arnie could hurt people pretty badly. Trying to prove himself he could ignore someone or appear condescending in conversation. He could talk over people, ignore what they were saying. Or focus exclusively on one person at the expense of another. So powerful was his attention and focus, that his ignoring someone could create rage and insecurity in that person. As close as we were, that person at times could be me.

Being pushed aside in a conversation, I might snap back in front of people, embarrassing him. Did this the other day with another close friend who pushed his body between me and someone I was having a conversation with and just started talking as if I wasn't there. He had done similar things before and we had spoken about it. But in this case, he had just done a reading and it was the host of the reading he did this with. So I embarrassed him and her and myself. I felt bad about it. He felt bad about what he had done. We spent the whole next day apologizing to each other.

But still there was no excuse on my part. My own anxiety, maybe jealousy, more likely insecurity had kicked in. It is just simply not a good thing to embarrass someone that way.

13

Arnie and I were two people thrown into turbulent waters, flailing away, terrified of drowning. Sometimes it was as if one of us was pushing the other's head below water so that the other could keep his own head above it. Most times though we would help each other stay afloat and at times, glorious times, we would swim spectacular distances together.

There is no more Arnie. His funeral and the memorial were quite extraordinary. Tributes to him, tributes to the world he imagined. A tribute to the smaller world we helped bring into being. With the magazine, with his statements on the radio, with his eloquence at public gatherings. To the discussions he worked so hard to bring about. At his funeral I looked out at the people in attendance, such a wide variety of people, and realized that Arnie finally had the discussion group he always imagined.

•

I can't think of a better way to end this piece than with Arnie's own words, an excerpt from "A Bitter Outburst," Arnie's last essay:

I wish to advance an oppositional culture. One which moves entirely outside the existing framework. I am not concerned with being so-called adjusted or mature. Existing cultural norms are often malignant. Even benevolent social democracy gives civil liberties and material well-being in exchange for efficient production and consumption. Highly disciplined wage-labor with concessions from the boss. The illusion of comfort. Severe anxiety underneath. We have a self essentially conditioned to fit the machine. I was involved with anarchist-pacifist politics, the sixties counter-culture, the early seventies social movements. We meant to turn things upside down. To foster the return of the repressed. Open fugitive spaces.

Political movements were reaching towards transcendence and ecstasy. Nowadays this is implicitly and explicitly ruled out by the left-liberal establishment. They are trying to reform the machine. We were trying to stop it. I ultimately come from a place where I do not fit in. I think a radical movement is ultimately internal as well as external. A breakthrough into a subversive consciousness. I wish to move outside the given. To negate the social order. I am not speaking of strategy or tactics. My disposition is rather mystical. I am exploring a different reality. Perhaps even an altered state. A move away from conventional notions of rationality. At one point we were taking emotional risks. Perhaps even playing with fire. At one level I might wish to withdraw from politics. Pursue an interior journey. Simply step out of the world. But paradoxically I also want to change it. To break the collective chains. To affirm the wild and strange. And reach towards the seemingly impossible.

What a ride this has been! Arnie I love you. ■

Rehab Romance

TERESA AT 102 YEARS old lives alone. She says people come by to look in on her. She is very self-sufficient. She works at the senior center which she walks to every day by herself. She was in the rehab center because her leg was broken. She was visited by an array of people, the super's son and his girlfriend among the most affectionate.

"How's my girl," she said to my mother as she dramatically pulled back the curtain separating their beds.

Her eyes always sparkled.

My mother, who had just turned 90, insisted that Teresa was having an affair with one of the aides. "She can do better than that. She's too good for her," my mother said. "That nurse is too rough and she is probably prowling the hallways looking for a doctor to marry."

And my God who would believe it. Just then the aide, a woman of about 35, came into the room. Teresa bolted upright in her bed and the two women, faces glowing, started throwing kisses back and forth at each other.

"We should write a book together called *Romances in the Rehab Center*," I said. "*Rehab Romances* would be a better title," my mother answered. ∎

Afterword by Myrna Nieves

The title of Robert Roth's *Book of Pieces* is more than a reference to the systematic organization of his written work for this publication. It is essentially a perspective on moments in time which can be glimpses at aspects of reality and their sum, forming a prism of the human condition. They point to the tragic nature of that condition, as well as its joys, beauty, contradictions, vagueness. All in all, this plural book seems to be a complex celebration of life from "an anarchist poet from the Village."

Robert's devotion to the literary magazine he co-founded, *And Then*, is not completely separate from *Book of Pieces*. His book includes his own work—essays, poems, conversations with people, letters to newspapers—as well as pieces written by others and with others (with the co-editor of *And Then*, Carletta Joy Walker, and with the late co-editor, Arnold Sachar) and interviews by him and of him. This conglomeration is very similar to the magazine *And Then*, now in its 18th issue. Being alive; stages of sexual development; good, bad and weird situations; as well as the process of aging and dying are all included here. His mother's life and her last days, and his interaction with her, provide the framework for the book and constitute an important leitmotif. The book opens with "Leading Lady," a tender and interesting piece in which the author plays along with his mother's fantasy in a hospital's emergency room. Later, towards the middle of his book, Robert describes the conditions of her last days and their painful, yet beneficial impact on him. The author closes the book with a conversation he had with her in a rehab center, planning future writing projects that they will undertake together. I think of Robert's book as the best homage a son can pay to his mother. This is a book of love. It is not always about love, but a product and affirmation of love.

The author describes old age, the breakdown of filters, sometimes delusions, but rarely the disappearance of intelligence. Again, in "Leading Lady," his mother is proud of her own resistance at being treated in a way that she cannot understand. Their interaction around the issue reveals that people may not lose their "spark" even under the direst of circumstances. Even when the serious implications that the family is facing are present, we have the impression that the author is enjoying his mother and glad to be able to "co-create" with her. In this and other pieces, we can grasp various issues about the dignity of life and preserving that dignity. Despite having to take action in an "uncharted territory," the author stays close to his mother's situation and even writes to newspapers, suggesting changes to the conditions in emergency rooms for older people, a suggestion that eventually bore fruit.

His father and other family members are also present in the pieces. Robert writes with great tenderness about a father whose life he admires. At the moment of his death, the author kisses his father's forehead while waiting next to him and quietly studying his own perceptions and feelings. His intellectuality comes into question, as he asks himself if examining his own thoughts at that moment reveals an acceptance of death or an inability to feel.

The author's constant inquiry into the truth of feelings and intentions forces many of us to look at ourselves and be as radically honest as he is. It touches deeply within and forces us to look at what has been suppressed, taken for granted, not noticed or avoided. In one of the first pieces, "Notes of an Unknown Writer," he states, "My whole life I have not allowed the full force of experience to affect upon me. I have always been too numb, too frozen by life-shock." We don't have to agree with the author all the time in order for the process of self-reflection to occur. In this piece, we can observe his anger at how aging is socially viewed and how people accept and morph into getting old. We are presented with the refusal to be passive or to acquiesce in situations in which a strong value of ours is challenged.

Many of the pieces are about the author's life as he relates to others, explores the world around him and takes care of himself. He pays attention to people, to social inequality, to madness, to his body, to marginal persons and random events. Robert is also aware of slips of attention; they are as meaningful as the main event unfolding in front of him. In the first part of the book, we see the author roaming the City, sitting in parks watching people and animals, meeting with friends, mourning the loss of the relationship with his lover, Akemi. He also describes his interaction with people who are famous and people who are not famous. At times, for me, some of the experiences that he describes border on danger. He also takes us to places where people struggle to remove the walls of outside repression and self-imposed repression. We have to be ready to read Robert's work, since, as he states, "Freedom unleashed is menacing and beautiful." Sometimes his book is quite scary. Powerful, and profound. Sometimes I caught myself making judgments. Most of the time I admired his capacity to be aware of the wide range of his humanity.

At one point in the book, the author states that although he does maintain a wide circle of friends, he saves for his writing what is truly happening in his life, but at times he feels depleted by doing this because his "thoughts lose vitality." Writing and the full expression of the self in social interactions are in tension here. This tension points to a balancing act that requires much caring, despite some resentment, but also a fierce commitment to literature.

Two outstanding pieces about friends share some characteristics: a piece about the feminist leader and artist Shulamith Firestone; and a piece significantly placed towards the end of the book, about Arnie Sachar, his great friend and the co-editor of *And Then*. The author describes two brilliant, passionate and creative persons who struggled with deep emotional issues or battled mental illness. The author demonstrates an enduring love of his friends and a loyalty that is truly outstanding. Painfully aware that in this City "you go mad in isolation," he never abandons his friends and walks alongside during the best and worst of times. Shulamith is described at times as "absolutely focused, and filled with ideas, theories and passion and categories," but also, at other times, she is described wearing disguises or scaring the hell out of the author when she was a bag lady in the street.

The piece about Arnie is a major one. Although the author focuses mostly on the hellish last days of Arnie's crisis at home and in the hospital, he also recounts the early years of their friendship, Arnie's eloquence and insights, their collaboration in the magazine as well as his friend's intense psychic pain at real or imagined social rejections. Moments of intense solidarity and camaraderie; others in which, as with Shulamith, the author had to run from the chaos and craziness of the last years with Arnie. Possibly as homage to Arnie, the author also includes an exceptional piece written by his friend, which is a delight to read. Arnie writes (excerpt): "I wish to advance an oppositional culture. One which moves entirely outside the existing framework.... We meant to turn things upside down.... To affirm the wild and strange. And reach toward the seemingly impossible." This is an important text; we can hear in these words the echo of Robert's activism and his core political values.

Sexuality occupies an important place in the author's writing as well. He describes the loss of love, the need of a physical experience, the comic attempts to relate, our relationship with our physical body and sexual situations with imagined or real persons of unknown gender. Rarely are detailed or graphic sexual interactions included. What's evident is the author's capacity for joy in most circumstances in which other human beings reach out to touch his body and heart, as in the "Conclusion" section of the piece "My Penis." In this piece, the author goes into what for some may be the most intimate areas of a man's life; his penis, herpes, circumcision, urinating. These topics could make another autobiographical writer feel vulnerable. Robert goes into these areas, and it is not that he makes them entirely comfortable, but his writing may make the reader aware of his/her body and that there is a huge complexity associated with this physical area of our existence. The author is aware of ugly sexual politics and views that make their way into our unconscious attitudes and behavior. With all that baggage and cultural prohibition, how can we have "deep explorations of desire"? There is no answer to this in Robert's book, but the question is there and points to the enticement of possibilities.

Not always are his pieces flooded by these tensions or by pain, nor does his writing have a sharp irony. In a delightful short story, "A June Wedding," a character observes human beings in moments of joy. Almost like a camera lens in a film, his eyes roam the room to find the gestures, the looks, the actions, the expectations present at a non-denominational, multiple wedding of one hundred and fifty "politically and culturally progressive orientation" couples, attended also by their families and friends. There is a certain "otherworldly" tone to this piece. In a beautiful description of the ceremony, the character states: "There is a rapt attention; no jokes or wisecracks, no uneasy glances. The couples now gaze into each other's eyes.... For these few minutes there is no feeling of cynicism or irony. No one will steal this moment from them." I surmise that in reality and fiction, as in love and war, Robert attempts to describe human beings at their worst and their best, with the author embracing all.

The above-described piece pulls our attention to some of the author's creative use of literary techniques such as the use of point of view and figures of speech. Many times the first person (the "I" of the author) narrates or a character narrates. In one piece, a second speaker comes in to confront the author (a fantasy or a "visitation"). At other times the narration is third person omniscient, such as the piece in which the writer's actions and feelings as he visits a museum are described. There are also points of view mostly focalized through the perspective of both the narrator of a story and one of his characters, a woman who looks at herself in a mirror, internally raging at her boyfriend and the narrator. We may also encounter in Robert's writing images (similes, metaphors) that are powerful and moving, as in "In the Audience," when the author describes the tense and paradoxical relationship between two of his characters, and states: "It was as if Allison had drilled two fingers through his chest, touching his heart for an instant, then pulled her fingers out as quickly as she could, leaving the part that she touched burning with love."

Interviews are also part of the text. At times, the author interviews people in the most awkward but critically important situations, such as his dialogue with a policeman when he is arrested for interfering with the questioning of a person in a street in New York, or in a hotel in Staten Island, his questions to a former foreign service man who worked in Chile during Pinochet's coup. Somehow people respond to his questions without feeling terribly judged or condemned, and are actually grateful to be able to tell their side of the story. These two are among the most intense and interesting pieces. I felt as if I was able to peek into what the Spanish philosopher/writer Miguel de Unamuno called *la intra-historia*, which describes the lives of people while the "big" events in the newspapers or in the "official" History play out. I see Robert mostly as a chronicler of the *intra-historia*. The reason for this is his love of people and their creative spirits. At one point in his book he states, "Basically I love the anarchic feel and unpredictability of what people do."

History as told in the newspapers is also included in his book. Several pieces are about international politics, such as the ones commenting on the world-wide involvement of the USA government in oppressive and destabilizing events. In "Out of the Ashes of the Warsaw Ghetto / Out of the Rubble of Jenin," he examines some of the intricate and disturbing aspects of the war between the Jews and the Palestinians. Robert concludes with the statement: "One thing I know for sure, any Homeland worth its name is not a place any person should want to live." The author also recognizes the oppression of the attacker and the victim (at one point in time), and that both of them could be in each other's place at another point in time, perpetuating the cycles of global violence.

What can we do when facing the world's conditions described above? Robert has created—with his friends—a response to it that is based in freedom of expression. He sees *And Then* as "a big communal gathering" and "a shimmering field of freedom." In his books, *Health Proxy* and *Book of Pieces*, we can grasp that the essence of his response is his behavior as a human being. The author is aware of how we all at one time or other may be part of that situation by participating in actions that oppress other people by alienating or embarrassing them. Robert is extremely concerned at all times with respecting life by not hurting people, and helping them flourish. To me, this is a foundation for peace.

Tragedy, irony, comedy and melodrama on a global and local scale are all part of this book; the pieces range from serious issues to simple concerns (of course, no concern is really "simple") and everything in between. Some pieces are truly hilarious. Two memorable ones for me include the one in his "Argentine Journal" in which there is a confusion about a woman who he thought was sexually interested in him but turned out to be a prostitute trying to make some money. Most of the time, amid serious worries, the author enjoys the absurdist character of life and runs with it. Sometimes "imagined" reality becomes "actual" reality, as in the first part of his "Argentine Journal" in which people often confuse him with a famous actor whom they cannot quite identify. Recently, the author has acted in several independent films. Some of his comments are memorable. In describing the kind of actor some people think he has been, the author writes: "Ghosts and lunatics all. My charisma is pretty intense."

Amidst political, social and cultural issues and concerns—and maybe because of them—this book is fundamentally about people, those very beings that Robert Roth describes as "a mixture of harshness and delicacy."

Book of Pieces is indeed an exploration of the terror and beauty of life. It has been a privilege to read this remarkable collection of many such moments.

Other And Then Press *Publications*

Improvisations on an Untamed Life
Louise Rader

Silence, Storytelling and Madness
Jane Heil Usyk

Mirror Mirror
Stephanie Hart

Another Version of Hansel and Gretel
Myrna Nieves

A Great Disorder
Frank Murphy

"The Closer It Gets to the Money..."
Advice on the Writing Life
Finvola Drury, edited by Sohnya Sayres

Made in the USA
San Bernardino, CA
02 September 2016